MW00873683

News Clippings from New Harmony, Utah 1898 - 1923

Compiled from the Washington County News (Utah), Deseret News (Utah) & Iron County Record (Utah) with contributions from other regional papers.

Often while working on family history (genealogy) I wonder about more than is listed on the pedigree sheets and am so grateful for their sacrifices and love for the generations to follow.

Some of the names include: Anderson, Barney, Bruppacher, Chinn, Condie, Davis, Englestead, Grant, Hammond, Imlay, Kelsey, Kirker, Mathis, Pace, Prince, Rance, Redd, Schmutz, Slack, Smootz, Taylor, Whipple, Williams, Woodward, Woolsey

Some of the articles are easier to read than others, please consider that they are nearly 100 years old.

Copyright 2014

No part of this publication (compilation) may be reproduced, stored in a retrieval system,
transmitted in any form or by any means without written permission of David Andersen,
Overton, NV, nor otherwise be circulated in any form of binding or cover other than that in
which it is published.

ISBN-13: 978-1502932419

ISBN-10: 1502932415

NEW HARMONY.

Jos. Worthen, Sr., and Jos. Worthen, Jr., of St. George, are here doing mason work.

The weather was quite warm here last week. On Saturday night we had a little rain shower.

Threshing commenced here on the 18th and is now in full swing. We will be through about next Thursday when the thresher will go to Kanarra to thresh there.

A social party was given on Aug. 14th, at the residence of Gottlieb Schmutz, to our Swiss friends from St. George. Swiss, French and American songs and picnic was the order of the evening and all enjoyed themselves.

New Harmony has been having a little building boom. New granaries, barns and some nice fences have been put up which gives the town a much nicer appearance. A neat meeting house is in course of erection; it is built of concrete and has the roof on, but windows, doors, inside finishing, etc., are yet to be made.

SWISS.

New Harmony, Utah, Aug. 21, 1898,

NEW HARMONY.

Chris Olsen of Leeds visited relatives and friends here on his return from Panguitch lake.

Prof. T. Isaacson, an optician, was in town on the 22nd. He is a pleasant gentleman who has been in several foreign countries and can talk several languages.

We had a nice rain here on Friday evening, which did much good, especially for late corn and third crop of lucern. Corn cutting and hauling has commenced; apple drying in progress; all other fruit ripening fast. Weather cooler.

Thos. John, of Provo, came here Friday trying to let the contract for carrying the mails between Hebron and New Harmony. So far no one in this place has taken the contract. $450 is the offer for a semi-weekly service.

Threshing finished here. Grain turned out excellent. The thresher left here for Hamilton near Cedar City.

SWISS.

New Harmony, Utah, Aug. 28, 1898.

NEW HARMONY.

Stubble plowing has commenced.

Plenty of plums and tomatoes ripe here

Miss Mabel Knell of Pinto is visiting friends here.

Corn cutting and hauling in full swing, corn a good average crop this year

James Prince took the mail contract carrying the mails between Harmony and Hebron.

Chas. and Nathaniel Baldwin, of Fillmore, are canvassing American and Spanish war books.

Geo. Spilsbury, of Toquerville, Asst. Supt. of Sunday Schools for this Stake, is here in the interest of S. S. work.

David Tullis was over from Pinto the first of the week for fruit. He said that the fruit crop in Pinto is a failure this year.

We had a severe wind storm on Sept. 1st which did lots of damage to the fruit crop. We had a slight frost on the morning of the 3rd inst., no damage.

SWISS.

New Harmony, Utah, Aug. 4, 1898.

NEW HARMONY.

Flies still all alive.

Health of the people good.

Harvey Pace has been putting up a neat rail fence.

Weather much cooler; last few days of last week quite hot.

Corn cutting and hauling nearly finished except the late corn.

Mrs. Martha Bairlocker went to Pinto attend the Knell-Palmer wedding.

Last week was a very busy one for the ladies here, botteling and preserving fruit.

Levi Pace and Louisa Mathis were among the wedding guests at Pinto from here.

Mrs. Annie Bradshaw and son, Benjamin, of Virgin City are visiting relatives here.

Bishop Reed and wife were among the conference visitors to St. George from this place.

Swiss, your correspondent went to Toquerville for grapes and fruit. He had a good social time with his many friends in the sunny south.

There will be a wedding here next Wednesday, the 14th inst. Enock Naegle of Toquerville will marry Miss Elnora Taylor of this place.

Neal and Miss Sophie Forsyth passed through her Friday enroute to their home at Pinto. They had been to Toquerville for fruit and to visit relatives.

Swiss.

New Harmony, Utah, Sept. 11, 1898,

NEW HARMONY.

Peach drying in progress.

Weather hot in the daytime, cool at nights.

Third crop of lucern being cut and hauled,

Ben Taylor started today for Milford for freight.

John Schmutz, of St. George, is visiting relatives here.

Mahouri Shapley of Kanarra was a visitor here Sunday, the 11th inst.

A surprise party invaded the home of the president of the Relief Society Mrs. M. D. Pace on the 12th inst.

The Misses Mary Reed, Villo Reed and Alice Reed left here Friday for Cedar City to attend the Normal School.

Mrs. Schlappi left here for her home at Middleton, near St. George, on Friday. She has been here several weeks for the benefit of her health.

Several loads of wheat were taken from here to the mill at Cedar City last week. 33 lbs of flour and 15 lbs of bran is given for each bushel of wheat.

What a mail service! I received a letter last Friday, the 16th inst., that was posted at Toquerville on the 5th inst. The distance is 20 miles between the two places, yet the letter had been through the postoffices at Leeds and Kanarra.

A wedding reception was held at the residence of Mrs. Julia Taylor in honor of her daughter, Lenora, who was recently married to Enoch Naegle. There were present from Toquerville, Mrs. Regula Naegle, John Naegle and wife, Mrs. Vilate Kleinaman, Joseph Naegle, Miss Edna Jackson, Mrs. Rose Lund and James Naegle. From Cedar City, George Wood and wife, and Mrs. Isaac Haight. Quite a number of Harmony people were present.

Swiss.

New Harmony, Utah, Sept. 18, 1898.

Washington County News
September 25, 1898

NEW HARMONY.

Roads dry and dusty.

Beautiful fall weather.

People busy drying fruit.

Frank Hyde was in from Hamblin Thursday.

Mrs. Eliza Milay of Panguitch is visiting relatives here.

The dairy cows are being got in from the mountain ranges.

Albert Taylor will start with some sheep for Chicago next week.

Lots of wire fencing being put up here. Nearly every field has a wire fence round it now.

Signs of approaching winter are seen in the changed color of vegetation on the surrounding mountains.

A few of the young folks attended a wedding dance at Kanarra on Friday night. It was given by John Berry.

Granville Pace returned from the Southern states mission field Saturday. He left Harmony in August 1896 and labored in Georgia and Louisiana.

SWISS.

New Harmony, Sept. 25, 1898.

Washington County News
October 2, 1898

NEW HARMONY.

Cedar mountains are covered with a mantle of snow.

3rd crop of lucern nearly all put up. Late corn hauling commenced.

Alfred Bauerlocker was in town from Leeds Monday visiting relatives.

Mr. Griffiths of Cedar City was in town this week fixing sewing machines.

We had a severe wind storm Friday night which did considerable damage to apples.

A fire was raging in the timbers on the mountains north of Harmony Friday morning.

Town nearly deserted, so many people have gone to Cedar City to attend the Iron county Fair.

Several horses of Harvey Pace got entangled in wire fences and were badly cut, one so badly that it had to be killed.

Last night was very cold. This morning there is a heavy frost with ice on standing water. Beans, squash, lucern and peaches are badly frozen.

SWISS.

New Harmony, Oct. 2, 1898.

NEW HARMONY.

James F. Prince and Albert Mathis left this town at noon on October 4th for the purpose of hunting deer. They camped that evening at a sheep camp, and started out early next morning leaving their horses in camp. They agreed to meet at noon at a specified place in the woods, but when Mathis arrived there he did not find Prince. Seeing deer tracks and Prince's foot tracks leading past the place of appointment, he concluded that Prince was after the deer and returned to the sheep camp. As Prince had not shown up next morning Mathis started out in search of him. He found Prince lying dead with his gun beside him. No wounds were observable and it is believed he died from heart failure. His body was brought in on Thursday afternoon, it having to be carried three miles as there was no roads through the woods. The sad affair is a severe shock to his wife, children and relatives. Funeral services were held in the meeting house on Friday, everybody that was able being in attendance. Joseph S. Berry of Kanarra, a recently returned missionary from California offered up prayer and very touching remarks were made by Elder Levy Pace. James F. Prince was born December 23, 1865. He leaves a wife and four children to mourn his loss. He was a cattle man and well known about this country.

Very cold mornings all last week.

Rance Brothers have their photograph gallery here this week.

Sheep are coming in from the mountains thick and fast. Second clip of wool being sheared.

Henry Kuhn was up here the fore part of the week from Grapevine Springs hunting cattle.

The Conference and Eisteddfod visitors from this place were Alex Pace, Wilson Pace, Bishop Redd and Venice Rohner.

SWISS.

New Harmony, Utah, Oct. 9, 1898.

NEW HARMONY.

Ice on the ditches here this morning

Wine making in full progress at Bellevue

Ben Ruppacher has gone to Cedar City on business

Alma Angel of Leeds has been here visiting relatives

School will start tomorrow with Mrs. Granville Pace as teacher.

George Anderson, from Anderson's range, was up with cattle Sunday

Corn and hay all hauled. Apples being gathered, a very fair crop. Potatoes being harvested and are very good

Thomas Judd and Miss Mary Morris passed through Bellevue Friday enroute to their homes in the sunny south

David Tullis and wife and Mrs. Thomas Platt were over here from Pinto Sunday visiting relatives and friends

James Taylor gave up the sheep herd of Eliza Kelsey. Joseph Prince and Reese Davis of Kanarra have taken it on shares

John M. Allen and family will leave their Dixie home in Bellevue on October 25th and make a home in Graham county, Arizona

SWISS,

New Harmony, Utah, October 16, 1898.

NEW HARMONY.

Very cold weather here now.

Emile Barlocker went to Cedar City on business Monday.

Potatoes nearly all dug, they are turning out fine in this locality.

Independence Taylor made a flying visit to Bellevue and back Friday.

Joseph Bryant and A. F. Gower, carpenters from Cedar City, are here putting up a building for Gottlieb Schmutz.

The Y. M. M. I. A. had a meeting here Friday night to put up a program.

Apple picking in progress—more on the ground than on the trees, the recent heavy winds having blown them off.

SWISS.
New Harmony, Utah, Oct. 25, 1898.

NEW HARMONY.

Politics very quiet here.

Mr. Wood is very sick with rheumatism.

A dance was held at Kanarra on the 5th inst.

Gottlieb Schmutz went to Cedar City on business Thursday.

Alexander Pace came in Tuesday with a load of goods for the Harmony Co-op.

Sam Dodge of Toquerville passed through here Monday enroute to Pine Valley.

The mountains north of Harmony had a light cover of Snow on Tuesday morning.

Arnold Graf returned to his home at Kanarra after an absence of three months in the east.

Nelson D. Pace, ex-bishop of Harmony is very sick. He was taken ill on returning from conference.

A Democratic meeting was held at Kanarra on Thursday evening. Mr. Baer was the principal speaker

John D. Morse of St. George is in Kanarra, plastering the new Co-op store building and the residence of James Davis.

August Cogin, former mail driver from St. George, passed through Kanarra Saturday evening enroute to his new home at Panguitch.

SWISS,
New Harmony, Utah, Nov. 5, 1898.

NEW HARMONY.

Hog killing has commenced here.

Many buildings have been reshingled this fall.

Sheep dipping has been extensively carried on here the past two weeks.

Jacob Schmutz, of Middleton near St. George, is here visiting relatives.

Joseph Taylor left for DeLamar on Tuesday with a load of chickens and produce.

John Mathis arrived from Price on Sunday to visit his father and other relatives.

Weather was nice and warm here all last week, but tonight it has turned very cold.

The roads between the bottom of the Black ridge and Toquerville are terribly rough.

James Naegle was up from Toquerville Monday visiting his many old-time friends.

Mrs. Julia Taylor went to Toquerville on Tuesday to visit her daughter and other relatives.

Today the surrounding mountains are covered with snow, and it is snowing here thick and fast.

John Ferris, an old resident of Washington county, is in Bellevue having recently returned from Marysvale.

Andrew Gregerson of Bellevue has taken the mail contract from Joseph Sylvester to run between Bellevue and Cedar City.

John Batty and son, Frank, of Toquerville passed through Bellevue on Thursday enroute home from a northern trip.

SWISS,
New Harmony, Utah Nov. 20, 1898.

NEW HARMONY.

Alma Angel of Leeds was visiting here Tuesday.

Will Pace of Harrisburg was here Saturday visiting relatives and friends.

Snow fell here all day Thursday, making the day very cold and disagreeable.

Mathew McMurtrie of Virgin City passed through here enroute to Pinto Thursday.

Mrs. Francis Prince has returned from Panguitch, where she has been visiting relatives.

Hog killing is in full progress, and betting on the weight of the hogs furnishes fun for the boys.

George Spilsbury, Asst. Supt. of Sunday schools of St. George Stake is here today in the interests of S. S.

Wilson D. Pace, ex-bishop of Harmony, is recovering from his sickness, and is able to get about a little.

Miss Mary Redd returned from the branch Normal school at Cedar City to spend the holidays with her folks.

Sam Roundy, an old resident of Harmony, came in from Cache valley this week to visit relatives and friends.

H. E. Eastman of Mill Creek, the agent for the Utah Nursery Co., was here Friday delivering fruit trees. Quite a large number came to this town, and before many years Harmony will have some choice fruits.

Thanksgiving day was quietly observed here. Your correspondent hoisted U. S. flags at two places in town. Schools closed at noon, and the little folks had a candy pulling in the evening at the residence of Gottlieb Schmutz.

SWISS,
New Harmony, Utah, Nov. 27, 1898.

NEW HARMONY.

Weather very pleasant here all last week.

Henry Mathis, Sr., went to Cedar City Monday on business.

Mrs. Louisa Mathis and her children have left for Loa, Wayne county, to visit relatives.

Ed Laub of Toquerville passed through here yesterday enroue home from a northern trip.

SWISS,
New Harmony, Utah, Dec. 4, 1898.

NEW HARMONY.

Saturday it snowed about four inches.

Mr. Owen, the Z. C. M. I. drummer was here Thursday.

Friday was a very cold day. Some potatoes were frozen.

Grand surprise birthday dinner at E. Barlockers residence today.

The weather has cleared up today and the sun is shining bright and warm.

George Batty of Toquerville was here on cattle business on the 5th inst.

E. Stout, representing the Studebaker Wagon Co., was in town on the 5th inst.

The children are anxiously asking how many days it will be before Santa Clause appears.

Dr. Middleton of Cedar City came in today to attend Miss Susie Taylor, who has been very sick since last Monday with the measles.

SWISS,
New Harmony, Utah, Dec. 11, 1898.

NEW HARMONY,

Weather nice and warm now, snow all gone.

Measles has broken out here, and is spreading.

A merry christmas to you, Mr. editor, and family.

A Merry Christmas to all the readers of the WASHINGTON COUNTY NEWS.

Orin Kelsey has sold his place here and will move next spring to White River.

William Roundy, from Cotton farm, near Washington, is visiting relatives in Kanarra.

Born—a son to the wife of William Watts, on the 13th inst.; mother and child doing well.

Ed Huber and Son of Rockville passed through Bellevue Tuesday enroute home from Beaver.

Joseph Platt of Pinto passed through here today, to start to drive the mail between Bellevue and Cedar City.

The St. George Stake Conference visitors from here are Emil Barlocker and wife, and Gottlieb Schmutz, president of the Y. M. M. I. A. of this ward.

Walter H. Pollack, an old resident of Kanarra, has sold out his place there and bought a place on the Cotton farm near Washington; he moved down to the sunny south last Tuesday.

There is much credit due to the road supervisor and working men of St. George for the good work done on the Black Ridge; the road is in fine condition, and is pleasant to travel over, except for the cold blasts that meet one going up in that direction.

SWISS,
New Harmony, Utah, Dec. 18, 1898.

NEW HARMONY.

Hyrum Duffin of Toquerville was here on business Monday.

Weather very pleasant during daytime, but very cold nights; no snow.

A happy new year to all the readers of the WASHINGTON COUNTY NEWS.

Frank Reeves has moved from his ranch near Kelsey's, to Harmony for the winter.

The students from the branch Normal school, and the branch B. Y. A., at Beaver, are visiting relatives and spending the holidays at the home fireside.

On December 24th, at 7 p. m., the Christmas tree festivities commenced, and the following program rendered: Music by Orin Kelsey and Levi Pace; song "Hosanna," by the Christmas choir; prayer by Bishop Redd; recitation by Eliza Prince; Christmas song by a group of small children, after which Santa Claus appeared and distributed the presents from the tree, on which parents, relatives, and friends had put the presents; Duet by Alice and Nora Redd. A dance for the children followed, and was hugely enjoyed. The committee having this affair in charge are entitled to much credit, they were: Francis Prince, W. Taylor, Emma Grant, Etna Dole, and Annie Prince.

SWISS,
New Harmony, Utah, Dec. 25, 1898.

HARMONY.

There was a dance last evening for the little children.

The M. I. A. missionary elders, Horsley and Wilcock, came here Friday from Pinto.

The Taylor brothers went to Toquerville to spend New Year's with relatives an the sunny south.

We had nice warm weather during the holidays until New Year's day, when it turned very cold.

Henry Mathis, Sr., has several of his range cattle dying today, caused through some kind of poison in the hay.

On the 27th some of our young folks went over to our friendly neighbor town, Kanarra, to play baseball and attend a dance. On the 28th our Kanarra friends visited us, played ball, and attended a bow dance in the evening.

On December 26th we had horse racing; a dance at 2 p. m. for the children, and a dance in the evening for the older folks. There was also a basket dance, the basket being put up at auction and sold to the highest bidder; some of them went as high as $1.50.

SWISS.

Harmony, Utah, January 1, 1898.

Washington County News
January 7, 1899

HARMONY.

Holidays are over and conditions are normal again.

Weather nice and pleasant, no snow; roads dry and dusty.

Jes. Woodard, of Harrisburg was here New Year's visiting relatives.

Alfred Barlocker of Leeds was up here on the 4th inst visiting relatives.

Co. Supt. of District schools, W. J. Snow, was here Friday in the interests of the schools.

Enoch Naegle and wife of Toquerville were here the fore part of the week visiting relatives.

A petition was taken round yesterday for signatures, asking that Harmony be annexed to Iron county.

A big fire was raging in the brush near town on the 2nd inst. Several men left town and put it out.

A big fire was raging in the brush near town on the 2nd inst. Several men left town and put it out.

The M. I. missionaries Horsley and Wilcock left for Pinto on the 5th inst., from there they will go to the Muddy.

Several of our young people went over to Kanarra on the 6th inst. to attend a missionary party that evening.

An old folks party was held here on January 2nd. Everybody was with it from the age of 16 up. It was held in the school house, which was tastefully decorated with evergreens and flags, while over the stand was the motto: "God bless the old folks." About 1 o'clock the old folks were brought in carriages to the school house, where everything good to eat was ready; all enjoyed themselves well. At 8 o'clock in the evening dancing commenced, being interspersed with songs, music, recitations, etc. Everybody helped to make this occasion a success. Some cooked at home, while others prepared the things in the school house. The committees and all who helped are deserving of credit for preparing such a pleasant party for the old folks.

SWISS,
Harmony, Utah, January 7, 1899.

Washington County News
January 18, 1899

HARMONY.

Orin Kelsey and John Mathis have gone to Milford for freight.

Benjamin Bruppacher went to Toquerville on business Wednesday.

Clarence Goddard, of Little Pinto, was here on business on the 16th inst.

Roads on the ridge very muddy. About three inches of snow in Bellevue.

Several of our people went to Kanarra on the 16th inst. to attend a theatre.

Will and John Reeves of Kanarra were in Bellevue Wednesday hunting cattle.

The ladies of the Relief Society have fixed up their meeting house and made it more home like.

James Russell has come home from herding sheep and is spending his vacation with his many friends.

Emil Barlocker has sold his home here to Henry Mathis, and will probably make a new home at Enterprise, where he has gone now to see about a place.

John Kinsley left here for Toquerville Wednesday where he will spend a week or two, and then go to the Switzerland of Utah, Santa Clara, and visit friends.

From two to three inches of snow fell here on the 15th inst. It is melting rapidly, barren places being visible. It is very cold in the early mornings, and lots of potatoes have been frozen.

SWISS,
Harmony, Utah, January 18, 1899.

NEW HARMONY.

E. M. Watts went to Toquerville on business Monday.

Alma Angell of Leeds was visiting relatives here Monday.

Mrs. Granville Pace of Harmony is visiting relatives in Pinto.

Lemuel Redd, a former resident of this place, is here from Mexico visiting old friends.

Mrs. George Wood and Sons of Cedar City came here on a visit and to attend the Mathis Wedding dance.

W. B. Davis of Kanarra and John Prince of Harmony visited the sunny south on cattle business last week.

The fruit trees have a sad appearance, frost having turned them yellow and brown; wheat is in fine condition.

Miss Rose Gregorson has quit teaching school at Kanarra, and is spending her vacation at the home fireside in Bellevue.

Gottlieb Schmutz and wife went to Cedar City Tuesday with their little son to have an operation performed on him. The operation was a success and the little boy is getting along well.

George Spilsbury of Toquerville was here with the superintendent of Sunday schools, and Dr. Karl G. Maeser and George Reynolds of the S. S. Union. Meeting was held at 6 o'clock in the evening and was well attended.

A wedding dance, in honor of John Arnold Mathis of Harmony and his bride, Rachel Cottam, one of the fair daughters of St. George, was held here on the 12th inst. All enjoyed the dance and good music until the early morning hours.

The Misses Alice and Molly Redd came home from the branch Normal school at Cedar City to attend the wedding reception. James Naegle of of Toquerville also attended. The music for the dance was furnished by Cosslett of Cedar City, and Sam Pollack, Jr., and A. Graf of Kanarra.

Washington County News
June 10, 1899

NEW HARMONY.

Charles Parker of Kanarra was here Sunday.

Miss Hannah Reeves is visiting relatives here.

The west mountains had a coating of snow Thursday.

Louis Balser left for Salt Lake City Monday to visit his father, who is very ill.

John Arnold Mathis and wife left for Price, Carbon county, Wednesday, where they will make their home.

Decoration day was observed very quietly here. Your correspondent hoisted National flags at two places in town in honor of the day.

The long-wished-for rain has come at last in our section. It rained on Thursday, Friday, and Saturday, the ground getting a good soaking. Farmers are jubilant as some of the wheat fields had nearly dried up.

Orin Kelsey and family left for Idaho, on the 1st inst., where they will make a new home. A farewell dinner was tendered them at the home of postmistress Taylor Sunday, and a farewell dance was given on Tuesday evening at which several Kanarra people were present.

Washington County News
June 24, 1899

LOCAL CHRONOLOGY

OF THE MOST IMPORTANT EVENTS RECORDED IN THE HOME PAPER FOR THE NEWSPAPER YEAR ENDING JUNE 17, 1899.

JUNE.

4. Joseph Crawford, of Springdale, died.

11. George Lenzie McAllister died.

JULY.

6. Willard R. Smith, of Harrisburg, died.

8. Mrs. Mary Lund Judd died.

10. Jacob Samuel Bowler, of Gunlock, died.

25. Susie Terry died. Twins born to the wife of Orin Woodbury.

29. Hottest day of the year, 115 degrees in the shade.

AUGUST.

8. James McArthur's left hand badly crushed, losing one finger and parts of others.

17. Jeppa Iverson, of Washington, died.

20. Mrs. Sarah Waite Pulsipher, of Bunkerville, died.

27. Orpha Leavitt, of Bunkerville, died.

SEPTEMBER.

4. Mrs Mary Ann Harrison, of Pinto, died.

9. Hazel Cox, of Overton, died, the result of an accident.

12. One-year-old son of Henry and Maria Spendlove drowned in the Virgin river at Grafton.

19. Mrs. Elzina Hepworth, of Springdale, died.

OCTOBER.

5. James F. Prince, of New Harmony, meets death by accident while hunting.

21. Mrs. Cora Keate Hartman, of Silver Reef, died.

23. Twins born to the wife of John D. Pymm.

28. James Macdonald loses an eye by being thrown from a horse.

NOVEMBER.

12. Samuel Dotson, of Overton, killed at Pine Valley by a tree falling on him.

14. Rudolph Frei, of Santa Clara, has his leg broken by a horse falling with him.

19. Mrs. Alice Lougee died.

21. Mrs. Caroline Bacon Rogers Hardy died, aged nearly 93 years.

DECEMBER.

1. Thomas E. Riding died.
11. Twin boys born to the wife of F. G. Miles.
20. Alvah Don Alger died.
21. Mrs. Jacob Hafen, of Washington, died.

JANUARY.

7. Eduardo Alvarez sentenced to two years imprisonment for grand larceny.
13. David J. Fuhrmeister died.
18. Mrs. A. W. Leavitt, of Bunkerville, died.
21. Mrs. Ella Jane Brown died.
26. John Bleak murdered at Hackberry, Arizona.
28. Twin boys born to the wife of Oscar Keate.

FEBRUARY.

1. Oliver Laub died.
10. Rex James Bleak died.
18. Mrs. Ellen Wood, of Grafton, died.

MARCH.

20. Rev. Galen M. Hardy died.

APRIL.

9. First carload of copper ore from the Apex mine, under new management, left for Milford.
13. Miss Leonora Cannon died. Mrs. Beata Eliza Cottam died.
16. John Henry Miller died.
17. Trains started running to and from Modena, on the Utah & Pacific railroad.
19. Slight shock of earthquake at Santa Clara.
22. Mrs. Susanna Keller, of Santa Clara, died. Slight shock of earthquake felt here.
26. Twins born to Mrs. Robert Gray, of Pine Valley.

MAY.

6. Twins born to the wife of Henry Frehner, of Littlefield.
10. Easton Kelsey died, leaving 16 children, 101 grandchildren, 41 great-grandchildren, and one great-great-grand-child.
11. Miss Louie Foster broke her left arm.
12. Smelter at Dixie mines started running.
13. Mrs. Walter Slack, of Toquerville, died after giving birth to twins.
16. Visit of President Snow and Church party.

JUNE.

2. Drouth broken.
4. Mrs. Anna Mary Reber, of Santa Clara, seriously injures herself by falling down a flight of stone stairs.
14. Franklin Turnbow Carter died.

Washington County News
August 19, 1899

OBITUARY.

JOHN MATHIS, son of Johanes and Dorathia Mathis, was born at Weidickon, Zurich, Switzerland, September 10, 1832. He joined the Latter-day Saints Church in his native land, and came to Utah in 1855 with the first company of Saints to leave Switzerland. Was married in Salt Lake City to Barbara Bryner March 20, 1856. Came to St. George in 1861, where he has since resided. Bro. Mathis had three wives, two surviving; they had twelve children, five of whom and twenty grand children are living.

Deceased was first taken ill with catarrh of the stomach about a year ago, since which time he has been quite broken down in health. This trouble finally caused his death, which occurred at New Harmony, where he was visiting, on the 29th of July. The body was brought to this city for interment. He had always been a very hard worker, and did considerable work in helping to build the St. George Temple.

Funeral services were held in the Tabernacle here Monday. The speakers, Elders D. D. McArthur, George Jarvis, James G. Bleak, James Andrus and Thomas P. Cottam made appropriate remarks. Bro. Mathis died as he had lived a faithful Latter-day Saint. A son, Wallace, is on his way home from the Swiss mission, where he has been for over two years.

Washington County News
April 14, 1900

Washington County News
April 14, 1900

HARMONY.

The new meeting house is so far completed that services are held in it.

Joseph Prince was among conference visitors from Harmony.

John Kinsley and Peter Anderson, of Toquerville, were visiting friends here on the 4th inst., while enroute to Salt Lake City to take in conference.

Snow fell here to the depth of three inches on the 4th inst. Not much grain has been planted this year on account of scarcity of water. Apricots and some peaches were frozen here this spring. Lucerne is up and looks promising. Stock wintered well.

Washington County News
May 12, 1900

Marriage licenses were issued by County Clerk Miles Tuesday to James Z. Naegle and Miss Anniss Jackson, both of Toquerville, and to Joseph W. Prince and Miss Vivian Pace, both of Harmony. Both couples were married in the Temple here.

Iron County Record
July 10, 1903

Over at Harmony the grass hoppers are damaging crops considerably in the fields, and at Little Pinto they are devouring the grass crop to an alarming extent and threaten to take the corn.

Iron County Record
July 14, 1903

HARMONY.

July 14, 1903.

At the school election held on the 13th, L. A. Pace was chosen to fill the vacancy in the school board.

A meeting was held here Tuesday for the purpose of incorprating the water.

Mrs. Rees Davis presented her husband with a new girl on the 10th. Mother and child are progressing satisfactorily but no hopes are entertained for the recovery of the father.

Gottleib Schmutz and Lorenzo Prince have gone to Panguitch for lumber.

Iron County Record
February 6, 1904

The Record extends sympathy to Mr. and Mrs. Henry Eddards, whose infant child died Thursday night.

Mr. R. A. Kerker and James Russel of the Harmony Coal mine passd through town this week on their way to Salt Lake City on business connected with the acquiring title to the coal land.

Bishop Wm. A. Redd of Harmony, who went to Canada a few weeks since accompanied by his son, for the purpose of locating a new home, returned a few days since. The bishop was surprised upon reaching Raymond to find that spring work was in active operation, and that farmers were busy in he fields. He at once made arrangements to take a hand and bought two or three hundred acres of land, a couple of good teams and suitable eqippage and set his son to work on his new holding, returning himself to settle up buisness in Harmony, preparatory to a permanent move. The bishop says that although the temperature has been tolerably low in that section during the past winter stock has lived out on the range the whole of the time, and there has been very little loss. A few of the new settlers have lost some stock through attempting to keep their animals up withomut being well prepared, but the older settlers who turned their animals out on the range have had no loss to speak of. The animals that have wintered out look as well this spring as the animals here did last fall.

ENOCH N. NAEGLE DEAD.

Bright Young Man of Toquerville Cut Down in Prime of Life— Biographical.

[Dixie Advocate.]

The many friends and acquaintances of Elder Enoch N. Naegle will read with surprise the announcement of his death, which occurred at his home Sunday night the 8th inst., of septic-malarial fever, after an illness of six weeks duration.

Elder Naegle is the son of Patriarch John C. and Regula B. Naegle and the youngest of his mother's children.

When a boy he removed with his parents to Mexico and returned to Utah to attend the Brigam Young academy at Provo and also the St. George Stake academy, and was well and favorably known among the teachers and students of these institutions.

At the age of twenty he left for a mission to Germany and Switzerland where he labored diligently for two years and nine months, and was one of the six of his father's family laboring in the Swiss and German mission at the same time. Shortly after his return from this mission he married Miss Lenora Taylor of New Harmony, and three children have been born to them, the youngest dying last July.

About three years ago Brother Naegle and his family removed to Emery county, locating at Price City, where he soon became very popular and was chosen to the positions of Stake secretary of Sunday schools, secretary of the 101 quorum of Seventies and teacher in the Theological department of the Price Sunday school. While faithfully performing the duties of these offices he received the ordination of High Priest under the hands of President R. G. Miller, J. H. Pace and Henry Mathis, and set apart as counselor to Bishop Horseley of Price.

One year ago he was released to return here to take charge of the affairs of his brother Joseph R. who had been called to fill a second mission and who left for the Northern States.

At the time of his demise Brother Enoch was in the presidency of the M. I. Association.

While in Mexico Sister Regula Naegle was called to mourn the untimely death of her son Hyrum, who was killed by a bear while out hunting, an account of which appeared in the Deseret News some years ago. Each of these boys were of splendid physique and robust constitution and the wonder is that their careers were so short. Sister Naegle has but two other children, Joseph R. Naegle and Francis R. Harmon. wife of Hon. Levi Harmon of Price, Utah.

Lafe McConnell moved his family yesterday from the residence ercently purchased by L. A. Pace of Harmony to the new Elliker home on Main street.

Iron County Record
October 20, 1905

ANOTHER SPLENDID VEIN.

New 5 foot Body of Coal Encountered in the Harmony Deposits.

R. A. Kirker, manager of the Harmony Coal Company, came in from the properties the first of the week, bringing some fine samples of hard coal from a five foot vein recently cross-cut by tunnel No. 4, three-quarters of a mile south of shaft No. 1, on the Iron county side of the line. The coal is of a splendid quality, suitable for smelting purposes.

One half mile north of shaft No. 2, on vein No. 5, a nine foot vein of splendid clean coal was opened up some little time since, and every week fresh bodies are being blocked out, and the value of the deposits increases accordingly.

The development of the Harmony semi-anthracite coal seems to offer a satisfactory solution for the fuel problem in the manufacture of iron in this county. Half coke and half coal from these deposits will make an ideal fuel for the smelting of iron, and one half the expense of transportation of coke will thus be saved.

The matter seems to be simmering down to this plain fact: Iron county has been endowed by nature with the natural facilities for becoming a great iron manufacturing center, and try as they will, capitalists cannot much longer stave off the inevitable. Somebody is going to take advantage of these resources and enjoy the profits.

If the corporations owning stock in the railroads that benefit by the tariffs on eastern-manufactured iron will not do it, it is only a matter of time until other capitalists will take the plum from between their fingers.

God never placed all these mammoth bodies of natural wealth here for nothing, and it is useless for men to try to stay the hand of Providence.

Iron County Record
June 22, 1906

Mr. Kirker of Harmony has been in Cedar employing men to work on his coal properties of Harmony.

New Harmony is putting in a waterwork system and has the pipe, etc, ready on the ground to go ahead with the work We congratulate the plucky little town for its progressive spirit.

COAL BEDS INSPECT'D

Government Expert Looks Over Southern Utah Field of Limitless Coal.

[SALT LAKE TRIBUNE]

The coal of southwestern Utah has been known since 1854, when the first mine was opened, but its remoteness from any large market has restricted its utilization to the supply of local demands, for which it has long been important. The construction of the San Pedro, Los Angeles & Salt Lake railroad has, however, brought transportation facilities within thirty-five miles of the important out crops, and a branch line from this road to the principal mines could easily be built Such railroad lines are said to have been surveyed, but no construction work has been done. The coal is in Colob plateau, east of Cedar City and Kanarrville and west of the plateau in the eastern slopes of Pine Valley mountain, near New Harmony.

The structure of the region is such that some of the coal crops out in precipitous cliffs bordering the plateau, 300 feet or more above the plains to the west, and some of it is exposed at the bottoms of canyons and near the level of the plains For this reason a knowledge of the geography, the stratigraphy, and the structure of the region is essential to a proper estimate of the value of the coal land With the purpose of gaining such knowledge, Willis T. Lee, one of the geologists of the United States Geological survey, made a reconnaissance survey of this Iron county field in the summer of 1906, visiting the principal coal openings, sampling the coal, and determining the position of the various coal-bearing rocks. A brief preliminary report on this work has just been published by the survey in bulletin No 316, which forms part two of "Contributions to Economic Geology, 1906," and contains the results of the government's investigation of coal, lignite and peat deposits This report may be obtained free of charge by applying to the director of the survey at Washington, D. C.

But little has been done in the Iron county field, partly because the coal has been used only in the small towns located near the outcrop, and partly because it is exposed at the surface at so many points along the outcrop. The workable coal of the plateau is probably all at the same horizon, though thin seams locally occur at several other horizons Mr. Lee calls special attention to the thin bed of limestone, containing many fossils, locally known as "screw shells," which lies about one hundred feet above the coal and is used by prospectors in locating the coal bed. Several prospects have been located in this way where the coal was covered with slide rock.

The first coke ovens in southern Utah were built near one of the mines of this region, and early settlers used the coke for smelting iron, but reports differ as to coking qualities of the coal from different parts of the field.

The proximity of this coal field to deposits of iron ore in the Iron mountains will doubtless prove a most important factor in its future development. The ore is too remote from existing smelters to be profitably utilized at the present time, but the iron properties are rapidly being acquired by large operators, and will eventually be productive It is possible that the coal might be used for smelting the iron ore near the mines The New Harmony coal, particularly, which is a semi-anthracite, may prove satisfactory for this purpose if it can be obtained sufficiently free from impurities This coal differs from the other coals of the region in its position in the lowlands, west of the plateau, and its occurance in several beds of workable thickness .

ELECTRIC RAILROAD

To Connect Coal Mines And Muddy River Settlements With Salt Lake Route.

Word has been received here that a company has been organized and financed in Los Angeles, California, to run an electric railroad from the Muddy river settlements through St. George to the anthracite coal mines near Pinto and New Harmony and thence to a connection with the San Pedro, Los Angeles and Salt Lake railroad. A representative of the company is expected here in a few days to attend to the *preliminary business

While this paper has every reason to believe the company means business, still we are not in a position to vouch for their intentions Should such a railroad go through here it will undoubtedly mean a great deal for the Dixie country. The coal is needed in Los Angeles, and will be shipped out in immense quantities once there is transportation facilities Our fruits will also be shipped out and find a ready market. We will have electric lights and power. Business will boom as never before, our population will be greatly increased, and St. George will be strictly in it. Whether this company put an electric line through or not, a railroad will surely tap this country in the not far distant future.

NEW HARMONY

New Harmony, March 17.—R A. Kirker is in town again after an absence of three months, which he spent in Los Angeles, California, in the interest of the Harmony Coal company. Mr. Kirker states that work will start up again next month at the mine

The weather has been very warm and pleasant the past week, but today is cloudy and looks stormy The men folks are all busy putting in crops

Our district schools closed March 13th with a fine entertainment and dance. All seemed to enjoy themselves

Miss Sadie Imlay has gone to Salt Lake City to visit her sister.

Work has been commenced on Henry A. Pace's new house

NEW HARMONY

New Harmony, March 30 —Lots of visitors in Harmony, Arizona people, Salt Lake people and lots of other people, to give names would take up too much room

House cleaning in full blast. You would think every dooryard was a second-hand furniture store. Had to take a chunk of wood and hunt a shady place to let you know what we were doing

Our sheep shearers are tying up their blankets to hit the trail for Modena this week We will be minus a round dozen big fellows for a month.

Harmony will be well represented at the April conference to be held at the metropolis, quite a number getting ready.

Look out for a big boom here soon, we'll be racing against Virgin, our coal against Virgin oil.

Farmers are about through planting the largest acreage this place has ever known

New Harmony, April 5 —Eight thousand feet of two-inch and one-inch pipe has just been delivered for our new waterworks system. Pipe laying will commence immediately under the superintendance of Judge Kelsey. Although nine tenth of the citizens have the finest wells with the best of waters, they have concluded to tap a fine mountain spring and bring the water right into their homes The next enterprise, electric lights, has been discussed. Nothing ancient about Harmony, just modern.

R A Kirker, the energetic superintendent of the Harmony Anthracite Coal company is getting ready for a summer,s campaign on the company's property; big developments are expected

A number of young ladies have arrived from the south to spend the summer; hope they will find it convenient to become residents in the future

Five men are employed on H A Pace's new eight-roomed house H A. expects to go to housekeeping in the new mansion about July 4.

Cold nights but very pleasant through the day. Gardening in full swing

New Harmony's Good Prospects

Albert Mathis, one of the progress- ive citizens of New Harmony, was in the city the latter part of last week, and left for his home Sunday Mr. Mathis informed our reporter that a party of California capitalists who are interested in the anthracite coal beds near New Harmony had been visiting that section and making tests of the coal, which they pronounced very satisfactory. The visitors are members of the com- pany recently organized to take over and develop the coal beds, and were Messers C T Inman, Peter Alder, F V Wyman and Dr G W Tape After getting such very sat- isfactory tests of the coal, they made some of their plans known, which consist of sinking a double compart- ment shaft and systematically min- ing the coal A railroad is talked of in connection with the coal de- velopment, and work is expected to be started on both propositions as soon as certain preliminaries are arranged The visitors arrived there on the 4th inst and spent some days in their investigations

Mr. Mathis says the new water- works installed at New Harmony is giving the best of satisfaction and is a blessing to the little town He reports general conditions prosper- ous and the outlook bright.

New Harmony, May 25.—At present the railroad from Lund to Harmony is the main topic of conversation We have heard (indirectly) that some of the promoters of the railroad will be at Harmony soon. We also understand that the engineers to survey the road will be here in a few days Prospects seem bright for the cross section to follow soon.

It would surprise some of the people of Southern Utah to know that our little town has the water system, and our women who have drawn water from wells all of their lives appreciate turning the tap in the house

Hyrum B Clark, the cattle buyer from Salt Lake city, has been in town recently contracting for spring and fall delivery of steers, he was also visiting relatives and friends.

Mr. and Mrs S A Pace while visiting at Salt Lake city recently, ordered a full line of goods for Harmony Co-op They had a very pleasant time while there

Harmony young people seem to be making things lively at present. Last Friday evening was spent very pleasantly at the home of Mr. and Mrs Henry A. Pace.

Mr. and Mrs Oren Kelsey and Mr and Mrs Wm P. Taylor are making preparations to go to St. George to work in the temple for a short time

Donald Schmutz returned home Sunday from Cedar city where he has been attending the Branch Normal the past winter

Due to the long spell of cold weather we have had, we are just getting in our late gardens

Mrs Berry Williams is in town visiting relatives.

NEW HARMONY

New Harmony, June 1 —In our last letter we were speaking about the railroad to Harmony, we now hear that the engineers have been delayed for unknown reasons A member of the Cedar City Commercial Club informs us that the Cedar people are doing themselves proud to have a railroad from Lund to Harmony via Cedar, where they expect to tap their coal mine and thus make a great opening in our section of the country

The Misses Viola and Alice Redd are here visiting their Aunt Moreah and other relatives and friends Miss Alice has planned to stop a day or more in Salt Lake city where she expects to go through the Salt Lake temple, after going through it will be permissible to call her Mrs Rich

Misses Annabelle Schmutz and Laverne Taylor, who have been attending the Branch Normal at Cedar city, have returned home We congratulate them on their success

On Sunday May 31, we had primary conference and a very pleasant time was had Pres U T Jones and wife were here and many more from Cedar and Kanarra.

J G Pace of Cedar city was in town lately Mr Pace is in the sheep business and is very busy at present

Some of our town people will be in attendence at court this term at St. George

Commissioner Prince is at St George attending to his official duties

Miss Minnie Pace was hostess at a social given in honor of the Misses Redd,

NEW HARMONY

New Harmony, June 7 —One of the promoters of the Harmony Anthracite Coal Co planned to be in Harmony at this time to begin business, but being unable to get engineers from Salt Lake city, he has been delayed.

Mr and Mrs Henry A Pace entertained the young people at their home Saturday evening Ice cream and cakes were served as refreshments and a pleasant time was the result

Henry A Pace's new building on the corner is nearing completion This building is a credit to Mr Pace and a beauty to the corner and street on which it stands

Miss Effie Pace from Thatcher, Arizona, who has been in Logan for the past winter attending the B Y college, is here spending the summer vacation with her sister

L. A. Pace has gone to St George to attend court Mrs. Pace accompanied her husband to the county seat where she will visit with relatives and friends

Mrs Joseph W Prince is in Cedar city consulting with Dr Robison relative to her health Mrs Prince has been in poor health for some time

The Harmony people will not vote for the weather man any more It is too cold to talk about.

Aaron Bordan, from Ohio, is visiting here with his cousin, Mrs Francis Prince

The Harmony men do not know where to go on account of house cleaning

Mrs Moriah Pace is in Cedar visiting with her son Granville and family.

NEW HARMONY

New Harmony, June 15 —Mrs. Francis Prince in company with her granddaughter, Florence Kelsey, and Mrs Orson Hammond have gone to Price, Carbon Co. on a short visit

Mr. and Mrs Wm P Taylor have returned from St George They report warm weather in Dixie

A committee has been chosen for the Fourth of July, we are looking for a pleasant time.

The farmers are beginning to cut their hay but, due to late frost, the crop is very light.

New Harmony, June 21 —We understand that R A Kirker of this place and I. L Shafer of Chicago, with others have gone to Los Angeles to consummate plans for the railroad and the Harmony Semi Anthracite Coal company

Prof. Tollestrup and company who have been taking a trip through our Dixie towns, give us a pleasant call, and we were highly entertained by their musical ability

We were much disappointed in not having apostles Lyman and Smith call on us

Commissioner Prince has made another trip to St George on official business

Due to the heavy south winds our farmers are unable to haul their hay

Mrs, Ann M. Pace has returned from Cedar

NEW HARMONY

New Harmony, July 5 —The 4th of July passed off very pleasantly The children were delighted in their races, jumping, tug of war and other amusements The young people indulged in a dance in the evening

It sets people wondering when they learn that some of our prominent young men spent the Fourth of July in some of our neighboring towns

A committee has been appointed for the 24th of July. We hope the committee and people will unite in making the celebration a success.

Lawrence Prince, who has been troubled with rheumatism for some time, has gone to the Warm Springs to spend a short time.

Francis Prince has made a trip to Cedar just recently. Mr. Prince has had a tumor taken from his face

NEW HARMONY

New Harmony, July 12 —We notice the farmers are preparing their binders to begin cutting the grain, already some are ready to start. Owing to the backward spring some of our farmers are now finishing up their first crop of hay

This will be a busy week for our people, they will be picking and bottling currants. People from outside settlements are contracting for them, our second crop will be on in about a month

Bp Schmutz and family have returned from Enterprise where they spent an excellent Fourth of July

At present Mrs Ann Moriah Pace is real sick, we hope for her speedy recovery.

We understand that the Harmony Co op has in a nice line of dry goods

NEW HARMONY

New Harmony, July 19 —Dr. Robinson was called to Harmony last Thursday, July 16, to see Mrs Ann Moriah Pace who is seriously ill. He diagnosed Mrs. Pace's condition and was unable to say exactly what the trouble was except a slight attack of bronchitis. At present Mrs. L. A. Pace and Mrs. Eliza Kelsey are nursing her, however, Mrs. Sophia Roundy, a trained nurse of Kanab has been sent for and is expected as soon as it is possible for her to get here

We often hear from Jas. W. Prince who is laboring in the Central States Mission. He is getting along nicely and reports things progressing. We are always glad to hear from our missionaries.

It is very convenient to have telephone communication between Harmony and Lund. J. G. Pace, president of the association sent a message over it just recently

Forest Ranger M L McAllister was here the last of the week on business.

NEW HARMONY

New Harmony, August 3.—Surrounding settlements have been damaged a great deal recently by floods, but we have been very fortunate till Sunday evening, we had a shower bringing down a large stream of water from the canyon north of town. Some damage was done in the way of tearing up fences and washing out dams.

During the severe illness of Mrs. Ann Moriah Pace, her children were called to her bedside. Mrs. Pace is now slowly recovering. Her son, W. W. Pace, returned to his home in Thatcher, Arizona, last Friday. Her two daughters from Idaho are still with her.

Mr. and Mrs Henry A. Pace in company with their neice, La Verna Taylor, have returned from the Kanarra mountain where they have been spending a few days out of the heat

New Harmony, August 9.—Of late much damage has been done by rain and floods. Much hay has been spoiled and large washes have been made in the fields

We understand that L A Pace receives letters regularly from the promoters of the railroad. Everything is moving along nicely.

Mrs Nora Naegle returned to her home in Toquerville yesterday Mrs Naegle has been visiting here for the past week

The Harmony Co-op has just received a nice lot of jewelry, which improves the looks of the show cases

Miss Florence Kelsey has gone to the Kanarra mountains to spend a short time out of the heat

Last Thursday Ashby Pace and Lawrence Prince took a flying trip to Cedar city on business

Harvey A. Pace has had his house repaired recently, it looks much improved

Due to the late rains, the binders have been obliged to stop work.

NEW HARMONY

New Harmony, August 16 —Elders Lngh and Wood from Cedar City were home missionaries in our ward today. Their talk in Sunday School and meeting was highly appreciated. Elder Wood has just recently returned home from a mission in the Central States, his reports of the work in the missionary field are excellent

George Angel of Leeds was here to take his son Charles home   Charles was taken suddenly ill after returning from Cedar.

Mrs. Minnie Blackburn, daughter of Mrs. Ann E Pace, and Irene Rhoner will return to their homes in Idaho.

Our Branch Normal students are making preparations to return to school again in a few weeks

Mrs Moriah Pace is now slowly recovering after several weeks of severe illness.

Our farmers are very busy putting up their second crop of hay.

New Harmony, August 24 —Dr Robinson was called here Saturday to see Mrs Rance, the daughter of A. M. Pace, and pronounced the disease typhoid, all probabilities are she was infected with the disease from nursing her mother who is now recovering from the same.

The farmers are now consulting one another about engaging a threshing machine as they are hauling the grain and it will soon be ready for threshing

Mrs L. A. Pace and Mrs. Eliza Kelsey are attending Mrs. Rance till further help comes, which is expected today.

Commissioner Prince has been complaining some the past week, but at this writing he is much improved

We were much disappointed in not having our home missionaries Sunday.

NEW HARMONY

New Harmony, August 31 —Co Com. Prince and his daughter Eliza Kelsey met met with an accident on their way home from Cedar city recently. They were driving along after dark when one of the clips of the single tree came of and the horses giving a sudden lunge pulled Mr Prince over the dashboard, but the plucky man held to the lines and finally quieted the horses down Then they mounted them and rode into town.

Mr. and Mrs Orin Kelsey and family have returned home from Fairview, where they spent a part of the summer visiting their daughter, Mrs Cox. Mr Kelsey tells us the people of that place are very enterprising

The Y. M and Y L M I A stake officers paid us a visit yesterday and organized the Y. M. Assn and filled vacancies in the Y L Assn

The stork visited the home of Mr. and Mrs Jed Woodward and left a nice baby boy August 30th the parties concerned doing nicely.

NEW HARMONY

New Harmony, Sept 1 —Saturday evening a doctor was called to see Miss Openshaw, who has been here for the past three weeks acting as nurse for Mrs. Rance. Miss Openshaw was attacked with hemorage of the stomach. With careful nursing she will be able to return home in a few days

We are proud to make note that some of our young people are going off to high school: Bert Grant left last Friday to go to Cedar to attend the Branch Normal; Lawrence Prince left last Tuesday to go to Logan, where he expects to attend the A. C College, and Anna Belle and Donald Schmutz expect to leave sometime in the near future to attend the Branch Normal at Cedar City.

Some of our boys and girls who went to the fair at St George have returned and they express themselves as having had an excellent time

We have been visited of late with a little spell of cool weather. Frost has paid us an unusually early visit this year.

Mrs Rance who has been very ill with typhoid is still very bad.

Com. Prince has gone to St George on business

Of late we have had a great demand for fruit.

NEW HARMONY

New Harmony, Sept. 21.—Our cow boys are rounding up their steers preparatory for delivering to Mr. Commerilh the fore part of October.

Bp. Schmutz is making preparation to build a neat picket fence in front of the bishop's office.

At this writing all the sick at the home of Mrs. Ann M. Pace, are slowly recovering.

A number of our people went to Cedar to attend quarterly conference

We are having beautiful weather for putting up our third crop of hay.

NEW HARMONY

New Harmony, Oct. 2 —Cold weather seems to have come to stay. Our third crop of hay is being hauled

S. J. Rance from Idaho, made a recent visit here to see his wife, Mrs Vinnie Rance, who is now recovering from typhoid.

Mrs Delta Hammond left the first of the week to go to Provo, where she expects to pay her daughter a visit.

Mr. and Mrs. Henry A. Pace left this morning for Salt Lake City. We wish them a pleasant time

Le Roy Grant is very ill at present. There has been no decision as to the nature of his illness

Eldon Schmutz who has had a long attack of rheumatizm is now getting better.

FROM OUR FILES OF TEN YEARS AGO

New Harmony correspondence:
James F. Prince and Albert Mathis
left this town at noon on Oct 4th
for the purpose of hunting deer
They camped that evening at a sheep
camp, and started out next morning, leaving their horses in camp
They had arranged to meet at noon
at a specified place in the woods,
but when Mathis arrived there he
did not find Prince Seeing deer
tracks and Prince's footprints leading past the place of appointment,
he concluded Prince was after the
deer and returned to the sheep
camp As Prince had not shown
up next morning, Mathis started
out in search of him He found
Prince lying dead with his gun beside him. No wounds were observable and it is believed he died of
heart failure. His body was brought
in Thursday afternoon, it having to
be carried three miles as there is no
road through the woods. The sad
affair is a severe shock to his wife,
children and relatives

NEW HARMONY

New Harmony, Dec. 21,—On Tuesday, Dec 15th, we had a nice snow storm which lasted about twenty-four hours About fourteen inches fell. Since the storm we have had some very cold weather.

R A. Kirker, Supt of the Harmony Anthracite Coal Co. who has been in Los Angeles for some time on business, returned a few days since He has put some men to work on the coal property.

Our students who have been attending the Branch Normal school are home for a few days They are pleased to be home again for a short time,

The young people of this place are looking forward to a good time during the holidays The committee met and made a program.

Mrs Ann M Pace died at her home on Sunday, November 29th, of general debility

Commissioner Prince has gone to St George to finish his work for the year.

Our New Harmony correspondent states that some men have started work on the coal property there belonging to the Anthracite Coal Co

Washington County News
January 4, 1909

NEW HARMONY

New Harmony, Jan. 1 —Since the cold wave passed by we have had nice spring weather, so much so that some of our people fear that the fruit buds will swell and be caught by another cold wave.

The holidays are a thing of the past The people had a very pleasant time, dancing and social entertainment. Now we will get down to earth again

A meeting is called for tonight to appoint an overseer of our pipe line, which is a success We wish all our neighboring settlements had a water system.

On Dec. 5, 1908, Mrs Sarah P. Davis gave birth to a nice baby girl, and on Dec 15, Mrs J. L Prince gave birth to a nice boy. All are doing nicely.

The school started today The students have had a nice rest and will get down to their work at once

NEW HARMONY

New Harmony, Jan. 11 —Chas. T. Inman and some of his associates in the promotion of the railroad, and owners in the Harmony Anthracite Coal Co , have been here looking over the property. They left Saturday morning via St. George for Los Angeles in good spirits and health The report of conditions of both the coal property and the railroad makes us all feel that there will be something doing in the near future

On Monday, January 4th, we held our pipe line meeting and elected officers for two years, as follows O Kelsey, manager and superintendent, Henry A. Pace, A F. Mathis and Wm P Taylor, the members of the board, L A. Pace, secretary and treasurer

On the 9th inst we had a nice warm rain. On the 10th inst the wind changed to the north and was quite cold

Joseph W. Prince of New Harmony, who recently returned home from a mission in Missouri, was a city visiter Saturday, on business Elder Prince says he enjoyed his mission, and values highly the experience gained in the field.

NEW HARMONY

New Harmony, Jan 17 —Some if not all of the Harmony people ask what is the reason we can't have a more direct mail route from here to St George. We think we could get a route from Cedar to St George by asking for it and with the support of the county papers

The party that left here for Los Angeles via St George arrived home all right but had a hard trip from St. George to Modena. Mr. Ramey, one of the party interested in the coal property and the railroad, writes us they got home o k. but very tired.

Spring weather. The snow is gone but we have plenty of mud; the frost is out of the ground and if this kind of weather continues, the farmers will soon be ploughing

The good housewives of our town are wondering what is the matter with some of our grist mills in the south, nearly every one of them complaining of sticky flour.

Mr. Kirker the manager of the Harmony Anthracite Coal Co is contracting for mining timber for the various tunnels and shafts

Prohibition is one of the talks on the streets, by the fireside and anywhere we get together.

NEW HARMONY

New Harmony, Jan 24 —A little excitement was created in this town the other night. The constable was attending a business meeting when in came the justice of the peace with a warrant for the arrest of a man who had been marking some sheep which did not belong to him. The constable immediately left to serve the warrant but his man had fled and although the constable followed him for more than twenty-four hours he escaped

Mrs Sadie Christensen of Twin Falls, Idaho, has been here for some time. She left for her home Friday morning, the young people giving her a very pleasant surprise prior to her departure

On Thursday the 21st inst we had a very heavy downpour of rain, every gulley was full, and old settlers say it was the wildest night they had known in the place

Encouraging word is received from the Los Angeles people about the coal property here and the railroad.

NEW HARMONY

New Harmony, January 31—On Monday, January 25th, Albert F. Mathis of. this place was on the desert looking after his sheep He went to put the blanket on one of his horses when the horse whirled and kicked Mathis' long absence caused the boys to go and see what was the matter. He was found lying in a pool of blood unconscious The boys got him into the sheep wagon and did all they knew how to do He was taken to Cedar where Dr Robison took twelve stitches in the wound. The doctor said a half inch lower would have broken his jaw, and a half inch higher would have struck in the temple and killed him At this writing he is getting along as well as can be expected.*

Saturday, the 30th, William Chinn met with a painful accident He was topping a large tree, and cut one limb off which knocked him out of the tree, fifteen feet or more. He is able to be out today on crutches and thinks he will be alright in a day or two

Jacob Duel of Idaho is here on a visit to see his mother, Mrs. M. O Woolsey. Mr. Duel tells us there are lots of people coming in all the time from the central states and settling in the state of Idaho

The sheep men say the sheep are doing fine this winter. The prospect for good prices for wool in the spring are good. Some have contracted their wool in the spring at a good figure

Mrs Delta Hammond has undergone an operation for some kind of a growth between her shoulders. She is getting along fairly well now

The committee on entertainment has made a nice program to be given on Washington's birthday

App. State School Fund

Apportionment of State School Fund of Washington Co , Jan 23, 1909. Springdale, school population 54, $162, Rockville, school population 88, $264, Grafton, school population 31, $94; Virgin City, school population 46, $138, Toquerville, school population 94, $282, La Verkin, school population 49, $147; Hurricane, school population 77, $231, Leeds, school population 50, $150, Washington, school population 180, $510. St George, school population 578, $1734, Bloomington, school population 17, $51;

Santa Clara, school population 103, $309, Gunlock, school population 42, $126, Pine Valley, school population 74, $222, Enterprise, school population 93, $279, Pinto, school population 21, $63, New Harmony, school population 37, $111.

Total school population 1634, total amount $4902

WILLARD O NISSON,
County Supt

NEW HARMONY

New Harmony, February 7—On Saturday the 6th inst three or four of our townspeople left here for Lund to assist in surveying the railroad from the Lund Station to this place. If it is storming there like it is here the progress will be slow.

Reese Davis came in last week with a load of Oregon shingles for his new house. He reports the roads very bad

A nice picket fence has been put in front of the bishop's office

Railroad Survey Started

The survey on the railroad from Lund to New Harmony is in progress. This is the railroad which is proposed to connect St George, the eastern settlements, Cedar City and Parowan with the Salt Lake Route at Lund

Bunkerville reports almond trees in bloom.

NEW HARMONY

New Harmony, February 28— Miss Ruth Whipple, who has been here since last November working for Mrs. L A. Pace, has returned to her home in Pine Valley. She had word that she had a new baby brother and was anxious to see him.

The surveying party surveyed the railroad close to our town and then went back home

Washington County News
March 7, 1909

NEW HARMONY

New Harmony, March 7.—Quite a number of our people have made applications for farming land on the east of town. They are interested in the dry farming plan

Reese Davis has the roof on his new house, which is quite an improvement to the corner

We hear from Elder Joseph W. Prince regularly; he is doing good work in the mission field.

NOTICE TO WATER USERS

State Engineer's Office,
Salt Lake City, Utah,
February 2, 1909

Notice is hereby given that Albert F. Mathis, whose post office address is New Harmony, Utah, has made application in accordance with the requirements of Chapter 108, Session Laws of Utah, 1905, as amended by the Session Laws of Utah, 1907, to appropriate ten (10) cubic-feet per second of water from Harmony Canyon Creek, Washington County, Utah. Said water will be diverted by means of a dam and a canal, at a point which lies 1,000 feet south of the north east corner of the south east quarter of Section 20, Township 38 south, Range 13 west, Salt Lake base and meridian and conveyed for a distance of 13,200 feet and there used whenever available during the period from January 1 to December 31, inclusive, of each year, to irrigate 160 acres of land embraced in Section 23, Township 38 south, Range 13 west, Salt Lake base and meridian. This application is designated in the State Engineer's office as No 1903.

All protests against the granting of said application, stating the reasons therefor, must be made by affidavit in duplicate and filed in this office within thirty (30) days after the completion of the publication of this notice   CALEB TANNER,
State Engineer.

Date of first publication February 11; date of completion of publication March 13, 1909.

NEW HARMONY

New Harmony, March 14 —President U. T. Jones, of the Parowan stake, and wife were here to visit us A very good meeting was had. his subject was "Be Good to All," and he quoted many remarks of the Savior on this subject.

The cold wave which lasted four or five days is past and we have nice weather now. Our farmers are farming

The cow boys tell us stock have wintered fairly well this winter

New Harmony, March 23 — Those who attended the quarterly conference at Cedar City report a very pleasant time. Minnie Pace, being one of them, reports Prof. Hickman's talk one of the talks of the conference,

Our boys who took up so much dry land east of town are anxiously waiting for the wire to arrive, they have the posts set now.

Ashby Pace met with an accident the other day by sticking a pitchfork in his foot; he will be able to be out in a few days.

Since our last report we have had lots of rain and snow; at this writing the ground is bare but very muddy.

Lurene P. Taylor has been confined to her room for some days but now is much improved

The sheep shearers are preparing to start to Modena soon

Assessor Harrison called to see us last week.

NEW HARMONY

New Harmony, April 11, 1909— Charles T. Inman and party are here finishing up the railroad survey which Mr. Weber left some time since. Mr. Inman talks like the road will be put through in the near future They intend running the line from Lund to Harmony via Cedar City The commercial club of Cedar has promised them a right of way and depot grounds in the city, which is now located The party will leave here for Los Angeles via St. George as soon as they get through the survey which will take them two or three days yet to finish

Our school is progressing nicely. It will be out some time in May. The students are anxiously waiting for Arbor day (15th) to set trees out

The past week was very cold, killing most of our apricots, but the other fruit was not far enough advanced to be injured much.

Our young people are figuring on having an ice cream party tonight in honor of Easter Sunday.

NEW HARMONY

New Harmony, April 18 —Arbor day was observed nicely here. Miss Minnie Pace, the school teacher, was out with her students planting trees and shrubs on the school grounds. The students thoroughly enjoyed the planting of their trees It so happened that the order placed with the nursery at Provo was delivered early on the morning of the 15th, so the town people as well as the students were busy planting trees

Mr. A J. McAdams of the U. S Geological Survey called to see the coal fields just north of town. He was very pleased with the showing He too thinks we need a railroad to develop the vast coal and iron fields of southern Utah.

We have had nice weather the last three or four days

NEW HARMONY

New Harmony, April 26 —Four teams loaded with barbed wire, for fencing the land taken up east of town, and merchandise for the Co-op store will be in Monday.

Henry A Pace is having some rock work done on a nice cellar.

California is proving a very profitable market for potatoe growers at Pinto and nearby settlements, which have been shipping potatoes this spring. When the new railroad is completed to Harmony, this branch of farming will receive a big impetus

Mr McAdams of the U. S Geological Survey, arrived here last Thursday, from San Francisco, on official business, and left for the Virgin oil field Friday. Mr. McAdams spent some little time at the New Harmony coal fields en route here, and will spend several days at the oil field.

NEW HARMONY

New Harmony, May 2 — W D Owen, the Z. C. M. I. dry goods salesman, and son, Ruben, are spending Sunday with us They spoke very nicely in Sunday school and in the afternoon meeting They expect to do business with the Co op store Monday, then start for St George via Pinto and Pine Valley.

The changable weather has caused bad colds and lagrippe, but at this writing there is much improvement in the health of the people.

We have had some very cold weather for this time of the year; we fear lots of our fruit has been killed.

Francis Prince has been feeling poorly for some time but is feeling much better at this writing

NEW HARMONY

New Harmony, May 16 — On Tuesday, May 11th, Jack Frost put the finishing touch on our fruit. We will have very little fruit this year, so we will depend on our friends in the sunny south to grow some for us.

Our sheep shearers have returned and report a very prosperous shearing The sheep men too feel well paid for their hard work for the last year.

Our school closed Friday the 14th, some of the students thought it was a long term (seven months)

Some of our people still have the grip

Washington County News
May 20, 1909

Albert Mathis, the New Harmony sheep man, arrived in the city last evening, on business.

Washington County News
May 23, 1909

NEW HARMONY

New Harmony, May 23.—Francis Prince and his grandson, J. L Prince, have closed out their stock business J. L figures on going to Idaho to look for a new home.

Wm R Williams of Kanarra was here last week with a load of goods for Harmony Co-op He will be in today with another load for the store

House cleaning is the order of the times Miss Ruth Whipple of Pine Valley is here helping Mrs L A Pace clean house.

M. L McAllister, one of the forest range riders, was here last week doing business with the stock men.

Henry Mathis, one of our aged townsmen, is quite sick with grip

Harvey A. Pace is having a new porch put in front of his house.

The cold weather hangs on well with us

New Harmony News

New Harmony, May 30—The Normal students have returned and report having had a profitable year at high school

Clinton and Vivian Milne of St George have been here the past week painting and papering for L A Pace

Our cowboys have gone to the winter range to round up their cattle and take them to the summer range

Mrs. Amelia Schmutz has been confined to her room for several days with the grip, she is improving

New Harmony Has A Good Lamb Crop

New Harmony, June 13.—Our sheep men are busy marking lambs and getting their flocks on the summer range. They all seem well pleased with their lamb crop this spring.

The hum of the mowing machine is heard now, everybody is getting ready for the first crop of hay, which is about average.

L A. Pace has a number of teams hauling hay from his ranch to Modena and Lund.

Miss Minnie Pace left on the 11th inst for Salt Lake City to attend summer school.

Mrs Mary Pace of Price, Carbon county, is here visiting friends and relatives

John W. Prince of Price, Carbon Co , is visiting relatives here.

New Harmony Railroad Encouragement

New Harmony, June 21—Apostle Richards and President Jones held meeting with us on Tuesday of last week. We had a good time and all who were at the meeting felt well paid for coming out. The apostle's plan is to visit all the settlements in the Parowan stake on his return trip to Salt Lake City.

We have encouraging reports about our railroad. Mr. Inman, the president of the company, was called to Los Angeles by wire on important business, so did not get as far south as he had planned. He expects to be with us soon again

Iron County Record
June 25, 1909

James B. Neilson of Monroe, and Emma A. Grant of New Harmony, were married by the County Clerk in his office on the 21st, Inst.

New Harmony Couple Have Started Right

New Harmony, June 27—James D Neilson jr. from Monroe and Miss Emma A. Grant of this place were married at the court house, Parowan They gave a dance the following Friday and a very enjoyable time was had, people from Pine Valley, Kanarra and other places taking part in the enjoyment.

The committee for the Fourth of July has a nice program prepared, and we anticipate a good time.

A wedding reception in honor of David H. Cannon, 3rd, and Miss Susana Wooley, married in the temple Wednesday, was held at the home of Pres. D H. Cannon last evening A large number of relatives and friends of the young couple were present and an enjoyable time was had. *

New Mail Route Pleases New Harmony

New Harmony, July 5 —Wm P. Taylor, one of our townsmen, got the contract to carry the mail from here to Leeds, so in the future we will have a direct route from here to St. George and up the river which is very pleasing to us

On Saturday, the 3rd, we had an electric storm which cooled the atmosphere a little. One of L A Pace's milch cows was killed by the lightening close to town.

The fore part of last week was extremely hot, some of our men in the hay field were nearly overcome by the heat.

Our celebration is going on very nicely today. We had a good time at the meeting this morning.

Typhoid Fever At New Harmony

New Harmony, July 19.—We are having some sickness in town now. there are three cases of developed typhoid fever and a number of others have symptoms of the fever. Mrs. Ann Taylor, wife of Independence Taylor, is critically ill at this time with a complication of diseases.

We hear the hum of the binder these days   Our crop of small grain is fairly good this year.   Our second crop of hay is being cut now, and bids fair for a good yield

We have had two or three nice little showers which have cooled the atmosphere off a little

Typhoid Fever Epidemic At New Harmony

New Harmony, July 27.—Our typhoid fever cases are not abating any, we now have nine cases. Dr. Woodruff thinks it wise to have a public meeting and locate, if possible, the cause of the fever. Dr. Woodbury was phoned to and given the symptoms, he, like Dr. Woodruff, pronounced it typhoid fever. We are at a loss to know where it comes from. There are a few more cases that have the appearance of the fever. We think it time that some move is made in the matter. We sent water to Mr Harms, the state chemist, and he will tell us soon whether or not it is in the water.

Miss Minnie Pace returned from summer school last Saturday. She tells us that the school is the largest summer school ever held in Salt Lake City.

We don't take kindly to having our WASHINGTON COUNTY NEWS go via Modena when it can come direct to us via Leeds.

On account of the sickness in our town, the 24th was not observed in a great time.

Hurricane and New Harmony correspondence was received by the News this (Thursday) morning—too late for insertion in this issue. Our New Harmony correspondent says there are now nine cases of typhoid in that town, he also complains about the News being sent via Modena instead of Leeds

Washington County News
August 2, 1909

Mrs. Anna Taylor Dies At New Harmony

New Harmony, August 2 —Today at 10 a. m funeral services were held, at the meeting house, over the remains of Mrs Anna Taylor, who died on Saturday, July 31, with a complication of diseases. One bad feature about the affair is she had a son and a daughter down with typhoid fever who could not be present.

We think the typhoid fever is abaiting a little. Dr. Woodruff will be here today to see Mrs Oscar Hammond, who is confined to her bed with a complication of diseases.

Typhoid Fever Abateing At New Harmony

New Harmony, August 9.—The typhoid fever is abateing. There are no new cases and the report today is that all the sick are improving.

Mr. Roundy was here unloading goods for the Co op this week, he reports some very heavy rains on the desert between Iron Springs and Lund.

We had a downpour of rain on Thursday, tho 5th, which cooled the atmosphere and makes us all feel better.

Our harvesting is done and the binders put away for the year. Our grain crop is good this season

FLIES THE CAUSE

Of The Typhoid Fever Epidemic At New Harmony—State Will Send Bacteriologist

With a population of only 100 people, the report comes to the state board of health that New Harmony, near Cedar City, in Washington county, has twenty-two cases of typhoid fever, with one reported death Thursday afternoon Dr T. B Beatty of the state board of health stated that in July there were a few cases of typhoid in the town, but that there was no epidemic at that time.

The cause of the epidemic, as near as can be learned from the slight information at hand, is flies. According to Dr. Beatty, the cases are not limited to the people who use flowing well water or to those who use pipe water, but are scattered indiscriminately from one house to the other Dr. Beatty said Thursday. "As near as I can learn from the slight information at hand, the epidemic has been caused by flies In the few cases which were reported during July, there could not have been proper disinfection. With the coming of hot weather and the accumulation of decayed matter, the flies have become thick, and have carried the typhoid bacilli from one home to another This is but a slight example of the great danger from flies, and the great necessity of keeping them from the home and also disinfecting all refuse matter."

Dr. John Sundwall, who at the present time is in Kanab, has been communicated with, and will go to the typhoid stricken city and give relief to the citizens.—Intermountun Republican

New Harmony Has Pure Water

New Harmony is afflicted with a typhoid fever epidemic, now fortunately abating, which has puzzled the inhabitants to account for, as the little town has good sanitary arrangements and believed they had the purest drinking water that could be obtained. They used to depend upon wells for water, and the place always had an excellent bill of health until the present epidemic About a year ago the enterprising little hamlet put in a waterworks system, piping the water from springs into the houses To ascertain if this water was the source of the typhoid, samples were sent to State Chemist Herman Harms at Salt Lake City by Mr. L A Pace of New Harmony. Passing over the technicalities of the analysis, we here print the summary of the Professor's findings, as follows·

"This water contains a rather small amount of solids consisting of the ordinary water constituents Calcium Chloride, Magnesium Chloride, Free Acids, Free Alkalies, Metallic Impurities and other objectionable impurities are entirely absent

"Organically Considered· The water is of 'ordinary purity.' No Nitrates or Nitrites are present. The amounts of Free and Albuminoid Ammonia as well as Oxygen Consumed are quite low. The residue does not emit a foreign odor upon gentle ignition, neither does it cinder, char or blacken The amount of Chlorine, respectively, Sodium Chloride is very small.

"All of the above tests amply confirm that no contamination by sewage, sepinge, drainage or other sources of pollution has taken place

"The water is bright, practically odorless and a pleasant taste, in brief, inviting to eye and palate

"From the above detailed examination, I am forced to the conclusion that the water submitted is 'perfectly safe and fit' for all culinary and drinking purposes, in fact, it forms a desirable one for domestic and technical purposes"

Thus Professor Harms does away with the fear that the typhoid exists in the drinking water at New Harmony, the water being pronounced as "bright, practically odorless, in brief, inviting to the eye and palate." The water being pure, and the surroundings good from a sanitary point of view, there is but one conclusion to arrive at as the cause of the epidemic, and that is flies.

Flies Not Numerous At New Harmony

New Harmony. August 15 — We have no new cases of typhoid. We have had one death here this summer. The cause of Mrs. Taylor's death was a complication of diseases, the main cause being heart failure. Mrs. Taylor has had a weak heart for years. Those who were closely related to her were not surprised at her death. We note from two or three pieces in the News that the cause of our sickness is flies. The people from out side settlements get the impression that we are carried away with flies. We have this to say: Our sanitary conditions were never better. People from the north say you people have only a few flies compared to what we have in Parowan, Cedar and other places. Traveling men from the south say we are glad to get away from the flies in Dixie, so there must be some other cause for the fever besides flies. We invite the people to come and see our sanitary conditions and see if we do not compare favorably with any town or city in the state. We will be very pleased to see Dr. John Sundwall whom Doctor Beatty is going to send to investigate the cause of the fever in our little town. We venture that when he comes he will not say that flies are entirely responsible for the fever. There is a cause somewhere besides the flies and when the doctor comes we hope he can locate it. From the reports, the people got the idea that we are a class of people that are too lazy to fight flies and sit down and let them carry us off bodily.

[Regarding what our correspondent says about the News attributing the cause of the typhoid at New Harmony to flies, we refer our correspondent to the articles in question and he will find that they were extracted from other papers. The disease is not caused by flies, they simply carry the germs from infected persons or places, and the number of flies cuts no figure in the matter, one fly being able to carry enough germs to infect a number of people. The less flies, however, there are the safer the people will be. There was no intention to convey the impression that New Harmony was not a perfectly clean little town, for according to our best information it is decidedly above the average of its size.—Ed.]

Miss Openshaw, a trained nurse from Parigoonah, is here with us. She thinks all the sick are improving. Dr. Woodruff, too, is quite encouraged at the conditions that exist at this time.

Carlisle Kelsey, son of Mr. and Mrs. Orin Kelsey, has been ill for some time; at this writing he is a little better.

We had a little shower last night which is pleasing to all.

Typhoid at Harmony Under Perfect Control

Dr. T. B Beatty of the state board of health received information from Dr. J. L. Woodruff of Cedar City, Utah, who has been attending the cases of typhoid at New Harmony, that the disease is practically under control. The infection, as the doctor had suspected, was caused by flies. The disease had its first origin from waste matter which had been dumped into the yards of houses where the disease had existed the previous year. The patients who have the disease at the present time have been screened from all possible contact with flies by means of wire netting and mosquito netting.—Herald-Republican.

Carlisle Kelsey Dies at New Harmony

New, Harmony, August 29.—
Thursday about 11 a m, Carlisle
Kelsey, of whom mention has been
made, died of typhoid and an acute
attack of appendicitis. All that
willing hands could do was done for
him. Funeral services were held at
the residence Friday afternoon.
The speakers were H. A. Pace,
Francis Prince and G Schmutz,
who spoke words of consolation to
those bereft of a bright son and
brother.

Dr. Woodruff will be here today
and hold a public meeting with our
Harmony folks; we look for a good
medical talk.

New Harmony Has Big Flood

New Harmony, September 5 —
Mrs. Minnie Pace Blackburn of Idaho Falls, Idaho, and her sister Vinnie Pace Rance of Sugar City, Idaho, are here visiting relatives and
friends and seeing to some business.

On Wednesday, Sept. 1, James
L. Prince with his wife and children were returning from Dixie with
a load of fruit. There was a large
flood at the crossing of north Ash
creek, and as Mr. Prince was driving across the flood the front wheel
struck a large boulder which threw
the little boy off from his mother's
lap and had she not had hold of his
clothes the little fellow would have
been thrown into the raging torrent.
The flood did much damage here
washing away fences, bridges, land,
etc.

Washington County News
September 9, 1909

Francis Prince of New Harmony
was in the city the latter part of last
week. He reports that his section
of country has had two weeks steady
rain, causing damages but to no
very serious extent. He left Sunday for return home, going by
Washington to visit relatives there

Washington county News
September 19, 1909

Every Body Busy
At New Harmony

New Harmony, Sept. 19.—Our
farmers are very busy these days
hauling corn, getting up the third
crop of hay, hauling grain, and preparing to get their winter supply of
coal from the mountain. The cow
boys are busy rounding up the steers
to be delivered the latter part of the
month.

Typhoid fever is about a thing of
the past. The patients are walking
around and the houses are being
fumigated so in a few days everything here will be moving along as
quietly as it ever did.

John W. Prince of Carbon county
is here assisting in gathering range
stock to be delivered the fore part
of next month.

Francis Prince and his grandson,
J. L. Prince, are closing out their
range stock.

New Harmony Desires Health Officer

New Harmony, Sept. 26.—Typhoid fever is about a thing of the past. Fumigating and house cleaning is the main business now; in our fumigating we have no health officer to direct the business, the health officer having gone to Cedar to do for her children while they attend the Branch Normal. If we had some one of experience to direct the fumigating we think it would be well.

Our school will start on Monday, the 27th. Miss Minnie Pace, the teacher, is anxious to get down to her teaching again.

Some of our young men are a little nervous about being asked what thought of receiving a letter from Box B.

We have been very busy the past week hauling hay and grain, but today we are having another rain

Will some of the correspondents to the NEWS tell us how to measure the rainfall?

The students at the Normal are registered and getting down to their work.

_____

We had a very heavy rain and hail storm, accompanied by thunder and lightning, last Saturday. Since then it rained more or less every day until Wednesday, when it turned out bright and clear, and we now have ideal Dixie weather. The rain will be of great benefit to the range

Harmony News

New Harmony, Oct. 17.—Leroy Grant of this place and Miss Mary Prince of Washington were married in the Salt Lake temple on the 8th. Their many friends are congratulating them.

We are very busy these days threshing grain, digging potatoes, etc. The new threshing machine is doing fine work this fall.

We are pleased to say we are holding Sunday school and meeting again after being discontinued for about three months.

New Harmony News

New Harmony, Nov. 9.—Today we are having a heavy rainstorm, the first rain for some months. We are very busy hauling coal and wood these days so when winter sets in we will be prepared for the cold weather.

Mrs Francis Prince has just returned from a trip to California, where she had been visiting her sister. Mrs. Prince had a very pleasant time and reports everything very pleasant in her travels.

Mrs. Vina Pace Throp of Thatcher, Arizona, is here visiting with her sister, Mrs. Vivian Pace Prince, and her mother, L. A. Pace. Mrs Thorp came on a business trip and to call on her relatives.

Lots Of Snow At New Harmony

New Harmony, Nov. 13—Heber C. Smith, state food inspector, from Salt Lake City, called on us the other day and gave us some very good talk about disinfecting our houses to prevent the typhoid fever from breaking out again next summer. *

We are having a snow storm today. The snow is now about ten inches deep. We hope the storm will not interfere with the Governor and party coming to see us.

Mr. Brown and family, from Arkansas, have come to make their home with us. They all feel well with their new friends and aquaintances.

W. D. Owen, Z. C. M. I's. genial traveling man, called and sold a nice little bill of goods to the Co-op store.

Our school teacher is desirous to hear the instructors of the U. of U. and will be at the institute.

New Harmony News

New Harmony, Dec. 5.—The Stake presidency and the Stake Supt. of Sunday schools are with us today. Their instructions were timely and we hope to profit by them.

Some of our towns people are making improvements in their dwellings by having them lined with adobies and plastered.

We are having a snow storm today and it bids fair for lots of snow.

John Condie's babe is on the road to recovery.

New Harmony News

New Harmony, Dec. 26 —Elder Joseph W. Prince returned last week from a mission to the Southern States. He is in good spirits and health. A welcome home was given him and a very pleasant time was had.

We understand that some of our people are putting bids to carry the mail from here to Toquerville and other places

We had about fourteen inches of snow last week. At this writing the weather is clear and cold.

Our students from the Normal are pleased to be home again.

Our holidays bid fair to be very pleasant.

Mr. and Mrs. Reece Davis and Mr. and Mrs. Berry Williams of Harmony were holiday visitors, the guests of Mr. and Mrs. J. L. Workman.

Heavy Snow, Harmony

New Harmony, Jan. 2—We have had two days rain, which melted the snow and caused much damage to our farms. The floods carried away much of our farming land. At this writing it is snowing and bids fair to be a heavy storm.

J. W. Clark of Springville, one of the Indian war veterans, has been here to visit with his sister, Mrs L A. Pace. He related some very interesting stories of his experiences in early times in Utah.

Our holidays passed off very nicely. Dancing was the principal amusement. People from Kanarra, Pine Valley, Toquerville and other settlements were with us to spend the holidays.

The students attending the normal have gone back to school; they think the time short at home this year.

New Harmony Notes

New Harmony, Jan 23—Mrs Peter Anderson is spending the winter with relatives and friends at Manti, her former home

The stock on the range have wintered fine, there being but very little loss so far.

The county road has been sufficiently repaired to make them passable

Several teams will leave in a few days for Lund for flour.

New Harmony

New Harmony, Jan. 30—John A. Mathis of Price, Carbon county, has been here visiting with his brother, Albert John H. Pace and Joseph and John W. Prince of the same place are here visiting their parents and friends. They report the Price people getting along very well, but lots of cold weather this winter

H. A Pace has a new porch in front of his house, which improves the looks of it very much

Reese Davis, Ashby Pace and Lawrence Prince have gone to Parowan for lumber.

Washington County News
February 13, 1910

New Harmony Notes

New Harmony, Feb 13.—President Lincoln's birthday passed off very nicely with us Horse racing, foot racing and other sports was the order of the day, and a good ball in the evening wound up the day's amusements

The Relief society gave a dance one night last week, with ice cream and cake Parties from Pine Valley, Kanarra and other places were with us.

Miss Cornelia Whipple of Pine Valley is here helping Mrs L A Pace in her house work.

Reese Davis and wife have gone to St George to work in the temple a week or two.

Washington County News
February 22, 1910

Mr and Mrs Reese Davis left for their home at New Harmony last Friday after spending about a week here doing Temple work.

Washington County News
February 27, 1910

New Harmony Loses An Aged Resident

New Harmony, Feb 27—Catherine Bruppacher, wife of Benjamin Bruppacher, died here of old age. She was past eighty years old. She died as she lived, faithful in the church. She leaves a husband to mourn her loss

We have had a very cold wave pass over us the last two or three days. There is an epidemic of coughs and colds taking the rounds. Everybody is coughing, especially the children, but none seriously ill.

The little child of Mr. and Mrs John Condie got bye the other day. At this writing he is getting along as well as can be expected.

Washington's birthday was fittingly observed here

NOTICE TO WATER USERS

State Engineer's Office,
Salt Lake City, Utah,
February 9, 1910.

Notice is hereby given that Robert Addison Kirker, Agent, whose post-office address is New Harmony, Utah, has made application in accordance with the requirements of the Compiled Laws of Utah, 1907, as amended by the Session Laws of Utah, 1909, to appropriate one fifth (1-5) of a cubic foot per second of water from Harmony Creek, Washington County, Utah. Said water will be diverted at a point which bears south 7 degrees 45 minutes west 2,850 feet from the southwest corner of the southwest quarter of Section 32, Township 37 south, Range 13 west, Salt Lake base and meridian, from where it will be conveyed by means of a canal and flume for a distance of 350 feet and there used during the period from January 1 to December 31, inclusive, of each year, for steam raising purposes in connection with the operation of the coal mines near New Harmony, Utah. As a secondary purpose, as much of said water as may be necessary will be used for domestic purposes during the entire year. This application is designated in the State Engineer's office as No. 2510.

All protests against the granting of said application, stating the reasons therefor, must be made by affidavit in duplicate and filed in this office within thirty (30) days after the completion of publication of this notice. CALEB TANNER,
State Engineer.

Date of first publication February 24, 1910, date of completion of publication March 26, 1910.

New Harmony News

New Harmony, March 6—Thomas Brown, from Arkansas, has bought the house and lot of James Russell, and will take possession this week.

Some of our young people went to Kanarra last week to see a horse race between the Harmony horse and the Kanarra mare Kanarra came off victorious.

Mrs Vivian Prince, wife of Joseph W. Prince, has been confined to her room for a few days but at this time she is much improved

Our farmers are busy these days putting their small grain in.

Harmony News Notes

New Harmony, March 21—Our farmers are very busy these days, they have the most of their small grain in; now they are very busy clearing the brush from the new land east of town for corn and potatoes The prospects for a grain and fruit crop are bright at this time. A nice rain would be very acceptable now.

John Whipple from Pine Valley is a visitor in our town this week

Our sheep shearers are preparing to start to Modena soon.

A. F. Mathis has just returned from a business trip in Nevada.

Washington County News
April 4, 1910

New Harmony Notes

New Harmony, April 4 — R. A. Kirker has just returned from a business trip to Salt Lake. He brings encouraging talk about a railroad through our country.

Dr. Robison was called to the bedside of Mrs Joseph W Prince. Mrs. Prince is some better but will necessarily have to go to Cedar for farther treatment.

Miss Maggy Pace of Price, Carbon Co, is here visiting her aged father Harvey A. Pace. She brings word that the people in that section are prospering.

Fighting House Fly At New Harmony

New Harmony, April 11—Teams are going to Cedar now after lime. We are cleaning up the back yards and other places and we are going to fight the house fly this summer in earnest.

Invitations were received by a number of our townspeople to attend the wedding reception at Washington of the Neilson-Barlocker couple. Those who went report a very pleasant time.

Our school will close on Friday, the 15th. Miss Minnie Pace, the teacher, is preparing a nice entertainment for the occasion.

Our sheep men are moving their sheep to Modena to have their coats taken off. They are looking for good prices this spring

Mrs A. E. Taylor from Price, Carbon Co, is here visiting her mother.

New Harmony News

New Harmony, April 17.—The school entertainment of the 15th was a complete success. Parties from Pine Valley, Cedar City and other places came to see it. The compliments Miss Pace got makes her feel good. Some of the townspeople wanted her to go to some of the out side settlements and show what talent we have.

Mrs Adair of New Mexico is here to visit with her daughter, Mrs Grant. She reports things in that part of the country prosperous, especially the fruit crop.

H A. Pace, one of our aged men, is under the weather, but nothing of a serious nature.

Miss Cecil Taylor has gone to Price to visit with her relatives and friends.

We are all glad to see The News come from St. George

Closing Exercises New Harmony School

New Harmony, April 18 —The evening of Arbor day, the closing day of the school term of the school of this place, came an eventful and an agreeable entertainment The exhibition presented by Mrs Minnie Pace, the teacher, was not only a success throughout but a treat which was appreciated by all in the crowded house Too much credit cannot be given to Miss Pace for the ability and qualification as an instructor and a disciplinarian No one who was present could gainsay it, nor could any one ignore the fact that great progress exists, and in the unusual brightness of the scholars make it a source of pride and the interest that the parents and all the people have in this school of such a small community. Order and quick action was noticeable with no delays The following program without a hitch or failure upon the part of any of the pupils was presented·

"The School Song," by all the school children

"Tom Thumb's Wedding."

"Ghost March."

Recitation, "Courtship Under Difficulties "

Song "The Merry Little Gypsies," Dialogue, "The Rival Orators "

Farce, "A Cure for Discontentment."

The unanimous expression of all, including visitors from Cedar City, Pine Valley and elsewhere, was that this exhibition would have been most creditable to any of the higher graded schools of any town in southern Utah Especially was it noticeable that the little tots, 5, 6, 7 and 8 years old, were beyond their years in the uniform self possession, delivery, manner of speaking and acting From the north end of our country under the shadow of Pine Valley mountains you need not be surprised if the little men and women will not be heard from sooner or later.

At New Harmony.

April 28, 1910.

Everybody busy and happy. Big fruit prospect. First crop of hay twenty inches high. All typhoid grounds plowed under twelve 'nches deep. Lime that thick you can smell it in your sleep.

New Harmony Briefs

New Harmony, May 8 —James L Prince and Wm P. Taylor have gone to Milford after lumber for Mr Prince's new house.

Mrs Jos W Prince, who has been at Cedar City under a doctor's care, is expected home today, much improved in health

Forest Rangers McAllister and Morris are with us today attending to forest service business

Carl Veters of Circle Valley was here buying cattle, paying good prices

Our sheep men are feeling good at the prices paid for wethers.

H A Pace is having a new coat of paint put oh his house.

Reese Davis is having his house plastered and painted.

Our farmers are busy planting corn.

Washington County News
May 19, 1910

Mr. and Mrs Alex Pace of New Harmony were in the city the fore part of the week.

Washington County News
May 22, 1910

New Harmony Notes

New Harmony, May 22 —Our sheep shearers and cooks have returned home from Modena all well and glad to get home again They report a very windy time but no rain to molest their shearing

Messrs Paco and Mathis have gone to Lund to deliver their wethers They got a living price for them.

Elders Wood and Macfarlane of Cedar City, home missionaries, delivered fine discourses at our meeting house last Sunday.

John Whipple of Pine Valley is a visitor in our town today.

Our sheep men are located on their respective lambing grounds They look for a good crop of lambs this season.

Iron County Record
May 27, 1910

Misses Annabelle Schmutz and Florence Kelsey, of Harmony, are visiting here this week.

Washington County News
May 30, 1910

New Harmony Notes

New Harmony, May 30 —Our students from the Branch Normal have returned and they are pleased to see their old friends They have a high per cent in their graduating exercises

Elder George Spilsbury of Toquerville delivered a good sermon to our people last Sunday. We are always glad to have him come and see us

Our stock men are very busy rounding up stock for Veter and Coumerilh.

Our townspeople are decorating the graves of the loved ones that have gone.

We understand that Lawrence Prince has bought Mr Russel's farm.

Some of the farmers are cutting hay.

_____

Grace, a little daughter of John Eardley, fell over with a chair yesterday and one of her arms was broken.

Harmony Jottings

New Harmony, June 13—Hans Anderson of Toquerville was here last week making arrangements to have his teams and drivers looked after. Mr Anderson has the mail contract from here to Toquerville for the next four years, provided we don't have a train to carry the mail before that time Bp Gottlieb Schmutz has the contract to carry the mail from here to Cedar City.

A party of young people from this place are going to Pine Valley next week; they will be joined there by a party of young people from Pine Valley and go fishing and have a general good time on the Pine Valley mountain.

Our farmers are very busy at present putting up the first crop of hay The yield is about an average.

We look for a pleasant time on the 4th of July, a nice program was read in meeting yesterday.

Tuesday evening Mrs. Roy Grant of Harmony, who has been here under the care of a physician for some time, succumbed to her trouble. The body was taken to Harmony Wednesday evening for burial. The young woman was a bride of only a few months. The citizens of Cedar deeply sympathize with the bereaved husband.

New Harmony Mourns Loss of Young Wife

New Harmony, June 26—We mourn the loss of one of our young women, a bride of eight months, Mrs Mary Prince Grant Mamie and Roy, as they were familiarly called, were married in the Salt Lake temple last October. Mamie died at Cedar on the 14th of June, a complication of diseases was the cause of her death. She was the daughter of Mr. and Mrs Richard Prince of Middleton, Utah. There was no lack of medical aid and kind nursing but for all that she had to go

The new mail contractors are making arrangements to begin their work this week Mr. Schmutz has gone to Lund to get a new buckboard to carry the mail with

Doyle Pace from Thatcher, Arizona, is here visiting relatives He reports the people in the Giba Valley prospering in spite of the drouth.

The young people who went to the Pine Valley mountain for a little outing have returned They report a very pleasant time

Mr. Anderson was up the other day from Toquerville to complete his arrangements in the mail business

Henry A Pace is going to the Kanarra mountain and take his family during the hot weather.

The carpenters are making a great showing on the new house of J. L. Prince

Mr. and Mrs Reese Davis have a child very sick with pneumonia.

Lemuel Hardison Redd, one of the founders of New Harmony and a member of the bishopric there for many years, died at Colonia Juarez, Mexico, June 9th.

New Harmony Notes

New Harmony, July 4—We had a very pleasant time today. Meeting and program at 10 a. m., sports for the children at 2 p m, dance for the little ones at 5 p m, and a dance for the adults at night. A committee was put in to arrange a celebration for the 24th We expect a good time then

It was a little amusing to the townspeople to see the two mail carriers rushing out of town on July 1st. "A new broom sweeps clean."

The little rain storm was good as long as it lasted, but too short to please the people.

The sick babe of Mr and Mrs Davis is much improved.

New Harmony Notes

New Harmony, July 11—Our school election went off quietly today, James E Taylor being elected to succeed L. A Pace Mr. Pace has been a school trustees for twenty years or more and retires with the good wishes of his fellow trustees

Elson Morris, one of the range riders, has been with us and reports everything in the Dixie forest range in good shape.

Our binders are very busy these days, the grain crop is good considering the drouth.

R A. Kirker expects to go to Cedar this week on business.

New Harmony Notes

New Harmony, July 26—On the 25th we had a very pleasant time. The committee did itself proud in the arrangement of the program which was well carried out A F. Mathis, the orator was highly praised for the delivery of his oration at the meeting in the morning. In the afternoon sports for all were indulged in One very laughable thing was the nail contest, six women over forty years contested for the prize and to see those women how serious they were in driving nails; Mrs L A Pace was the winner.

- We had at our celebration people from Pine Valley, Cedar, St George and other surrounding settlements

J. G. Pace and family are here from Cedar visiting relatives and friends.

We had a very heavy shower here today.

New Harmony, July 31—T. J. Clark from Silver City, New Mexico, and Newton Adair from Luna Valley, N. M., are with us today. Mr. Clark is here to visit his sister, Mrs. L. A. Pace, whom he has not seen for twenty-seven years. These gentlemen are early settlers in the south who took an active part in early war times against the Indians They go from here to Cedar City to lay their claims before the commissioners for a pension for their services It is interesting to hear them tell of their experiences on their trips after the Indians Mr. Clark was one of the company when their leader was killed by the Indians and helped to bury him in that lonely spot.

H. A. Pace has gone to the Kanarra mountains to bring his family home who have been there during the warm weather.

We have been having some very nice showers lately which have done much good but the floods took our dams out.

LOST—Between Leeds and Anderson's ranch, a parcel containing a shirt, summer underwear, razor, khaki trowsers, and toilet articles Finder please forward, C. O. D to F. K. Nebeker, Jr., New Harmony, Utah.

Washington County News
August 7, 1910

New Harmony Notes

New Harmony, Aug. 7—Prof Hickman from Beaver and Prof. Peters from Provo gave us very good talks on education, Mr. Hickman representing the Murdock Academy, Mr. Peters from the B. Y. U. at Provo

We have had showers nearly every day for the last week; some of the second crop of lucern is bleached.

Our threshing machine will start soon if we do not have too much rain.

Washington county News
August 11, 1910

B. F. Anderson, writing The NEWS from Echo Farm, New Harmony, says: The fruit crop is good again this year and operations will soon be going on in the fruit yard. Third cutting of hay is all up and fourth cuttin growing nicely. The water supply has held out very good, we have had no rain to help the crops.

New Harmony Notes

New Harmony, Aug 15—The second crop of lucern is all up We are very busy hauling and threshing our small grain, the machine started this morning with William Fawcett of St. George in charge of the business

Doyl Pace who lives in Thatcher, Arizona, has been here this summer. He has gone to Idaho to see his sisters.

The Y. M and Y. L stake officers were with us Sunday. We had a very pleasant time.

New Harmony Notes

New Harmony, Aug 22—Bp Macfarlane from St George was here last week to get teams to work on the road north of the Black Ridge.... He got one man and team to help in this good cause He tells us that the road up the Harmony canyon will be fixed in good shape so that the people from the Dixie land will be able to go through the canyon without any trouble

Yesterday Freeborne Jones from Cedar was the speaker in our Sunday services. Elder Jones is a late returned missionary from South Africa His talk was very pleasant, giving his experience among the people in that far off land.

We have had ideal weather for threshing, we are through now and the thresher has gone to Kanarra We have had some nice showers the last few days.

Our young people are preparing to get off to school, some to Provo, some to Beaver and some to the Branch Normal.

We have blue plums this season, more than we will consume so we invite our neighbors to come and get some

Mrs Lusene Pace Taylor who has been suffering with rheumatism in her back is on the road to recovery.

We had a few people from Cedar and Enoch here to get plums Our plum crop this season is fine

Miss Minnie Pace starts next Sunday for Richfield to teach school; she takes the 5th grade

Our meeting house is recently illuminated by gas light.

New Harmony Notes

New Harmony, Aug 28—Our third crop of lucerne is ripe and some is in the barns, it is uncommonly heavy this year.

Messrs Hansen and Eggertson, traveling salesman called on the Harmony Coop last week.

We understand Miss Ruth Sterling from Leeds will be our school teacher this winter.

Arthur Jones and his sister Effie came down from Cedar to get fruit today.

New Harmony Notes

New Harmony, Sept 6—County Road Supervisor I. C. Macfarlane of St. George was here yesterday inspecting the roads up the Harmony canyon. Mr. Macfarlane thinks it will not cost much to repair the road up the canyon so that it will be a good road for the general travel. He will soon put a force of men at work to repair the road from here to the Black ridge.

We understand that funeral services will be held today at Kanarra over the remains of Owen Williams, 11 years old, who was struck by lightning last Saturday on the Kanarra mountain. The boy is a son of Wm. R Williams deceased, and Mary Roundy Williams. The mother is in a critical condition over the accident.

Our cowboys are preparing to gather their cattle for delivery on or about Sept. 20. They are getting a fair price for their stock.

Our south bound mail from Cedar had to stop over night in Kanarra Saturday on account of floods.

We had rain storms the 2nd and 3rd which did much good to the country.

Washington County News
September 26, 1910

New Harmony Notes

New Harmony, Sept 26—The students who have gone to high schools have settled down to their work in ernest. Some have gone to the Branch Normal, some to the Murdock and some to the B. Y. U.

Miss Minnie Pace who is teaching school in Richfield writes that she is getting along nicely. She thinks the Richfield people are very nice.

Miss Annabelle Schmutz has been confined to her room for a few days We hope her sickness is not of a serious nature

Mrs Eleanor Condie presented her husband with a nice 10-pound baby boy, all getting along very well

We are having very nice fall weather, no frost yet.

Harmony's Good Crops

New Harmony, Oct 10 —The hum of the mower is a thing of the past for 1910 Our fourth crop of hay is in the barns The Harmony people have nothing to complain for this year; the barns are full and lots of hay is stacked outside; the stack yards are full of shock of good corn; our potato crop is better than the avarage, so we invite our Dixie friends to come and bring the good molasses and get good potatoes

Mrs Jed Woodard gave birth to a nice eleven-pound girl on Sunday morning; the mother and babe are getting along very well.

Harmony Happenings

New Harmony, Oct. 17.—A farewell party will be given in honor of Elder J. L Prince, on Friday Oct 21. His field of labor will be in the Eastern States People from surrounding settlements are expected to attend.

Our district school started last Monday the 10th. Miss Sterling, the teacher from Leeds, reports every thing moving along all right.

We have had a nice rain which will fix the farming land in a good shape for plowing.

New Harmony Notes

New Harmony, Oct 31.—What might have been a serious accident terminated with little loss William Williams, who is hauling coal for L. A. Pace from the Kanarra mountain, was coming down the other day on the worst hill on the road when the break shoe broke and about fifteen feet farther the lock chain broke. Had he not had a strong harness and good team to hold the chanches are he would have gone off the grade which would have been good bye to him and his outfit

Carl Phiffen from Carey, Idaho, and Miss Florence Kelsy of this place left here this morning Their business will be a trip through the St. George temple We wish them a prosperous journey through life

Last night the young people had a very pleasant Halloween party at the home of Henry A. Pace.

Washington County News
November 17, 1910

New Harmony Notes

Dr. Robison was called to the bed side of Frank Prince last week   He pronounced the case blood poison Mr. Prince is now on the improve

Our nimrods are bagging some nice deer during the game season, the largest one dressed 250 pounds. Fresh venison has ceased to be a rarity.

Carl Phippin with his young bride have gone to the Gem State to make a new home, the Y L M I A, gave them a farewell party.

J L Workman and wife of Hurricane have been with us visiting relatives and friends and doing some business

We have been housed up the last two days by gentle rain

New Harmany Notes

New Harmony, Nov. 20 —We
Harmony people note what your
Toquerville correspondent says also
what Mr. Spilsbury says relative to
the smallpox. Miss Anderson spok
en about "home on a visit," left the
Branch Normal school and went
home under a quarantine flag for
smallpox She broke the quarantine,
came to Harmony and was met outside of town by the health officer,
was fumigated and went to Cedar,
where Dr Robinson placed her
under quarantine and had the driver fumigated and vaccinated before
he could come back. We will be
pleased to have some explanation
from the Toquerville people We
think Drs Woodbury and Robinson
have acted wise in this matter.

We have had another nice rain
and now we are having some cold
weather.

Harmony Happenings

New Harmony, Dec 1 —The Parents' class had a nice program made for Thanksgiving, but got nervious about the smallpox and gave it up

Albert Mathis, who went with the health officer to stop two ladies, who had jumped quarantine, to prevent them from entering town, was quarantined here this morning for the same disease. He is reported to be feeling fairly well at this time.

Miss Iva Slack, who has been here from Toquerville all summer will soon go to Salt Lake City to have an operation performed on one of her legs

Mrs Sarah Wolsey from here will go at the same time and be operated on for gall stones.

Our Sunday school and all public gatherings have been closed for the present.

Our farmers are plowing and sowing now, so we have fine weather.

Harmony Happenings

New Harmony, Dec. 11.—Victor E. Huntzicker from Salt Lake was here a day or two last week talking about the railroad business and looking over the coal property. He is highly pleased with the coal outlook. Development is all that is lacking now in the coal fields.

Mrs Woolsey left this morning for Salt Lake. We wish her a safe return after her operation.

Roy Cox and wife, who was a Miss Kelsey, are here visiting with their friends and relatives.

It was a mistake about our public gatherings being discontinued.

We have no new cases of smallpox.

Estray Notice

State of Utah, county of Washington, in the New Harmony precinct of said county.

I have in my possession the following described animal which, if not claimed and taken away will be sold at public auction to the highest cash bidder at my corral on the 29th day of December, 1910, at the hour of 10 o'clock a. m.

One red muley bull about eight months old, no mark or brand visible.

Said animal was taken up on the 19th day of December, 1910

HENRY A. PACE,
Poundkeeper.

Harmony Happenings

New Harmony, Dec. 25.—Our students that have been gone to high school have come home to spend the holidays. Miss Minnie Pace, who has been teaching school at Richfield is home feeling well, she speaks very highly of the Richfield people, especially her students. Miss Eva Pace from Salina came with Miss Pace to spend the holidays with her relatives and friends here.

The students and their friends who have come to spend the holidays with us have been vaccinated and fumigated and a doctor's certificate of purity so we feel reasonably safe.

Mrs Jos E. Taylor presented to her husband last week a nice boy; this is the eighth baby of Mrs. Taylor, seven of them being boys.

The committee for holidays has a nice program made out so we look for an enjoyable time if nothing unlooked for happens.

Miss Ruth Sterling, our school teacher, left today to spend the holidays with her folks at home at Leeds.

Last week we had about eight inches of snow and at this time it looks like we will have more soon.

The smallpox flags were taken down this morning, so we are all well again.

Harmony Happenings

New Harmony, Jan. 9 —Our holidays are over with once more. We had a very pleasant time, dancing, socials, and family dinners were the order of the times The extremly cold weather interfered some with enjoyment but for all of that a general good time was had

Bert Grant while jumping the other day, burst a blood vessel in his head and nearly bled to death before the blood could be checked. He has gone to Cedar for medical treatment.

Mrs. Bud Heyborn from Idaho is is here visiting with her sister, Mrs. James L. Prince She reports the people in that part of the state are in a prosperous condition.

President Marsden of the Parowan Stake and others were with us last Sunday holding ward conference. They gave us some very good talk.

Miss Iva Slack, from Toquerville has returned from Salt Lake It was not necessary to amputate her leg, as was feared at one time.

Cornelia Whipple, one of our holiday visitors, had her ears nipped a little by frost coming over.

Henry A. Pace left here this morning to attend some business at the court in St George

School started here this morning again everything in the school is moving along nicely.

Mrs Sarah Woolsey has returned from Salt Lake feeling fairly well after an operation

The students have all gone back to school except Laurence Prince.

We are having a nice rain storm today.

Henry A. Pace of New Harmony is in the city, on business.

Harmony Happenings

New Harmony, Jan. 15.—Last week we had a great rainstorm, a six quart milk pan was set out in the open it was filled three times. Will some of our correspondents tell us about how much rain fell? The pan was straight. Now we are having another rain. ∗

James E. Taylor and Roy B. Cox are doing very well this winter trapping, Roy caught a very large eagle the other day in one of his traps

Mrs. L. A. Pace has been indisposed for the last two or three days but at this time she is on the improve.

Bert Grant is improving fairly well now. The blood vessel was in the back part of his head.

FOR SALE—About 9 acres of good land with plenty of water. 6 acres in alfalfa, small orchard, good 5-room brick house with spring water piped into it, good grazing, corral and stables. For further information write to, or call upon, Wm. P. Taylor, New Harmony, Utah.

Harmony Happenings

New Harmony, Jan. 29 —Last week J. H Ramey from Los Angles was here looking over the coal fields and doing business with R A. Kirker. Mr. Ramey owns stock in the Harmony Coal Co. and is looking forward to the development of the property.

We are having warm rainy weather. Sometimes the mails gets in late and sometimes they get in the next day.

Independence Taylor has been indisposed for a few days, the Dr. says he is getting along now very well

Mrs Eliza Kelsey is confined to her room with the grip

Harmony Happenings

New Harmony, Feb. 20 —We have had about eight inches of snow since last letter and the coldest weather of the season and today we are having another snowstorm

John W. Pace of Price is here visiting his parents He reports things in that part in a prosperous condition.

Ashby Pace, Laurence Prince, and Eldon Schmutz have gone to Dixie to look after their cattle.

We have had some railroad talk lately which is quite encouraging

Harmony Happenings

New Harmony, March 19 —The following people went to Hurricane to attend the funeral of Jacob L. Workman   Mr and Mrs L A. Pace, Mr and Mrs Wm P Taylor, Independence Taylor and daughter, Julia, Mr. and Mrs Reese Davis   Mrs Davis is a sister to Mrs Workman   Some of them made the remark they "wished President Snow's speech at the services could be put in the WASHINGTON COUNTY NEWS "

Two of Mr. and Mrs. Geo F. Princes' little boys were chopping wood when one cut the forefinger of the other's hand off   The doctor put twelve stitches in and now the little fellow is getting along very well

Mr and Mrs James D. Neilson buried their first and only child last week.   The little one died of canker in the stomach and throat   The entire ward feels to sympathize with them in the hour of their grief.

At last our farmers are preparing to go to farming.

Harmony Happenings

New Harmony, April 3 —Last week Dr. Robinson was called to the bed side of Mrs J L Prince The doctor pronounced her case pneumonia. At this writing she is a very sick lady,

We are pleased to state that our new water system is in, and we are highly pleased with the same Our townsmen today put the water in to the home of J L Prince who is doing missionary work in the Eastern States

Harmony Happenings

New Harmony, April 10 —Our farmers are about through putting their small grain in, they are busy preparing corn ground now. The sheep shearers have gone to shear.

The primary ward conference was held here last Sunday under the direction of President Susan E Pace Mrs Pace is deserving of great credit for her untiring efforts in the Primary, she has two very good aids to help her.

Henry Mathis who has been to Price for more than a year returned home this week. Albert F Mathis who was to Salt Lake to conference has returned feeling well paid for his trip

Mrs Amelia Schmutz is confined to her room The doctor thinks her illness is not of a serious nature

Roy B Cox and family who have been here all winter will start for his home at Fairview this week

Mrs George Worthen, Jr, and Mrs Frank Penrose entertained at a party in honor of their brother, Irvin McQuarrie's 20th birthday, Tuesday evening, at the home of Mr. and Mrs. R. G. McQuarrie.

Harmony Happenings

New Harmony, April 16 —The cold wave that has just passed killed the most of our fruit The thermomiter registered 20 above on Friday morning

Mrs Prince and Mrs Schmutz, spoken of as being under the doctor's care, are on the road to recovery nicely now

Quite a number of our men folks have gone to haul wool to Lund from the shearing pens west of Kanarra

Our young people and children observed Easter by going to various places with their picnic.

Arbor day was remembered by our citizens A number of nice trees were set out.

Washington County News
April 23, 1911

Harmony Happenings

New Harmony, April 23 —Francis Prince, who sold hundreds of dollars worth of fruit from his orchard last year, said he would take five dollars for all the fruit he will raise this year, not very encouraging

Willard Corey of Cedar City, representing the Con W. and M Co, is doing business with our farmers today.

Mr Alexander of the Alexander Optical Co was fitting glasses for a number of our town people last week

Laurence Prince was thrown from a horse the other day and hurt but not seriously.

Harmony Happenings

New Harmony, May 15 — We notice in traveling out of this county into Iron that the Iron county roads are in good repair and not a lick done on the Washington county roads. We wonder what is the matter.

Miss Minnie Pace who has been teaching in Richfield this last school year returned home last week. She speaks very highly of her students and their parents and the Richfield people in general.

Our school closed on the 28th of April The teacher, Miss Ruth Stirling, took her students for a walk and picnic, they report a very nice time

We have had a nice little shower of rain which did much good to the crops

Harmony Happenings

New Harmony, May 22 — Chief Engineer Weber of the Dixie Route was doing business with some of our townspeople last week. Mr Weber talks very encouragingly of the railroad

Henry A. Pace and Albert F Mathis have gone to St George to attend to some land business

John L. Whipple of Pine Valley was a visitor here last Sunday.

The past week has been dry and cold.

Harmony Happenings

New Harmony, May 28 —Our cowboys have returned from Dixie where they have been attending the roundup Eldon Schmutz got his arm broken between the elbow and wrist caused by his horse running against a cow; he was taken to St George where Dr. Woodbury set it He is doing very well.

Quite a number of the townspeople are going to Cedar to the commencement exercises to be held there this week. Some of them will take the horse races in while there

The farm products do not grow very well, on account of cold dry winds during the day and frost at night.

Forest Ranger M. L McAllister was in town last week doing business with the cattlemen.

Albert Mathis, Henry A. Pace and James Russel of New Harmony were business visitors in the city Tuesday.

Washington County News
June 8, 1911

Prince-Whipple

Mr. Geo. L. Prince of New Harmony and Miss Ruth Whipple of Pine Valley are in the city going through the temple, where they were married yesterday. They are an estimable young couple of highly respected parentage and have a host of friends who will wish them a life of unalloyed happiness.

A wedding reception will be held at the home of the groom's parents Monday evening, June 12th.

Harmony Happenings

New Harmony, June 11.—Eldon Schmutz, the boy that got his arm broken on the roundup, is home from St George. He is feeling fairly well, he had the misfortune to get his ankle sprained while his arm was in a sling

Our students from the B N. S. have returned all feeling well and in good spirits Donald Schmutz, one of the students, has gone to Salt Lake to attend summer school.

We are having spring weather at last Some of our farmers are putting up the first crop of hay; they report a light crop

A committee has been appointed to get a program up for the 4th and 24th of July.

We have one case of measles here, Ray Grant being the victim.

Miss Ida Pace is here on a visit from Price, Carbon Co

Stake Supt. of Sunday schools is with us today.

Harmony Happenings

New Harmony, July 3 —Daniel Barney and family of St Thomas come to stay with us this summer, they are busy clearing new land for Francis Prince

Orin Kelsey has gone to Lund to take Mrs Charlotte Angell, the widow of the late Alma Angell She will spend the summer in Lehi with her daughter.

Eldon Schmutz, who had his arm broken six weeks ago is not doing very well The doctor says he will not be able to do any work for three months.

Ashby Pace and Laurence Prince have returned from their cattle round up in Dixie, they think it very warm down there

L A Pace was poisoned by eating canned fish the other day, at this time he is feeling fairly well.

Edward Vincent and family of Leeds have moved into our town; he will make this his home

We are very busy with our hay, which will be a light crop

Everything is in readiness for a good time on the 4th.

Harmony Happenings

New Harmony, July, 10—We had a very pleasant time on the 4th, a meeting in the grove on the meeting house lot was fine While we were gone to dinner a very nice shower passed over the town which made it nice and cool for the afternoon sports, which consisted of foot races, horse races and other amusements

Miss Mildred Pace entertained her crowd of young people Sunday night; they had a very good time if singing and laughing is a sign of a good time

Some of our townspeople are talking of going to the Panguitch lake to spend the 24th while some are going to the Kanarra mountain and other places

Our dry land grain is being cut now, it is a very good crop considering the small amount of rain since the fore part of March

We are having very warm weather now. Sunday the 9th, the register stood 98 in the shade at 3 20 in the afternoon

A program was read in the meeting for a celebration on the 24th

Mrs Sylvester Earl and children have returned home from New Harmony, where they have been visiting the past week with her mother, Mrs Annie Bradshaw

Washington County News
July 31, 1911

HARMONY

New Harmony, July 31.—Mr and Mrs L A. Pace have just returned from a trip to Panguitch and Cannonville, where they have relatives They speak highly of the roads through Iron and Garfield counties and say that prosperity is apparant all along the line, although the floods have done some damage to hay and grain

We had a very nice time on the 24th. The committee who arranged the programs for the 4th and 24th are deserving credit for their untiring efforts in seeing that all had a good time.

We have been having quite a number of showers and floods, the floods did some damage, taking out fences, bridges and flumes, quite a lot of our farming land also went down

The binders are busy these days taking care of our grain. Our second crop of lucern is ready now for the mower.

Louis Root has been painting Albert F. Mathis' new fence, which is a credit to the town.

John Condie was in St. George last week filing on some land as a homestead.

HARMONY

New Harmony, Aug 10 —Some of us were talking of going to St. George at the homecoming time but the diptheria excitment has caused those who were counting on going to hesitate

Ed Vincent and family have returned from Leeds where they had been to visit with Mrs Vincent's parents Mr and Mrs Jolley.

G Schmutz came in late last night loaded with goods for the Co op store, he reports the roads spongy after the late rains

H A Pace one of our aged citizens has been on the sick list for a day or two but at this time he is on the improve.

Wm P Taylor has sold his home to Francis Prince Mr Taylor is going next week to look for a new home

Mr and Mrs Carl Phippen of Carey, Idaho, are here visiting Mrs Phippen's mother, Mrs Eliza Kelsey.

Some of our people are figuring on going to Hurricane to attend the peach day.

The harvesting is about all done, and some grain is in the stack

Washington County News
August 13, 1911

HARMONY

New Harmony, Aug 13 —The stake presidency of the Parowan stake are with us today. Their talk was instructive and timley, encouraging all to live up to our duties.

John W. Imlay and family from Panguitch are visiting with relatives here, they are going to Hurricane to the Peach day festival

Joseph W. Prince has planned a trip to Kansas City with his sheep James W. Imlay of Hurricane will ship sheep with him.

Quite a number of our townspeople are going to the Peach day doings at Hurricane

Independence Taylor, who was stunned by lightening, is feeling fairly well at this time.

Washington County News
August 20, 1911

HARMONY

New Harmony, Aug 20 —The people who attended the Elberta Peach day at Hurricane are home Their praise of the fruit exhibited was fine, extremely so The hospitality of the people of Hurricane is beyond the expression by pen, such a brotherly feeling is seldom felt in a community

Mrs Frances Prince has been ill for the last week with cholera morbus, but at this time she is on the road to recovery

A F Mathis and Ashby Pace have gone to New Castle to visit with friends

Some of our townspeople are going to Dixie for fruit to put up

We are having dry warm weather, the warmest of the season

NEW HARMONY

New Harmony, Aug 27 —Some of our enterprising men have fixed the road up the Harmony canyon so our Dixie friends and others can go by Harmony and not have to go around the mountain.

Miss Sarah Roundy from Kanarra was here today in the interest of the Murdock Academy She put up a good talk in behalf of the school

Yesterday we had a nice shower which did much good to our dry land corn and cooled the atmosphere off wonderfully.

Elders James Stapley and John Reeves from Kanarra were home missionaries here today

Mrs John Condie is at Cedar City having her babe medically treated.

Miss Anna Slade from Panguitch is here visiting friends

HARMONY

New Harmony, Sept 4,—We now have a nice foot bridge across the gulch that goes through town. The bridge is made of wire and is about a 90 foot span.

Our farmers are very busy these days clearing and plowing their dry farms preparatory to the seeding time

Mrs Dr Shipp from Salt Lake City is here giving a course of lectures to the woman and girls; she is spoken of as handling her subjects very well

Dry Farm Corn

L A Pace, one of New Harmony's progressive and enterprising citizens who is here attending the Homecoming, brought The NEWS office some "white flint" corn that he had grown on his dry farm at New Harmony There are ten ears which average a foot each in length and are plump and heavy Mr. Pace says this corn has never been irrigated That corn can be grown to such perfection under these conditions proves that the soil and climate around New Harmony must be pretty near perfect

HARMONY

New Harmony, Sept 18 —Wm P. Taylor and wife, Independence Taylor and daughter, Julia, who have been on a visit connected with business, have returned, all feeling well There trip was to the Sanpete valley

Some of our students have gone to the B N S and some are going to the B Y. U this school year

Those who attended the Homecoming at St George speak of it as the time of their life

Our farmers are very busy, with their corn and the third crop of hay,

New Harmony, Oct 8 —On the first of this month we had a killing frost, thanks to the weather man for putting it off to that date

An entertainment will be given this evening at the meeting-house for the purpose of starting the young men's and young ladies' associations for the winter.

We had a very heavy rainstorm in 48 hours or less 4 23 inches of water fell and the floods did some damage, but not a great amount

Our sheep men are very busy moving their flocks from their summer to their winter ranges and selling wethers

Our cowboys are busy rounding up cattle to wean calves and sell steers. The delivery will be Oct. 10

Sarah Prince Davis has been very sick, but at this time she is on the road to recovery.

Born, to Mr. and Mrs Phiffen, a daughter; mother and babe doing nicely

The farmer is very busy turning the soil over after the rain.

NEW HARMONY

New Harmony, Oct 15 —School has been going two weeks Miss Minnie Pace, the teacher, has her hands full with all the grades, but she is getting along very well now

A party from Los Angeles is expected here to look over the coal property near here with a view to buying.

The last of our students, Ashby Pace and Frank Kelsey, have gone to the Brigham Young University

We are having cold weather now, it makes us wonder where we are going to get our coal this winter.

Miss Mary Knell of New Castle is here visiting her friends for a week.

NEW HARMONY

New Harmony, Oct 22 —After waiting some time for the threshing machine it has arrived here; the driver had the misfortune to turn the separator over but after a day and a half work on it the machine does good work We find some of the grain spouted into the stack.

James E. Taylor has a boy very sick with typhoid. A doctor has been twice called from Cedar to see him

Potato digging is the order of the day, the crop is good

Co Clerk Woodbury has issued marriage licenses is follows. Nov. 21, to Lorin C Smith of Summit and Miss Pricilla Benson of Parowan; Nov. 22, to Delbert T Woolsey of New Harmony and Miss Hanna Slack of Toquerville.

New Harmony, December 3rd — We had ward conference here to-day All the officers were sustained in their various callings. Susan E Pace, who has been president of the Primary for twenty years, was honorably released with her aids, with a vote of thanks, Miss Ruth W Prince was chosen to fill the vacancy.

Delbert Woolsey of this place and Miss Hannah Slack of Toquerville were married in St George last week, Bp Isaac C Macfarlane performed the ceremony.

Thanksgiving day passed off quietly here, most of the people observed it in hearty social dinners and other ways

We have been having cold dry weather, the ground is frozen so that farmers had to stop plowing

Ranger L A Harris has been here looking up the lines and posting new notices

New Harmony   Dec 31 —We
are having cold weather and some
snow which interfers somewhat with
our holidays but for all of that the
young men have swept a track so
we have some horse races foot races
and other sports

People from Pine Valley Cedar
New Castle and other places are
spending the holidays with us and
enjoying themselves very well   (

Delbert Woolsey had his ankle
sprained the other day in a wrestl
ing match   At this time he is get
ting along very well

Jesse Whipple of Pine Valley had
his ankle sprained today in a wrestl
ing match

New Harmony, Jan 8 —The students have all gone back to their respective schools The district school opened today with a full attendence Everything is settled down to normal conditions

The sheep men are rejoicing over the snow storm, it gives them a chance to get out from their old watering places

The thermometer hovered around zero the Christmas week; at this writing we are having pleasant weather.

L A. Harris, the forest ranger, was here last week looking after the stock on the reserve

Mrs Orin Kelsey left here yesterday to visit her daughter, Mrs Roy Cox, at Fairview

The holidays are things of the past; we had a very pleasant time.

New Harmony, Jan. 14 —The Relief society had read today a nice program for a benefit party for missionaries to be given next Friday Jan 19

R A Kirker starts east this week for the purpose of trying to get some capital interested in his semi anthracite coal located five miles from here

We have been having some trouble with our water pipes freezing up. Some of us carry water a block or more now.

Joseph W. Prince and wife start to St George tomorrow to work in the temple.

Mis Nancy Prince is quite sick with the grip

Jos W Prince a prosperous sleepman of New Harmony was transacting business here the latter part of last week leaving for home Sunday Mr Prince reports every looking prosperous in the New Harmony section of country

Washington County News
January 29, 1912

New Harmony Jan 29 —Frank
Kelsey who has been attending the
B Y U at Provo will have to quit
school and return home on account
of having erysipelas in his eyes

Wm P Taylor has been confined
to his room for the last three or
four days but at this time he is con
valescing nicely

The entertaining committee has
made arrangements to have a char
acter ball on Washington s birthday

Washington County News
February 3, 1912

New Harmony Feb 3 —Benj
Bruppacher has been ailing for some
time Sunday it was thought best
to send for a doctor at this writing
he is some better

Our farmers are busy these days
clearing off new land and plowing
some are sowing grain some repair
ing fences everything has the ap
pearance of spring

A baby girl came to the home of
James D Neilson Jr on the 2nd
Mrs Neilson and babe are getting
along nicely

Washington County News
February 19, 1912

Jos W Prince of New Harmony
was a city visitor Monday He was
moving his sheep from the Hurri
cane valley to the desert west of Mo
dena and reports them in good
shape

New Harmony Feb 19 —Elder J L Prince has returned home from a mission to the Eastern States he returned a little sooner than he would have done on account of the ill health of his wife Mrs Prince will go to Cedar to be under the care of the doctor for a while

Miss Minnie Pace dismissed her school to attend the teacher s institute at Parowin she reports over the phone they had a good time in the institute

Mr Gould from Cedar is with us doing blacksmith work he is a good smith and doing satisfactorily

Mrs Jane Whipple from Pine Valley has been here visiting her daughter Mrs Ruth Prince

Washington County News
March 4, 1912

New Harmony, March 4 —J G Pace and wife from Cedar were here last week visiting L A Pace They have just returned from a trip to southern California and Arizona They speak very highly of the country they have seen Mr Pace thinks the Imperial valley a nice place to make money

Jos W Prow and Sons have been here putting in gas lights and did good work they go from here to Toquerville Hurricane St George and other places in the south

Our character ball given on Washington s birthday was a success quite a number of people from other settlements were with us

Last week we had a rabbit hunt which did much good the losers gave a dance and picnic

Washington County News
March 11, 1912

New Harmony March 11 —We
have had a nice rain at last Satur
day night the rain fall was 2 75
inches

L A Harris the range rider re
ports stock dying in the parts where
he has been riding

Lurene D Taylor is very sick
with neuralgia and is under a doc
tor s care

Washington County News
March 17, 1912

New Harmony March 17 —Presi
dent Marsdane and Counselor A
F Lyman of the Parowan stake
were with us today   They honor
ably released Gottlieb Schmutz from
being bishop of this ward and his
counselors with a vote of thanks
for their untiring efforts in doing
good   Henry A Pace was sustained
as bishop with Albert F Mathis
and Joseph W Prince as his coun
selors James L Prince was chosen
as ward clerk

Some of our men have gone to
shear sheep at Gould s ranch where
there is a nice shearing plant es
tablished

Since our last letter we have had
about six inches of snow

New Harmony Mar 25 —Last week all of our able bodied men except two got out with their teams plows scrapers picks shovels and other tools and fixed up the streets and sidewalks so that our little town looks quite respectable a storm came on before we got through but the work will be finished

Bp Henry A Pace and counselors Mathis and Prince attended the quarterly conference at Cedar where they were set apart to their high calling by Apostle James E Talmage They report a very good time

Mrs Lurene P Taylor who was spoken of as being under Dr Lenard s care will be taken to the hospital at Cedar tomorow where the doctor can look after her a little better

There was quite a good turn out to th conference last week the old bishop and his counselors and the new bishop and his counselors and others went

Some of our school boys have chosen up for a hunt they are seeking the scalp of gophers rats chip monks and other animals that are a pest to the farmer

Today John A Condie is moving into his new house on his farm about a mile from town

Washington County News
April 2, 1912

New Harmony April 2 —Mrs Rhoda B Prince who underwent an operation at the hospital in Cedar for appendicitis is home feeling very good again

The hunt the school boys got up came to an end today there were 149 to 130 Max A Pace got 48 he is proud of his record

The total precipitation for the month of March was 8 16 in registered by Geo F Prince with a government instrument

Quite a number of our townsmen are going to shear sheep out near Kanarra

Washington County News
April 14, 1912

New Harmony April 14 —Last week several parties at different times came to inspect the semi anthracite coal deposits in Pace s canyon five miles north of here in Washington and Iron counties

Forest Rangers McAllster and Moody Supervisor Raphael and Mr Rynolds of Ogden were here three or four days last week they did not accomplish the work they came up to do on account of stormy weather McAllister and Moody returned to St George Mr Raphael took Mr Rynolds to Lund where he took the train for Ogden The storm lasted from Tuesday until Saturday morning

Mrs Emeretta Kelsey who has been spending the winter at Fairview with her daughter Mrs Cox is proud of her new grandson which was born while she was there While she was in Salt Lake she got a little boy from the orphans home a nice little fellow eight years old

Saturday morning the thermometer registered 18 degrees of frost the result is we will have a shortage in our fruit crop

We are having some sickness among the children but nothing of a serious nature it is a kind of grip

New Harmony April 21 —The farmers are having a time to get their small grain planted some of them have their grain sowed and disked in but no water marks made to irrigate it some have it sowed and not covered at all either with the disk or harrow Last week it rained or snowed a little every day but one now the wind is blowing from the north and is quite cold

The young ladies and mens meetings will be discontinued tonight for the summer they have had an enjoyable and profitable time this winter and feel well paid for the time spent at the meetings

Lurene P Taylor who has been to Cedar for three or four weeks in the hospital is home again she is feeling better every day now and we hope she will regain her usual health again

Miss Lottie ballard from Grafton who has been working for Mrs Rhoda Prince has had a serious time with quinsy but her throat broke and at this time she is much improved

Arbor day was fittingly observed by Miss Minnie Pace and her students setting trees out and doing work on the school grounds

Our school will close here this week the little ones think seven months is a long time to go to school

Benjamin Bruppacher is quite sick again he is an old man and about worn out

John Whipple from Pine Valley is here working for Henry A Pace on the farm

New Harmony April 28 —Our sleep men have had their sheep sheared they report a fairly good clip Those who contracted their wool before shearing are the loosers of about three cents a pound The shearers will finish shearing in another week if the weather is fair Last week five teams went to Lund with wool and loaded back with wire and machinery they report the roads good

The Schmutz boys Donald and Andrew have bought a brush grubber which will cost them about $225 to $250 put down here we hope it will be a success as there are hundreds of acres of new land taken up here in the last year or two

At the close of school last Friday Miss Minnie Pace gave an entertainment assisted by Miss Cecil Taylor the entertainment was very nice and was highly spoken of by those who were there

Robert A Kirker has returned from the east where he has been trying to get men of means interested in the coal here

Doctor Leonard was called to the bedside of Mrs Vivian Prince who has been very sick but at this time she is much better

Miss Lula Whipple of Pine Valley is here doing domestic work for Mrs Melissa Hammond

We are having very cold weather freezes every night

New Harmony May 14 —Your correspondent has been to Parowan and noticed the good roads the Iron county people have and they are making them better all the time there is a force of men and teams grading between Cedar and Parowan We think the people of Iron county are fairly well converted to dry farming judging from the amount of dry land grain they have in I was talking with some of the sheep men in Parowan they tell me the flock ma ters are out about $30 000 on wool contracted too early in the season

Quite a number of the sheep men are in a bad box for lambing ground, the cold backward spring prevents many of them from getting to their regular mountain lambing grounds About thirteen herds will try to lamb their sheep on the mountain north of Harmony where usually there are not more than three or four

The Harmony sheep shearers are home again after an absence of more than a month they were longer than they figured on account of too much falling weather

Mrs Annie Imlay Lee and her daughter Maggie are here from Panguitch visiting relatives and friends

Washington County News
May 26, 1912

New Harmony May 26 —Some of our stock men are closing out their cattle this spring the delivery will be about June 1 they are a little discouraged with the conditions that exist at this time some of them say they cannot get permits to range their stock on the reserve so they will be forced to sell

Today our local primary officers went to Kanarra to meet the state officers to transact some business for the advancement of the primary cause

J M Moody the forest ranger was here rounding up stock and doing business with the stock men last week

We are having cold windy weather a little discouraging to the farmer

Washington County News
June 2, 1912

Mr and Mrs Orin Kelsey of New Harmony were in the city the fore part of the week taking steps for the adoption of a child before the district court

Albert Mathis one of New Harmony s enterprising citizens was a city visitor Monday Mr Mathis reports everything looking prosperous in his section considerable land has been taken up for dry farming and past experiments prove this to be a profitable occupation on the rich soil in the vicinity of New Harmony

New Harmony June 2 — The students who have been attending the Branch Normal have returned they are glad to get home again we are proud of their record in school they think the B N S is the School to go to they are proud of their teachers and the equip ments there Miss Verna Taylor a 4th year and Miss Annabelle Schmutz a special passed out with high honors It sounds good to hear them talk of their school life

Memorial day was observed by our townspeople in decorating and fixing up the graves of the dear ones that have gone to the other side every grave in the cemetary had attention, so it looks like we think of the ones that are gone

Washington County News
June 9, 1912

New Harmony June 9 —James E Taylor one of our enterprising farmers has just returned from Lund with a hay press which cost about $385

We are having windy weather now which seems to cause the crops to stop growing in the last week can t see that there is much ad vancement in the growth

Delbert T Woolsey who has been living at Martin Woolsey s ranch has moved in here for the summer

Some of our sheep men have marked their lambs they say the lamb crop is not very good this spring

Mrs John W Prince of Price Carbon Co is here visiting rela tive and friends

We are pleased to know that our southern friends have their hay in the stack

New Harmony June 16 —It is reported that Johnie Adams the stock buyer went through the valley with 2 000 head of cattle the main party of them so we understand came from up the river and Toquerville

Some of our cow boys have gone to Antelope spring Arizona to round the mustangs up they deliver the horses at Lund the boys think they can do fairly well in this enterprise and we wish them success

J M Moody the range rider was here last week seeing that the stock men put out salt and attending to other business pertaining to the reserve

A committee has been appointed and a program made for the celebration of the 4th we look forward to a good time

Joseph W Prince one of our sheep men is reporting his lamb crop is well pleased with his marking

The cold wave is on at this writing north wind today

Flag day went by without much excitement

Washington County News
June 23, 1912

New Harmony June 23 —The
Primary Assn here gave an enter
tainment consisting of songs recit
als etc   Ice cream and cake were
served   A dancing party for the
little ones was much enjoyed by
them   The entertainment was a
success from beginning to finish

At last we hear the hum of the
the mowing machines Our farmers
are busy putting their first crop of
hay up they are having quite a
time on account of the heavy south
wind

Gottlieb Schmutz and his son
have had quite a strenuous time the
last six weeks gathering stock for
delivering looking after the farm
and carrying the mail to Cedar

The boys who went to Antelope
to roundup mustangs have returned
they report having done fairly well

Washington County News
June 29, 1912

New Harmony June 29 —We
have had two or three nice rains
this week something out of the
usual for June there was quite a
lot of hay in the fields at the time
of the rain but the farmer thinks
now he is ahead a little

Quite a number of our towns peo
ple attended the quarterly conference
at Pine ran Bp Henry A Pace
reports a very pleasant time the
attendance was not as large as usual
on account of so many people being
away from home

Dr Clark was called to see Miss
Clara Woodard The doctor thinks
she will get along all right now

New Harmony, July) —The 4th of July was fittingly observed here meeting in the forenoon, afternoon sports consisting of foot racing with the children and the young people horse racing and a dancing party for the little tots a dance at night for the adults The Barney Bros from the Sevier furnished the music There were people from the sur rounding towns here to participate in our sports

Mr and Mrs Ed Whipple were over last week from Pine Valley visiting with their daughter Mrs Ruth N Prince

The school election passed off quietly George F Prince the post master was elected to succeed Al bert F Mathis

Quite a crowd of our young peo ple have gone to the Pine Valley mountain for an outing

Miss Ruth Stirling from Leeds was here to spend the 4th and visit with friends

New Harmony July 14 —Presi
dent L N Marsden and Counselor
W H Lyman of the Parowan Stake
and James Allerton stake superin
tendent of Sunday schools were with
us today   They reorganized the S
S here this morning   Wm P
Taylor was chosen Supt   Orson
Hammond 1st and James L Prince
2nd assistant   The three brethern
spoke in the sacramental meeting
in the afternoon   their remarks
were timely and were highly appre
ciated by a good sized audience

Albert F Mathis took your cor
respondent out to see his dry farm
It is a marvel to see the crops grow
ing there without irrigation   He
has 20 acres of as nice corn as any
body wants to look at his wheat
and oats are fine   The Parowan
visitors were indeed surprised as
well as the rest of us to see such
fine crops

The young people who went to
the Pine Valley mountain for an
outing have returned they report
having had a very pleasant time

Miss Sadie Imlay of Tooele is
here visiting friends after an absence
of four years at one time this was
her home

J M Mo ly the forest ranger
was here last week doing business
with the stock men

New Harmony July 21 —Effie
Pace from Thatcher Arizona is
here visiting relatives and friends
She feels and looks sad having bur
ied her mother on the 17th of June
She tells us the fruit crop in Thatch
er this season is light   She said it
froze ice there some time last winter
which is uncommon for that climate

This afternoon Elders Wall er
and Mendenhall from Cedar occu
pied the time in our sacramental
meeting their remarks were good
and highly appreci ted by a very
attentive audience

We have had so ie very nice
showers lately which lid much goo l
to the growing crops but not so good
to the hay piled up in the field

We lool for a nice time on Pion
eer day   The various committees
have been very busy arranging
things to that en l

James F Taylor and Orin Kelsey
have gone to Luna with baled hay
they will load back with goods for
the Co op store

Washington County News
July 31, 1912

New Harmony July 31 —The
Pioneer day passed off very nicely
Meeting in the forenoon afternoon
sports for young and old dance in
the afternoon for the little ones and
a dance at night f r the adults

Saturday night Miss Minnie Pace
entertained her young friends with
ice cream and cal e an informal pro
gram was carrie l out without a hitch
All who attended expres ed them
selves as having a very pleasant
time

Our new Bishopric have had the
meeting house bl cl fenced with a
n ce fence and had the grove trim
med and the grounds cleared up
which mal es the place look very
nice

J Granville Pace and family were
here this weel visiting with relatives
and friends

Our harvesting is on if the rain
will allow the binder to run

We have had some very nice rain
showers the last week

Washington County News
August 5, 1912

New Harmony Aug 5 —Friday
Aug 2nd we had a hail storm for
about fifteen minutes which damag
ed our crops fruit was knoel ed off
from the trees and vines by the
wagon loads and that left on was so
badly bruised that it is not valuable
at all grain was threshed out by the
bushels corn was torn into ribbons
and not a garden is left in the town
The damage was about $1 500 quite
a loss for a little town lil e this

A close call for a fire Lightning
followed the telephone wire into the
office the other day burned the
curtains up scorched the wall pa
per and chared the ceiling It the
people of the house had not been
home their house would have burn
ed to the ground

A little boy of Mr and Mrs Geo
F Prince was playing on the thresh
ing machine he fell off and a piece
of iron weighing 75 pounds fell by
him and cut an ugly gash back of
the ear at this time the child is
getting along alright

We have had lots of rain the last
week or two our farmers trying to
put up the second crop of hay find
it uphill work

Miss Minnie Pace will teach school
this school year at Grantsville if
nothing happens to change the plans

New Harmony Aug 12 —Since the hail storm Aug 2 we have had fine haying weather the farmer has not been slow to take advantage of it the second crop of hay is being put in the barn in good shape

Will you please answer through The News whether or not everybody of age will have to register this year or only those whose names are not on the registration list

[Replying to this question Sec 8 of Chap 2 Election Laws for State of Utah 1910 reads No person shall hereafter be permitted to vote at any general special municipal or school election without having first been registered within the time and in the manner and form required by the provisions of this Chapter Prior to the time for registering voters the county clerk prepares an official register transferring to it the names of all persons who voted at the last general or municipal election As we understand the law the persons whose names are thus transferred are not required to register unless they have changed from one precinct to another It is well to examine the register and see that your name is properly on it —Ed]

It is reported that the threshing machine will start to thresh grain here this week we look for one half more small grain this year than we had last year

The Registration officer has been in his office today

Mrs. Joseph Prince of New Harmony underwent a double operation at the Southern Utah hospital Tuesday morning, one being for appendicitis and the other for a minor trouble. Dr. Leonard was the attending surgeon. The patient is recovering nicely.

NOTICE TO WATER USERS

State Engineer s Office
Salt Lake City Utah
August 5 1912

Notice is hereby given that Al bert F Mathis whose postoffice address is New Harmony, Utah has made application in accordance with the requirements of the Com piled Laws of Utah 1907 as amend ed by the Session Laws of Utah 1909 and 1911 to appropriate one tenth (1) of a cubic foot of water per second from Limestone Spring Washington County, Utah Said spring is situated at a point which bears north 4 degrees 17 minutes east 6 740 feet distant of the south west corner of Section 11, Township 38 south Range 13 west Salt Lake base and meridian from where it will be conveyed by means of a flume ditch and a pipe line for a distance of 7 856 feet and there us

ed during the period from January 1 to December 31 inclusive of each year to irrigate 10 acres of land embraced in Section 14 Township 38 south Range 13 west Salt Lake base and meridian This applica tion is designated in the State En gineer s office as No 4354

All protests against the granting of said application stating the rea sons therefor must be made by af fidavit in duplicate and filed in this office within thirty (30) days after the completion of the publication of this notice

CALEB TANNER,
State Engineer

Date of first publication August 15, 1912 date of completion of publica tion September 14, 1912

New Harmony Sept 1 —On Wed nesday Aug 28 Frank P Kelsey of this place and Miss Lottie Ballard of Grafton were married in the St George temple We wish them a prosperous journey through life

Dr A N Leonard was the speak er in the sacrament services this af ternoon his subject being the ne cessity of killing the fly which was lis tened to by a very appreciative audience

This (Sunday) morning Albert F Mathis left here for Pine Valley where Lula Whipple will join him They will be married in the Salt Lake temple on Wednesday Sept 4

Elders Leigh and Granger were with us today reorganizing the Y M M I A Miss Ethel Ashdown was here in the interest of the Y L M I A

Mrs Joseph W Prince who un derwent an operation for appendict is a little time since came home to day feeling well as can be expected

We have had some nice rains but at this writing it looks like we are going to have a nice spell of weather

Today R L Wrigley and Misses Decker and Brown were here in the interest of the Branch Normal school

The threshing machine has start ed at last the company had some trouble in getting the extras in

Miss Minnie Pace leaves here this week to teach school at Grantsville this winter

John Schmutz returned Sunday from New Harmony and bought back with him some fine ears of corn that had been grown on the dry land farm of John Mathis Mr Schmutz speaks highly of what is being accomplished in the way of dry farming about New Harmony oats grown by this method going 35 bushels to the acre and wheat 25 bushels

Pine Valley, Sept 2 —A bridal party left here at 5 o clock this morning consisting of Albert Mathis of New Harmony and Miss Lula Whipple of this place and Mrs E J Whipple They have gone to Salt Lake City

New Harmony Sept 8 — On Tuesday Sept 3rd Frank P Kelsey gave his wedding reception Every body in town was invited to attend all had a very pleasant time

Rogers Hardy of St George who has been here driving stage for Gottlieb Schmutz underwent an operation last Wednesday Sept 4th for appendicitis at Cedar Mrs Schmutz who was with him reports he is getting along as well as can be expected at this time

We are through threshing The hail storm of Aug 2nd threshed out more grain than we thought it had one stack that looked to have 400 or more bushels in turned out 107 bushels and other stacks equally as bad or worse

Albert F Mathis has just returned from Salt Lake He and Miss Lula Whipple were married in the Salt Lake temple He will give his reception tomorrow (Monday) after noon

Mrs Harriet Root from Lund and Mrs Ada Root Stewart from Cedar have been here putting up fruit they were shocked to see so much damaged fruit

James E Taylor has gone to bale hay for the Mt Carmel boys at the Mt Carmel ranch Elmer Taylor and John A Condie will assist him in the work

Miss Josephine Kelsey scalded her foot the other day which is not serious but very painful she is not getting along as well as we hoped she would

Some of our townspeople went to Cedar today to attend the convention of Y M M I A

New Harmony Sept 16 —On Monday Sept 9 Albert F Mathis gave his wedding reception and a dance at night People from Pine Valley, Pinto and other towns were here and all seemed to have a very enjoyable time

This evening the Parents' class entertained nearly all the married people of the ward at the home of Bp Henry A Pace A very pleasant evening was spent all expressed themselves as being well paid for coming out No doubt but the enrollment in the class in Sunday school will be large and the attendance better in the future

Mrs Della Redd Ivins from Lund Nev and Mrs Lewella Redd Adams from Parowan are here visiting relatives and friends this is the first time Mrs Ivins has been back to her old home for twelve years they are both well pleased to see their old friends again and we are all glad to have them with us

On the night of the 4th frost killed the corn and potatoes in the lower fields but in the higher parts everything is green yet

The stockmen are busy gathering beets for the Panguitch Commission Co from Panguitch

Corn hauling is on now with all the farmers

New Harmony Sept 29 —Last week Clark Pace the 12 year old son of Mr and Mrs L A Pace was racking hay when the horse ran away with him and headed for a gulch 12 or 15 feet deep just before reaching the gulch the horse turned and threw the boy off fortunately the boy escaped without being hurt only a little shaken up The horse escaped alright but the harness and rake were badly broken

Dan Barney and Julia Taylor from this place were married last week in St George Bp McArthur married them The townspeople gave them a bundle shower Tues day night and all had a pleasant time

Mrs Goddard Jolley from Idaho is here to see her mother and to visit with relatives and friends she will take her mother back to Idaho to live with her for a while

Robert A Kirker has a force of men at work cleaning the tunnels out of the coal mines here preparatory to the inspection of mining experts from Salt Lake

Quite a number of our townspeople will attend conference and the state fair this fall

Washington County News
October 3, 1912

Wm Taylor of New Harmony is here buying cattle   He is the guest of his aunt Mrs Peter Neilson

Gile Hardy left Saturday for New Harmony to visit with his brother Rogers for a few days

Washington County News
October 14, 1912

New Harmony   Oct   14 —The cow boys are rounding up their stock to wean the calves and get them on their winter ranges

James D Neilson and wife left to day to be gone all winter   Mr Neilson expects to get work on the Sevier this fall and winter

We are having beautiful fall weather since the storm   The pre cipitation for this month up to the 13th is 4 00 inches

The conference people have re turned from Salt Lake feeling well paid for the time spent

The M I A started their meet ings last Sunday night with a fairly good enrollment

The people are busy picking ap ples digging potatoes hauling hay etc

School started this morning   Miss Verna Taylor is the teacher

Iron County Record
October 25, 1912

AGED WOMAN BURNED TO DEATH

A most distresisng accident occurred at Lund Tuesday evening, by which Mrs. Margaret Pace of that place lost her life.

Mrs. Pace was the foster-mother of Mrs. J. A. Root, wife of the postmaster at Lund, and had resided for years. She was aged and a partial invalid and because of the care and quiet required for her comfort she was given a room in a building separate and apart from the premises occupied by the family.

On Tuesday evening, about 8 o'clock, Mrs Root left the room occupied by the old lady to prepare supper for her. As she was on the point of returning she heard the cry of fire, and rushing to the door of her own house discovered the room occupied by Mrs. Pace to be on fire.

Frantic efforts were made to rescue her but when found she was dead, death being caused partially from the effects of burns received and partially from smothering. When Mrs. Root left the room, as above stated, there were a number of quilts near the stove and by some it is thought these caught fire, the flames quickly spreading and preventing the escape of the unfortunate woman.

The body was taken to New Harmony, where funeral services were held Thursday and the remains laid to rest. The sympathy of the community goes out to Mrs. Root in her hour of bereavement and distress.

New Harmony Nov 3 ---Mrs Margaret L Pace one of the settlers here in 1862 died October 23rd of general debility She was the wid ow of the late William Pace She joined the Church of Jesus Christ of Latter day Saints in her native coun try in her youth and lived faithful to the cause to the end

Mary Ann Goddard one of our 1862 settlers left here a short time since to live with her daughter Mrs Hannah Goddard Jolly Mrs God dard is 77 years old and she took her first ride on the railroad train at Lund on her way to Idaho

The Misses Mildred Ice and Rosalia Schmutz gave a Halloween party to their crowd of young peo ple at the home of the former they had a very pleasant time

Born a daughter to Mrs Lurene P Taylor October 24, a son to Mrs Ruth Whipple Prince October 30 Both mothers and babies getting along nicely

We have been having lots of rain and some snow Wood hauling and coal hauling would be the order of the day if the roads were not so muddy

Rogers Hardy returned home Fri day from New Harmony where he has been working

New Harmony Nov 17 —Some of the farmers have their dry land corn shucked It is a wonder to see what has grown here without irrigation oats 32 bushels to the acre wheat 15 bushels and potatoes larger than a man s hand The fall grain on the dry farms look s fine

Elders Adams and Holyook from Parowan were here today looking after the high priests their talk in the sacramental meeting was timely and to the point

Some of the men working on the state road were here today They report that they are getting along fine on road at the head of the black ridge

The nice weather is pleasing to our farmers they are very busy fall plowing and hauling wood and coal

Born a daughter to Mr and Mrs George F Prince all concerned doing nicely

New Harmony Nov 24 —Lawrence Prince will move into his ne home this week Geo F Prince s ad dition to his home is finished Reese Davis new hou e is nearing comple tion L C Grant s new house is progressing nicely John Dove of Cedar City is assisting our home car penters do the work on the various buildings When it is all complet ed our little town will be much im proved in appearance

Independence Taylor is not feeling very well these days and the doctor wants him to go to Cedar for treat ment

The farmer is taking advantage of the fine weather preparing the farm for next season

Washington County News
December 1, 1912

New Harmony Dec 1 —One of
the coal miners working on the
coal property here thinks it too bad
that we have to haul coal from the
kanarra mountain and from Cedar
when there are mountains of it with
in four or five miles of us

Bp Henry A Pace s family has
been under quarantine for the last
six weeks for chicken pox the little
ones feel like a bird set free from its
cage since the flag has been taken
down

Our cowboys are now making
their final fall roundup in the Dixie
land they expect to bring the stock
from the south that will not winter

Washington County News
December 8, 1912

New Harmony Dec 8 —Presid
ent Marsden and Counselor Wilford
Day of the Parowan stake were with
us and held ward conference All
the officers were sustained without
a dissending vote The ward clerk
James I Prince is undergoing an
operation at the hospital at Cedar
for appendicitis this afternoon The
doctor has an appointment in Salt
Lake hence the operation on Sun
day

Our fine weather suddenly came
to an end last Tue day night It
has been snowing some and is very
cold

Mrs Luth Whipple Prince has
gone to Pine Valley to live this win
ter

An entertaining committee was
put in today to act for one year

Washington County News
December 23, 1912

New Harmony Dec 2o —John H Pace and James S Mathis from Price Carbon Co have come in to spend a part of the holidays with their relatives and friends It is pleasant to see them here again They report things in their part in a prosperous condition

Mrs Minnie Pace who has been teaching school in Grantsville is home to spend the Holidays with us she reports a pleasure in her work and also a good word for the people in Grantsville

A cold wave is passing over us the thermometer registering 10 degrees this morning

The students are returning from their respective schools to spend holidays with us

We wish The News A Merry Christmas and a prosperous New Year

Washington County News
December 26, 1912

Rogers Hardy left Tuesday for New Harmony where he intends to spend holidays

Washington County News
December 29, 1912

New Harmony Dec 29 —Holidays are passing quietly Ball playing horse racing and lancing is the order of the times The committee had a Christmas tree in the school house for the children which was very pleasant for the youngsters The married men played base ball with the single men for a dance the married men winning the game

There are quite a number of young people here from outside settlements spending the holidays All seem to be having a good time

We have had some cold weather but no snow

Washington County News
January 6, 1913

New Harmony Jan 6 — Holi days for 1912 are a thing of the past The students have gone back to their schools The people who came to visit us have gone back We are pleased to know that they got back before the cold wave struck us This morning we have zero weather

The mail boy had a little experience Saturday morning One of the convicts knocked him off from his horse The boy went to the camp and asked for a guard The convict was rounded up later at the Gregerson barn just at night fall It seems his object was to get the horse and get away

The school trustees are installing a heater to heat the school house with hot air

Washington County News
January 20, 1913

New Harmony, Jan 20 —Albert F. Mathis has three or four men engaged digging a well on his dry farm, his object is to get water for his stock.

Quite a number of our townspeople are sick with grip A doctor was called to our town to attend Mrs Lottie Ballard Kelsey, she is feeling much better

We have a case of mumps here that is quarantined; the school trustees are undecided weather or not to dismiss the school for a time

Our farmers took advantage of the dry weather we have had by ruling and burning brush from their new farms

Last week we had four or five inches of heavy snow, at this writing the weather is fine

Washington County News
February 2, 1913

New Harmony, Feb 2.—The nice springlike weather we have been enjoying for the past ten days or more suddenly came to an end This morning there is a stiff wind from the north with just enough snow to cover the ground and make it very cold.

W D Owen Z C. M. I's. genial salesman was here doing business with the merchants in our little town. He expects doing a very good business. He tells us the roads are dusty all along the line

Miss Minnie Pace, who is teaching school in Grantsville, writes that the town got a good exposure to the smallpox; all the students will have to be vaccinated.

Gottheb Schmutz who has been under the weather for two months or more is on the improve, he says he knows how to sympathize with Job

We have two or three cases of mumps here all under quarantine; it is in a slight form and we are doing our best to keep it from spreading

The sheep men say their sheep are doing fairly well considering the dry weather they are having where they have their herds

A rumor that one of the convicts well armed had left camp caused some of the women folks to get quite nervous for a time

J. M. Moody, genial forest ranger, was here last week transacting business with the stock men.

Washington County News
February 9, 1913

New Harmony. Feb 9 — Last week Dr Clark was called here twice, once for Geo. A Grant (Bert), who ruptured a blood vessel of his head and bled at his nose until his strength was about all gone; the other was for a 10-month old baby of Mr. and Mrs Orson Hammond which ate something that sent it into spasms. Bert went to Cedar with the doctor for further treatment, and the little one of Mrs Hammond is apparently alright again

Forest Ranger J. M. Moody thinks if the bounty on the cougar and other destructive animals is not raised that all the increase of the deer, the horse and cattle will be taken; he tells us he saw where seven deer, one or more of the horse kind and two or three cattle had been killed lately in his travel through the mountains.

The following men are making arrangements to have the telephone put into their houses Bp Henry A. Pace, L. A. Pace, James E. Taylor, E O Grant and Reese Davis Others are talking of having it put in later.

We have had a nice rain since our last letter which is encouraging for us all

Washington County News
February 10, 1913

Pine Valley, Feb 10.—Mrs Ruth Whipple Prince of New Harmony is here visiting her parents Her babe was taken with a bad cold and finally they sent for a doctor who found it had pneumonia It is a very sick child; Dr. Woodbury was here yesterday to see it.

Washington County News
February 23, 1913

New Harmony, Feb 23 —Since our last letter we have had changeable weather. Some of the farmers have sowed wheat but since that time the thermometer has registered 8 above zero, at this time we are having a snowstorm.

James D Neilson, jr , and family have returned from Sevier county, where they have been for the winter; they report things prosperous in that part of the state

The entertainment committee arranged for a good time on the 22nd, but as there were so many who could not attend it was postponed for the present

The mumps are abating, there being but two flags up now.

New Harmony, Mar. 2 —Since our last correspondence we have had snow and rain to our pleasure, but at this time spring weather is at hand, the snow is about three inches deep, and melting rapidly.

The men, young and old, have been out on a rabbit hunt, after the snow storm they killed 200 rabbits, which will be a help to the farmer.

New Harmony, Mar 10 —Two of our young men, Wm. P. Taylor and Frank P. Kelsey, chose sides for a rabbit hunt to last until the 1th of April, the losing side to give a dance.

Myrtle Duffin underwent an operation today for appendicitis at the hospital at Cedar.

Quite a number of our townspeople are down with grip but none seriously ill

The farmers are just starting work a little on the dryest parts of their farms.

Washington County News
March 16, 1913

New Harmony, Mar 16 —We thought we had the mumps under control, but at this writing we have four or five mild cases

We have had some cold weather, last week the thermometer registered 18 and 20 above nearly all week

The postmaster said he could hardly distinguish the names on the WASHINGTON COUNTY NEWS

Mrs Lawrence Prince, who has been in Pine Valley all winter, came home last week.

Mrs James E. Taylor is confined to her bed, but is on the improve.

The latest in the parcel post was eggs, sent from the south

Washington County News
March 31, 1913

New Harmony, Mar. 31.—Our sheep men report their sheep have done better this winter than they have done for a number of winters, the sheep are in a thriving condition. The farmers are all busy now putting in spring grain clearing new land and preparing for a prosperous season, and some of them have cleared forty or more acres during the winter and now are plowing and fencing

It seems that we have spring now. Last week the coldest morning was 16 above, we had snow about three inches deep

New Harmony, Apr. 13 —Some of our people are asking why the forest reserve has been extended to the town and some of the farming land taken into the reserve

John E Whipple has taken up some dry farming land and is here working on it Mr. Whipple expects to go to Pine Valley to put in his spring crop

John S Woodbury, Supt of the Iron Co telephone line, has been here installing phones in a number of houses.

Quite a number of our townspeople have an attack of the grip but nothing of a serious nature.

We are having spring weather at last, still the mornings are a little frosty.

Some of our farmers have cleared 50 acres and are now plowing it.

New Harmony, Apr 21 —Arbor day was fittingly observed by our townspeople, especially the school teacher, Miss Verna Taylor and her students, who were busy in the forenoon planting trees and pruning the old ones in the school grounds In the afternoon she took the children for a pleasant little walk to gather some flowers, they report a very pleasant time

Mrs Varona Bryner Redd, from Alberta, Canada, widow of the late Bp Wm A Bedd, is here visiting her old friends and relatives Mrs Geo. Wood, sister to Mrs. Reed, is here

Some of our men folk have gone to shear sheep near Kanarra, they are a little disappointed as some of the sheep men went to another pen to shear at the last minute

Our farmers are busy planting corn, some of them figure on having 50 or more acres of new dry land corn this spring

Forest Rangers Moody, Sorenson and Woodbury were here last week locating the new lines on the reserve

New Harmony, Apr. 27.—Mr. and Mrs John Bennet of Pennsylvania are here staying with their friends, Mr. and Mrs J L Prince. Mr. Bennet and wife are in Utah for the purpose of doing temple work. They have been to St George for that purpose and are well pleased with their treatment in the St George temple.

We feel a little metropolitan, having two phone lines in our little town, both giving good service.

Born, April 23, a son to Mr and Mrs Henry A Pace; all concerned getting along nicely.

Quite a number of our men are hauling wool from the Kanarra shearing pens

This is a busy time with the farmers, corn planting, irrigating lucerene, etc

New Harmony, May 4 —Last week Wm Chinn of this place and Miss Olive Leavitt were married in the St. George temple. The young people gave them a bundle shower and all had a very good time. They have many warm friends to wish them a pleasant and prosperous journey through life.

Mr and Mrs. John Bennett left this morning for their home in Pennsylvania. The townspeople gave them a farewell party, a very pleasant time being enjoyed.

L A Harris, one of the rangers, is here doing business with the stock men. Our sheep men are very busy now getting their flocks on the lambing grounds.

We had two or three freezing nights last week.

New Harmony, May 11.—Miss Velva Prince, daughter of Mr. and Mrs Joseph W. Prince, underwent an operation for appendicitis, the doctor says it was one of the worst cases he ever had. She now is at home again feeling as well as can be under the circumstances

Mrs. Eliza Kelsey has gone to Carey, Idaho, to spend the summer with her daughter, Mrs Carl Phippin Miss Josephine Kelsey has gone to Fairview to visit with her sister, Mrs Ray Cox and to pick berries.

Miss Myrtle Duffin, who has been here living with her grandmother, Mrs Delta Hamond, has gone to her home at American Fork.

Francis Prince had the misfortune to sprain his ankle severely.

Our school closed last Friday.

New Harmony, May 18.—This week there will be nearly a carload of wire brought from Lund for the purpose of fencing new land put in to grain this spring.

John Raphael and L. A Harris were here Saturday doing business with the stockmen   They report that the Pine Valley people will be ready to have their cattle counted about the 20th.

Last Sunday Elders Jones and Jones from Enoch were here is home missionaries; their remarks were along the line of temple work were highly appreciated by those present

The heavy south winds of the last ten days are not very encouraging to the dry farmer.

Some of our eighth grade students were taking the examination last week.

House cleaning is the order of the day; it is hard to get help to do the work

New Harmony, May 26 —Last Sunday we had with us at our sacrament meeting the officers of the Primary. They held their yearly ward conference We also had home missionaries, Elders T B. Wood and Edward Palmer so we had a good spiritual feast All seemed to be highly pleased with the remarks of the elders and the children's exercises.

Miss Mildred Pace has gone to Grantsville to meet her sister, Minnie Floyd Frint went also They will take Salt Lake City in and other places of interest before returning

Mrs Sarah Barnum from Cedar City and three of her children were here last week visiting with friends and relatives

Roy Robison from Paragooah was a visitor to our town last week.

Estray Notice

State of Utah, County of Washington. In the New Harmony precinct of said County.

I have in my possession the following described animal, which, if not claimed and taken away, will be sold at public auction to the highest cash bidder, at my corral, in New Harmony Precinct, on Friday, the 30th day of May, 1913, at the hour of 5 o'clock p m.

One red 10 months old bull calf, no marks or brands visible

GOTTLIEB SCHMUTZ, Deputy Poundkeeper of New Harmony Precinct

Dated at New Harmony, May 20 1913.

New Harmony, June 2 —Bp Henry Pace and wife entertained at a musical Saturday evening Prof. Durham and Miss Ada McGregor from Parowan furnished the music, all present spoke of being highly pleased with the music. Those present were President Marsden and his counselors Day and Lyman, Mr. and Mrs A. F Mathis, Martin L McAllister. Miss Minnie Pace, Misses Mildred Pace and Rosalia Schmutz Messrs Coal Taylor, Andrew and Eldon Schmutz and Floyd Grant.

Last week was a bad week on growing crops; there was lots of south wind which seemed to stop the growth of the crops, however, the latter part of the week a little rain fell which brightened things up some

Miss Minnie Pace returned home last week from Grantsville, where she has been teaching school since last Sept.; she speaks very highly of the people of the town; she figures on teaching there the coming school year.

Forest Rangers McAllister and Woodbury were here last week. They built a neat little house to put the salt in so that the stock men will be able to house the salt required of them all at the same time

Quite a number of our towns people attended the M. I. A day at Cedar last week. All speak of having a nice time.

The presidency of the Parowan stake was with us last Sunday, their remarks were timely and highly appreciated by all

Washington County News
June 8, 1913

New Harmony, June 8 —Eldon Schmutz while stretching wire fence had the misfortune to have his thumb cut off. He was taken to Cedar for medical treatment We hoped to report a favorable condition, but we learn that Dr. Leonard went to Salt Lake without undoing his thumb

Last week Bp Henry A Pace asked the people of the ward to come out and clean the cemetary up, every able bodied man and boy responded to the request It took them two days to do the work. Now the cemetary looks clean, a nice fence around it and all the rubbish cleared away.

Our women folks that have nice flower gardens are ready to declare war on the cottonwood tree.

Allen Cameron of Salt Lake City is here on business.

Washington County News
June 16, 1913

New Harmony, June 16 —The students from the B N. S. have returned. We are glad to have them home again. Some of them think the B. N. S is good enough, they don't take kindly to the new name but they say all is well that ends well.

Harvey A. Pace, one of the pioneers to Dixie, is getting the geneology of the pioneers to Utah in the early days to be published in the book of the early settlers of Dixie and the state

The entertaining committee has appointed a committee for the 4th of July so we look for a pleasant time We understand that there will be no dangerous firing of guns on the 4th.

Verna Taylor, one of our progressive school teachers has gone to Salt Lake to attend the summer school; she will be gone about eight weeks.

Maeser Dalley of the Dalley Sons Co , was here four or five days last week surveying canals and locating corner stones for our farmers

Miss Cecil Taylor has gone to Price to visit relatives and friends a month or two

Mr. and Mrs. Lawrence Prince was here on the 15th of June and took Mrs Jane Whipple home with them to New Harmony.

New Harmony, June 21 —Last week while Mrs Jane Whipple was coming from Pine Valley, she was thrown out of the buggy and painfully but not seriously hurt

The young women have organized a sewing club, they plan to meet every Wednesday afternoon The officers of the club are, Miss Minnie Pace, president; Lurene Taylor, vice president; Emma Neilson, secretary

Profs Evans and Sharp were here in the interest of the B A. C Their talk was highly appreciated by an attentive audience, all seemed pleased that they came and think that good will result of their visit

We had a nice rain on the 17th; there was quite a lot of hay piled up in the fields, the farmers think it did a great deal more good than damage

Haying is the order of the day everybody is very busy putting up the first crop of hay, which is much better than was expected.

New Harmony, June 29 —Some time since Gottlieb Schmutz's barn caught fire The boys got home from the dance just in time to extinguish the flames One pair of horses got scorched a little

Lurene P Taylor entertained the O. B B club last Wednesday afternoon; dainty refreshments were served. . They report having had a very pleasant time The by laws passed by the club were of an elevating nature

Last week was not a very good week for making hay, heavy south wind and just enough rain to keep the hay damp At this writing the prospects are now good for fair weather,

Leroy Grant from here and Miss Sadie Imlay from Tooele were married in the Salt Lake temple on June 25,

New Harmony, July 7.—The celebration of the glorious 4th passed off pleasantly. We had two days celebrating. the 5th was a day of foot racing, horse racing, etc The following are the winners in the various contests on the 4th paper cutting, Perle Pace; peanut shelling, May Pace, teaspoon drinking, Goldie Prince; needle threading, Erving Prince, cracker eating, Gladys Grant; rainy day race, Minnie Pace, patching contest. first Mrs L. A Pace, second Mrs Geo, F. Prince; pole vaulting Antone Prince.

The O. B Bs were entertained at the home of Mrs Emma G. Neilson on Wednesday of last week. Mrs Neilson did herself proud in entertaining the club

Born, to Mr. and Mrs A F. Mathis, a sweet little girl; all concerned getting along well.

Frances Prince is under a doctor's care; the nature of her illness is not known

Washington County News
July 13, 1913

New Harmony, July 13 —E. C Grant met with an accident coming down the Kanarra mountain with a load of lumber. He has a badly crushed foot. Wm Gunn, while assiting Mr Grant had the misfortune to have a team run down the mountain, his wagon was broken badly but the team escaped without injury

Mrs Harvey A Pace entertained the O B B club last Wednesday; one interesting feature was the initiation of a new member, which was very pleasing to the members, refreshments were served. A very enjoyable time is reported

Leroy Grant and his bride have come home from their honeymoon trip. They have the good wishes of a host of friends.

Floyd Grant had the misfortune to run a twentypenny nail through his foot and has gone to a hospital for treatment.

Francis Prince is on the road to recovery, his illness was caused by the heat while he was hoeing in the garden.

A committee for the 24th has been put in, the program has been made so we look for a good social time

Mrs Julia Taylor Barney has given birth to a nice baby girl. Mrs Barney is very weak.

Jos W. Prince underwent an operation for appendicitis, he is improving nicely.

The hot wave has gone and we now are having cool winds from the north

We hear the binders now. The fall grain crop is fairly good.

Reese Davis has gone to St George on land business

Washington County News
July 22, 1913

New Harmony, July 22 —Messrs Wrigby and Sharp of the B A. C were here in the interest of the school. They have been over some of our dry farms and speak highly of the soil and crops.

The O. B. B's. held their regular weekly gathering, they were very nicely entertained by Mrs Flora Brown. They discussed the reading of high classed literature in club

The school election results are James E. Taylor to succeed himself for three years, Gottlieb Schmutz to fill the unexpired term of Bp Henry A. Pace, resigned

We have had a few nice rains which is pleasing to the farmer who has his hay all in the barn. There are a few who have hay piled up in the field

Ranger L A Hurns of the Dixie national forest was here doing business with the stock men.

New Harmony, Aug 4 — The 24th of July was fittingly observed here. Our young people think one day is too short so they usually take two days. This year the 25th was spent in horse racing, foot racing, boxing contests, etc.

Last week Mrs Lottie B Kelsey entertained the O B B club. They planned an entertainment to be given in the near future, the proceeds to be used for public purposes

Miss Laverna Taylor returned home today from Salt Lake City where she has been attending summer school at the U. of U.

B Jarvis, jr., was here last week in the interest of the canning plant at Leeds. He seemed satisfied with the business he did here.

Mrs Ballard and her son, Afton, have been here to visit with her daughter, Mrs Frank Kelsey.

The harvesting is nearly all done and the farmers are busy with their second crop of hay

New Harmony, Aug 17.—Some of our sheep men are preparing to ship some of their wethers. Joseph W. Prince starts this week to Kansas City with five carloads; some of them belong to Bp Henry A Pace. Mr Prince thinks it will take him about three weeks to make the trip

Some of our townspeople are figuring on going to Hurricane to attend the good time at the Elberta Peach days

The threshing machine started work here last Saturday.

Washington County News
August 24, 1913

New Harmony, Aug 24.—The people that attended the Elberta day at Hurricane report having had a very pleasant time. They are loud in praise of the hospitality of the Hurricane people

Elders T. J. Jones and Hillman Dalley were home missionaries to our town today. Their talk was good and highly appreciated by the audience.

Last week Gottlieb Schmutz was knocked down by lightning. The bolt struck about 8 feet from him.

The O. B. B. gave a benefit party for an amusement hall which was a success financially and socially.

The threshers have finished their work here and gone to Dry Creek to thresh.

Iron County Record
August 29, 1913

HEAVY RAIN WASHES OUT STATE ROAD

Friday night a heavy rain storm in the mountains south of this city caused the canyon streams to overflow with the result that the state road was badly washed and damaged in several places between Cedar City and New Harmony. It is said the large concrete culvert about half a mile east of New Harmony was not large enough to hold one-fourth of the water that poured down against the grade, with the result that the water broke over the road bed, washing deep gulleys in the newley-made grade.

If a repetition of the damage is to be prevented additional culverts will doubtless have to be constructed.

New Harmony, Sept. 7.—On Monday, Aug. 25, we had a hail storm lasting about twenty minutes which did much damage to gardens and other growing crops.

Joseph W. Prince has returned from Las Angeles where he has been with a train load of wethers; he reports a very pleasant trip and was agreeably surprised at the price he received for sheep.

Mr. Benett of Arkansas is here visiting friends. He is on his way to Oregon on business and stopped here to visit some of his old acquaintances. He is quite well pleased with the west.

The O. B B was entertained by the misses Minnie and Mildred Pace; the regular club work was changed into a social; they report having had a very pleasant time.

Miss Minnie Pace entertained at a social last Thursday evening. A jolly crowd was present; water melons were served during the evening.

Washington County News
September 14, 1913

New Harmony, Sept 14.—President Lyman of the Parowan Stake and his wife are with us today. Mrs Lyman is here in the interest of the Relief society. They gave us a good talk.

James L Prince is hauling lumber from the Panguitch lake, he reports the roads in bad shape over the Parowan mountain and lots of rain on his last trip

Donald Schmutz has been afflicted with boils for the last month or more, he has been almost as patient as Job was of old; he is recovering

Quite a number of Cedar people are here getting fruit; they seem pleased with the fine quality they are getting

Elder Herbert Haight from Cedar was here in the interest of Religion class work; his talk was to the point.

Some of the boys are on the Kanarra mountain gathering horses from the summer range.

Wm. P. Taylor went to St George last week to attend to some land business

Reese Davis is recovering from an accident he had in handling a wild horse

Washington County News
September 22, 1913

New Harmony, Sept. 22 —James E. Taylor returning from the quarterly conference at Cedar with some others in his buggy had the misfortune to tip over in the darkness Mrs Amelia Schmutz one of the passengers was thrown violently to the ground and painfully but not dangerously hurt.

Some of our stock men are wondering where they are going to get off, with the high taxes, the forest reserve expenses and the damages their stock do to the farmer. Ranger L. A. Harris has been here doing business with the stockmen.

Last week Misses Mildred Pace and Rosalia Schmutz entertained a crowd of young people; ice cream and cake was served; they all had a very pleasant time.

Wm. Prince and wife from Panguitch are here visiting with their brother, Francis Prince, and other relatives and friends.

Donald Schmutz and brothers leave here today for Kanab, where they will get a bunch of goates.

Miss Laverna Taylor has gone to Hurricane where she expects to teach this school year.

Elmer Taylor left here this morning to attend the B A. C. at Cedar.

Joseph Sterling left for new Harmony this morning after cattle.

older young people. The following have secured positions as teachers in the schools mentioned. Leonard Slack, New Harmony, Linda Slack, Pine Valley; Fan Kleinman, Enterprise, Isabel Jackson, Milford; and Ruby Naegle at Tooele.

In Memoriam

E. L. Taylor, a son of Wm. and Julia Taylor, of New Harmony, died at Elba, Idaho, on August 27, 1913, from a complication of diseases.

He was reared at New Harmony, Washington County, but moved from there to Cache county about fifteen years ago, and from which place he filled a mission to the Central States, and about four years ago he removed to Idaho.

While in Idaho he served as a Bishop's counselor, and was quite prominent in Church affairs generally. He leaves a widow, Sophia Parker Tayor, and four children namely, Otho, Marion, John and Ivie.

The neighborly assistance proffered by the people during his illness, and the attendance and large cortege at his funeral attest the esteem in which he was held by the people of the community where he passed his last years.

New Harmony, Oct 6 — We had a little excitement in our little ward the other day. Four or five small boys, unbeknown to their parents, went off to get pine nuts The alarm was phoned over the town that the boys were lost; the townspeople turned out en mass to took for them The children returned about 5 o'clock in the afternoon. One of the little tots said, "I didn't have any dinner either."

The farmers are busy now with their third crop of hay. The cowboys are off on the regular fall round-up, the boys from Toquerville and Leeds have joined them They expect to gather all the stock that has gone from their regular ranges and put them on the winter range.

The Young Ladies M. I. A. convened at the meeting house last Sunday for the purpose of taking up their course of study for the winter. They expect to have an enjoyable and profitable time this winter as they have done in the past.

The women folk are doing their fall cleaning and putting the heaters up, none too soon as the nights are cold

Some of the men folk are taking advantage of the chance to hunt deer, most every one has been successful

School started here this morning with Leonard Slack from Toquerville as teacher.

All the tender garden stuff has felt the thorney hand of "Jack Frost."

New Harmony, Oct 20 —Last week more than 30 tons of coal were brought to town from the Kanarra mountains. More teams will leave this week than last week. The road in the mountain is good so our men are taking advantage of the nice weather and rushing their coal hauling.

John Bennet is with us again. He reports the farmers in his part of Pennsylvania have grown good crops this year.

Potato digging is still on, some as nice potatoes as one would wish to see were grown by James L. Prince on a dry farm.

John Raphael, the forest supervisor, was with us last week doing business with the stock men.

The threshing machine will be here today to thresh lucern seed.

New Harmony, Oct 26 —Some busybody has started a falsehood about our bishop killing deer. The rumor has it that he killed five deer. The truth of the matter is he killed one large fat one and sent his neighbors a nice mess to taste. He wants it plainly understood that he killed one and one only.

John Bennett and Thomas Brown have taken their traps and guns and gone into the Pine Valley mountains to try their luck in catching cougars, bears and other animals that kill so many of our calves and colts every year. We wish them success.

Joseph N. Prince returned today from Parowan where he has been to get a bunch of full blood sheep. He says he got a good bunch and will increase the value of his flock.

Bp. Henry A. Pace started to Lund this week with fifty fat hogs; he will ship them to Los Angeles from Lund. Sam L. Pollock of Kanarra will ship with him.

Rufus Lamb and his brother-in-law of Toquerville are here clearing ground for G. Schmutz. They will clear and plow seventy acres or more.

The threshing machine is through work for this season; some of the farmers were disappointed in the yield of their lucerne seed.

The boys that went hunting deer were successful, that is most of them were.

New Harmony, Nov. 2 —Evelyn Prince, son of Geo. F. Prince, had the misfortune to cut his foot with an ax; he is painfully but not dangerously hurt.

Wm. J. McConnel from McConnel farm has been plastering a number of new houses The new buildings improves the looks of our town.

Mrs Wm Lunt from Cedar was here last week and took home a load of apples. The potato crop is good this year.

Martin L McAllister, the ranger, is here doing work with the stockmen

The drouth is broken at last, we are having a nice rain today.

New Harmony, Nov. 17.—Last week we had about 2 6 inches of rainfall which makes the farmer, the sheepmen and stockmen all rejoice

The O. B B. club was entertained by Mrs Melissa Hammond last week. They report they are going to take up some study for the winter.

The ward entertainment committee has planned for a public dinner and a grand ball on Thanksgiving; we look for a good time.

Mr. McCune from Panguitch has been here buying beef stock; he paid a very fair price for them.

A. Y. Milne and Sons are here painting and paperhanging for a number of our townspeople

New Harmony, Nov. 30 —President Marsden from Parowan and former President Jones from Cedar are here today holding ward conference. Some changes were made in the Sunday School. The talk of the brethern was highly appreciated by the people of the ward. The ward entertaining committee was honorably released with a vote of thanks for their untiring efforts in their calling, a new committe being chosen to act for the next year.

Thanksgiving day was fittingly observed here. A public dinner was given at which every family was represented except two. A ball was given in the evening for the children and the adults. Everything went off without anything to mar the pleasure of the participants.

Students are returning to their various schools after spending Thanksgiving at home; they all report getting along very well and are fully satisfied with their schools.

The teachers and students are pleased to be home for a holiday; they all go back to their work with renewed vigor.

The stormy weather hangs on about as long as the drouth did in the summer. It is snowing today.

New Harmony, Dec 6 —During the past week we have had little snow but lots of freezing weather; the farmer's plow is housed for the present; cow boys are busy rounding up their cows from the fields and getting them in the yards to feed, the flock masters are rejoicing that there is snow on their winter ranges

The new entertaining committee has arranged for a Christmas Tree at the school house Christmas Eve; after the tree is undressed there will be an entertainment for both old and young consisting of songs, recitations, dancing, etc

L. A Harris, the forest ranger, is here doing business with the stock men and looking after things in general pertaining to the forest service.

Mrs. Melissa Hammond's little girl fell against the red hot heater and was badly burned but not seriously.

Iron County Record
December 12, 1913

New Harmony

We are pleased to note that after the storm the farmers are able to get out and prepare the ground for spring crops, and those who are not plowing are working on the canal which is being constructed north of Harmony. Those who are working on the canal say that if they have one week more of fair weather they will have the worst part of the work done.

Mr. Harris, one of the forest rangers is here in interest of the forest getting cattle that belong to the other end of the reserve, and has surveyed the canal.

Lawrence Prince and John Whipple are hauling straw from Kanarra to feed cattle which they have bought.

The annual meeting of the pipe line company was held on the 8th of December for the purpose of electing new officers for the year and transacting other business.

The O. B. B. Club was held at Mrs. William P. Taylor's. She served very nice refreshments, and they decided to postpone the club until the first Wednesday in May on account of the winter being so cold and stormy.

Washington County News
December 14, 1913

New Harmony, Dec. 14.—Some of our enterprising young men are making a pond four or five miles long to use the high water that goes by in the spring, they report that they are progressing very well on their work.

Some of our townspeople, so we understand, have put bids in for the mail contract from here to Cedar and also to Toquerville. We hope their bids are high enough to justify their caring to carry passengers from Cedar and Toquerville.

Mrs John Bennett from Penn., who has been spending a few weeks with her daughter in Idaho, joined her husband here a few days ago. Mr Bennett is a prosperous farmer in Penn. but feels at home among the Saints in the west.

Some of our townspeople are figuring on going to Pinto to attend the funeral of Mrs James G. Knell. Mrs. Knell's death, so we understand, was caused by a sudden attack of pneumonia.

Elders Jones and Mathison from Cedar City are here today as home missionaries, their talk was highly appreciated by the audiance.

We are having pleasant weather, farmers are busy plowing, the nights are quite cold but not cold enough to stop the plowing.

Iron County Record
December 19, 1913

New Harmony

As holidays are nearing we are pleased to see the faces of our school teachers and students.

Miss Laverna Taylor who has been teaching school in Hurricane is home for a week or two.

Mr. and Mrs. Mathew Batty from Twin Falls, Idaho, are here spending Christmas with their daughter Mrs. James L. Prince.

Our sheep men have just returned from the Hurricane valley where they have been taking a load of provisions and report the sheep in first class condition. There is plenty of snow and feed and they feel quite elated over the winter prospects.

Anna Bell Schmutz and Donald Schmutz, one of whom is teaching school in Leeds and the other going to school in Cedar, aren't with us yet but we hope to see their smiling faces in the near future.

At this writing we have learned that Elder John Pace of Price will be here to spend holidays with his aged father Harvey A. Pace.

Washington County News
December 23, 1913

New Harmony, Dec. 23.—Mr. and Mrs Ed. Whipple from Pine Valley moved here for the winter to get their children in school and to improve their farm here. Mr. Whipple has taken some land here and is busy now fencing and clearing the same.

The parties who attended the funeral of Mrs. James Knell. are loud in their praise of the hospitable way they were treated by the good people of Pinto There was a large attendance at Mrs Knell's funeral from the surrounding settlements

Miss Minnie Pace. who is teaching school at Grantsville this year, and Miss Laverna Taylor, who has been teaching school at Hurricane are here for the holidays

Since our last letter we have had a change in the weather. this morning the thermometer registered 10 above, the coldest we have had this fall

Leroy Grant went to St George last week on business pertaining to ranging stock on the reserve

Some of the students who have been attending high school are home for the holidays.

Washington County News
December 25, 1913

John Whipple of New Harmony
was a business visitor Monday.

Iron County Record
January 2, 1914

New Harmony

We are having a splendid
time during holdiys. Last Monday night a crowd of eleven boys
and girls from Gunlock came
over to spend the remainder of
the festivities with us.

Mr. Ray Robinson who has
been spending the holidays here,
has returned to his home in
Paragonah, and Mr. John Pace,
who has also been visiting here,
has returned home to Price.

Mr. and Mrs. William Chinn
have returned home from Gunlock, where they have been
spending Christmas with Mrs.
Chinn's mother and attending
the wedding of her sister.

New Harmony, Jan. 4.—Eldon Schmutz, a son of Bishop Gottlieb Schmutz was accidentally shot in the side of his head and neck, December 30th. Citizens were on a general rabbit hunt when the accident happened. Dr. Macfarlane attended the boy, who is about 16 years old, and dressed the wounds. He extracted some of the shot and does not anticipate serious results. With this exception the holidays passed off very pleasantly, some of the young people from other settlements participating. 230 rabbits were killed during the rabbit hunt Tuesday.

L. A. Pace and his daughter, Miss Minnie, went to New Castle to be with James G. Knell and family during their time of sadness in the loss of their mother and wife; they are kindly remembered by many friends sending letters of condolence, which they appreciate very much.

The teachers and students who have been home to spend the holidays have gone back to their various schools; all have had a pleasant time at home.

The music furnished during the holidays by Arnold Graf and Sam L. Pollock from Kanarra was highly appreciated by our townspeople.

Mr. and Mrs John Hall from Hurricane have returned to their home after spending a few days visiting with relatives and friends.

John H. Pace from Price, Carbon county, is here visiting his father, Harvey A. Pace, and other relatives and friends.

Among the visitors are numbered several of our former residents, Horace L. Slack of Provo, Mrs. Hannah Woolsey of Harmony, accompanied by her husband; John H. Batty of Bingham, Archie Bringhurst of Riverton, John A. Kinsley of Salt Lake, other visitors are R E Fletcher, of Enterprise, Mitchel Smith of Hamilton's and Floyd Grant of New Harmony.

New Harmony, Jan. 12 —The men working on the new canal are taking advantage of the nice weather and pushing the canal to a finish.

The officers and teachers of the Sunday school went to Kanarra last Sunday to meet with the Stake Supt. of Sunday schools. They report having had a very profitable and pleasant time.

The county superintendent of schools, Chas B Petty, is here to-day visiting schools, he seemed fairly well pleased with the conditions that exist in the school.

Eldon Schmutz who was recently shot in the head is able to be out to his regular work again.

Mrs Vivian Prince underwent an opperation for gall stones this morning at Cedar City.

Mrs John Bennett has gone back to Idaho to look after her daughter, who is very ill.

Mrs. Lottie Kelsey of New Harmony was at Grafton last week visiting with her mother, Mrs , Ballard.

New Harmony

Mrs. Jo'n Bennett left here Saturday for Idaho. She went to attend her daughter, who is ill.

Mr. and Mrs. Joseph W. Prince are in Cedar City. Mrs. Prince underwent an operation recently at the Southern Utah Hospital for the correction of a trouble involving her liver. She has been troubled more or less with it for some years.

The Harmony Sunday School officers and teachers went to Kanarra Sunday to attend the Sunday School Union held there.

We are glad to see Eldon Schmutz about again. He has recovered very nicely from the accident that he met with recently during the rabbit hunt.

New Harmony, Jan. 29.—We are having our share of rainfall. The precipitation since the 15th to the 25th has been 6 86 inches, and it is still raining, some days the south mail fails to get here on account of high water.

There is an epidemic taking the rounds among the school children here in the form of sore eyes They are out of school about two days then their eyes apparently are all right again

Last Friday night the officers and teachers of the Sunday school gave a dance and sold lunch for the benefit of the S S   A very enjoyable and profitable evening was spent

Mrs Vivian Prince is still in the hospital at Cedar City, but she is slowly recovering, she will be home this week if everything goes well with her.

A number of our townspeople are having telephones put into their houses, more than half of the people have them in now.

Roy grant is home again after an absence of two or three weeks, working on a reservoir in Hurricane valley.

New Harmony, Feb 2 — The weather has cleared up at last and is now fine. The precipitation for January was 7 86 inches The sheep and stockmen are highly elated over the late storms and the farmers are wearing a broad smile owing to the fine prospects next summer

Elders Adams and Mathison from Parowan were with us last Sunday They were down in the interest of the High Priests and remained for the afternoon services Their remarks were highly appreciated by the audience

Some of the cow boys have gone to the Iron mountain to look after their cattle that have drifted away from their ranges

New Harmony, Feb 10 —Some of our townspeople went to Kanarra last Sunday to attend the funeral of Riley B Will, who died last week at Cedar of pneumonia.

Mrs Vivian Prince who has been in the hospital for the past five or six weeks returned home today. She stood the trip home very well.

Quite a number of the school children are out of school on account of bad colds accompanied with fever

The cowboys have returned from their trip to Iron mountain

Gottlieb Schmutz of New Harmony is a business visitor here

New Harmony, Feb 16—The men interested in the long canal north of town have begun work again   they report that one more week will finish the job if the weather remains favorable

Some of our stockmen are so dissatisfied with the arrangements of the forest reserve they think they will have to go out of the business

There are so many of the school children sick with grip or something similar that it is hard to keep the school going

Our farmers will soon be plowing if the weather remains like it has been the last week or ten days

Quite a number of our citizens are talking of going to the Farmers Roundup at Cedar next week.

NEW HARMONY.

New Harmony, Utah, Feb. 18, 1914.

We are very glad to see Mrs. J. W. Prince back home again and getting along as well as she is.

Dr. E. Smith, the dentist, is in Harmony and has been doing quite a lot of dental work for us. He has been here nearly two weeks, and when he is through here he will go to Kanarra and spend some time.

Mr. Page has been here this week with his moving pictures, which have been very good and greatly enjoyed by everyone present at his exhibitions.

We have been enjoying spring weather for about two weeks, but it is raining again now.

We are sorry to see so many of our people sick with bad colds, but are fortunate in not having any cases of pneumonia here as yet.

New Harmony, Feb. 22 —The death of George Reed of Mexico, a former resident of this place, was sad news to us all

Since our last correspondence we have had some rain, the precipitation was 4 38 inches, the rain storm wound up with snow from the north, at this writing the sun is shining as bright as a May morning

We have had no mail from the south for three days; the mail from the north came all right but a little late

The epidemic of grip hangs on to our people, one day there were only eight students at school.

Many of the people who figured on going to the Farmers' roundup have given up the trip

NEW HARMONY.

March, 3, 1914.

We are again having some very cold and stormy weather. The precipitation for the month of February was 4.96 inches.

* * *

Dr. E. Smith, who has been here for nearly three weeks left last Thursday for Kanarra where he will remain for a short time.

* * *

Mr. Mace and Ferron Gardner of Pine Valley were here for a few days last week gathering cattle.

* * *

J. W. Prince is in the Hurricane Valley looking after his sheep. He will be gone for a week or ten days longer. His wife is getting along nicely now.

Melva the little eight months old daughter of Mr. and Mrs. A. F. Mathis has bronchial pneumonia, she has been quite a sick babe but is very much better now.

* * *

Last week a convict at the convict camp in Dixie made a break for his liberty. He lay in a secret place for a few days and Saturday last the mail driver from here to Toquerville met him coming north. He intended to telephone to the guards when he reached Bellevue, but he met two of the guards on the road, and it was not long until the convict was in custody again.. It has been reported here that after he had been captured the man tried to commit suicide by cutting his throat with a piece of sharp glass, but did not succeed in his purpose. It has not been learned here what has been done with the convict.

New Harmony, Mar 8 —The New Harmony Reservoir and Irrigation company held their annual meeting the 2nd inst The following were elected· Henry A Pace, president; L A. Pace, secretary and treasurer; Independence Taylor and Gottlieb Schmutz, directors, Albert F. Mathis, Watermaster.

L A. Harris, the forest ranger, is here doing business with the stockmen and locating a drift fence which will be put up at once with the assistance of the stockmen of this place

We understand the mail contract is open for bidders to carry the mail from here to Cedar. The bids that went in were too high for the government

The parties making the long canal north of town will suspend work this week on account of having to work on their farms

George A. Grant(Bert)and his wife came home last week They spent the winter in Payson where Mrs. Grant's parents live.

Mr McCune, representing the Panguitch Commission Co , has been here buying stock. He paid a fairly good price for stock.

Those who attended the Farmers' Roundup at Cedar are well pleased.

County Assessor Jacob Frei called on us last week

Iron County Record
March 18, 1914

NEW HARMONY.

March 18, 1914.

Mr. and Mrs. James Neilson from Monroe are here visiting their son. They will remain until next Fall as Mr. Neilson is going to do some prospecting.

A crowd of young people from Kanarra were over to the dance Tuesday night.

* * *

Mrs. O. Hammond, who has been very ill, is now on the improve.

* * *

Mr. Frank Kelsey has been down with a bad attack of LaGrippe, but is getting along nicely now.

* * *

Miss Ethel Leavitt from Gunlock and Miss Dell Prince are visiting in town for a few weeks.

Washington County News
March 22, 1914

New Harmony, Mar. 22.—The Relief society remembered the organization of their society by giving a dancing party with songs, recitations, etc One feature of the entertainment was a song by the older members of the society, which was rendered in a pleasing manner The president, Mrs Sarah Prince Davis, with her counselors are to be commended for their active work in the association.

The grip hangs on with some of our townspeople, it is hard for some of the older ones to shake it off Orrin Kelsey is able to be out again after a spell of the grip

We are having spring weather. The farmers are busy with their spring work, cleaning and repairing canals, planting small grain, etc

John E. Whipple who has just returned from a business trip to St George, reports everything lovely and prosperous in the Dixie country.

Schmutz Bros are about through shearing their goats and are fairly well satisfied with the clip.

The flock masters are busy these days with their sheep getting them on to the spring ranges

Washington County News
March 29, 1914

New Harmony, Mar. 29.—The past week has been windy and cold The apricots have been injured considerably by frost. We are now having a nice rain storm, which is good for the farmers, the flock masters and all.

Mr Kerr is here with his steam plow and grubber for the purpose of clearing and plowing some of the new land; it is reported he is doing good work.

Bishop Henry A. Pace has gone to Ogden or somewhere near there to get a bunch of full blooded sheep, he is expected home soon with them.

W. K. Drouillard representing the Merchants Protective Association is here doing business with some of our townspeople.

Mrs. Melissa Hammond, who has been quite sick for the last month or more, is able to be out again

Washington County News
April 5, 1914

New Harmony, April 5 —Bp Henry A. Pace has returned from Ogden with a nice bunch of full blood ewes

James D Neilson and wife are here from Sevier Co Mr Neilson is a professor on the violin and furnishes good music for the dancing parties. Our young people had a nice time here on the 1st of April, the young ladies gave the young men the slip and left them to have it all their own way.

New Harmony, April 15, 1914.—
Monday April 13, the stork visited the
home of Mr. and Mrs. Frank Kelsey
leaving them a nine pound boy.
Mother and child are doing fine. Dr.
Leonard was in attendance.

* * *

Mr. Reese Davis returned from
Cedar City yesterday where he was at
tending to business. Mr. L. A. Pace
and son also have been to Cedar City
on business.

* * *

We had a fine time on Easter every
body took their lunch and went up in
the meadows, after lunch was served
everyone joined in the games. To
wind our day up, Mrs. Thomas Brown
gave a party in the evening and ice
cream and cake were served.

* * *

The steam plow has been here for
two or three weeks at work and they
report doing very nice work.

* * *

Mrs. Berry Williams of Kanarra has
been over here visiting her mother,
relatives and friends.

* * *

Mr. J. W. Prince has returned home
from his herd where he has been for
several weeks.

Joseph Prince of Harmony is in Cedar today. He reports a good deal of
activity at Harmony this year in the
matter of arid farming. Mr. Kerr,
the traction engine man, is there and
has signed up to do a good deal of
plowing in that locality.

Washington County News
April 19, 1914

New Harmony, Apr 19 —The last week has been changeable; we had a little rain and two or three days of cold wind from the north, some ice, but the freeze was not hard enough to kill the fruit

The parties interested in the long canal have it finished; they worked all winter on it when the weather would permit and have a good canal This is a high water project.

Arbor day was observed by our townspeople, planting trees, etc The school teacher and his students were busy putting trees out and cleaning the school grounds up

On the 15th a nice baby boy came to the home of Mr and Mrs Frank Kelsey, all concerned are doing nicely.

Easter Sunday was observed by our townspeople in going off for picnics and other amusements.

Washington County News
April 26, 1914

New Harmony, April 26 —The last week we have had some nice showers, which is a great benefit to the farming and other industries. We had 1 48 inches of precipitation this month.

The stockmen are figuring on making a pasture to hold their cattle in before they are counted on to the summer range They are having a little trouble in keeping stock out os some of the fields where there is not much of a fence

Miss Verna Taylor is home from Hurricane, where she has been teaching school. Donald Schmutz is also home from Leeds where he has been teaching school They both spoke in the sacramental meeting today.

Mrs Florence Phippin of Carey, Idaho, is here visiting with her mother, Mrs Eliza Kelsey. Mrs Phippin reports things in a prosperous condition in the part of Idaho where she lives

The sheep men are shearing; they report a fairly good clip this spring Quite a number of our men are now hauling wool from Iron Springs to Lund

School closed last Friday. The students are well pleased with their record this school year.

Our Go to Church Sunday was fairly well attended today.

New Harmony, May 3 —Our farmers are having a lay off while the ground is drying out a little, we have had 3 25 in of precipitation during the month of April Frost has injured our fruit crop some but there is enough fruit to supply our homes left yet if we have no more freezing weather. Quite a number of the farmers are putting corn in where the fall grain winter killed. Rabbits are doing quite a lot of damage to our small grain, we are trying to kill them with strychnine by mixing salt, flour and strychenine together but up to this time we have not killed as many as we hoped to do.

Bishop Henry A Pace has some experience in shearing and lambing on his farm but he thinks he will try it again next season The stormy weather was a little hard on his flock

The schmutz Brothers have sheared their goats, they had an offer of 28 cents per pound but thought they could do a little better so shipped their crop east.

W. D. Owen, representing Z C. M. I. is here doing business with the merchants, he reports a favorable business

J. G Pace was a town visitor from Cedar City last week, doing business with the farmers

Ammon Jolley left for New Harmony recently to drive mail from Harmony to Cedar.

Iron County Record
May 5, 1914

New Harmony, Utah, May 5,1914.
Mrs. Florence Phippin of Carey,
Idaho, is here visiting relatives and
friends.

* * *

Bishop H. A. Pace has been shearing his sheep up at his farm. The
shearing is now completed, but on account of the stormy weather and the
scarcity of feed he has lost a good
many of his lambs.

* * *

We have had some very stormy
weather of late, but it is fine at present ,and all of the farms are looking
fine.

* * *

Miss Lenora Ballard is here visiting relatives.

* * *

We are very glad to have our school
teachers back home with us again.
Miss LaVerna Taylor has been teaching in Hurricane, Utah, and Mr. Donald Schmutz has been employed at
Leeds, Utah. They report having
spent a pleasant winter.

New Harmony, May 10.—J
Thomas Kerr, the traction engine
man, is doing good work clearing
and p'owing our new land. He had
quite a close call the other day. A
man weighing about 200 pounds
was swinging an eight pound ham-
mer when the head flew off from the
handle and knocked Mr. Kerr's hat
off, two inches lower and he would
have been a man of the past

Our sheep men report that their
prospects for a crop of lambs is good
this spring The late rains has done
them a wonderful lot of good.

The last week has been dry with
more or less wind from the south
Our farmers are very busy putting
in corn and potatoes.

A baby girl came to the home of
Mr and Mrs Lawrence Prince,
mother and babe are getting along
nicely.

Mr. Page and wife are here again
with their moving picture show
They are putting on some nice pictures

Lawrence Prince has the mail
contract from here to Cedar

New Harmony, May 24 —We had home missionaries last Sunday from New Castle, Elders Donald Forsyth and John Tullls; their remarks were timely and highly appreciated by an attentive audience

The stork visited the home of Mr and Mrs William Chinn last week and left a nice baby boy at their home, mother and babe getting along very well.

Miss Minnie Pace has returned home from Grantsville where she has been teaching school the past school year

Mr. and Mrs. Thomas Brown have gone to Lund to meet some of their friends from Arkansas

We have had very high south winds the last two or three days

The town of Harmony, with a population not to exceed 200 souls, situated just over the line in Washington county, but embraced in the Parowan stake of Zion, is one of the most energetic and progressive little settlements in Southern Utah, and has a great future before it in an agricultural sense. The valley, while not very large, is one of the most fertile tracts of land in this entire country, and one of the best adapted to arid farming. The rainfall is heavy, the soil is deep and loamy and already arid farming has been conducted there on quite an extensive scale with excellent results. Besides this, there is an abundance of high water there, and dams and canals have recently been constructed to bring a much larger area under irrigation.

Within the past year several hundred acres of new land has been brought under cultivation, and at the present time Mr. T J Kerr is busy with his caterpillar traction engine, grubber and plows on contracts for the clearing and plowing of fully 600 acres, and this will likely be increased before he finishes in that locality. Among those who have let contracts to Mr. Kerr we learn of the following

Mr. Ernest	..	..160 acres
Bp Harvey A. Pace	.	. 80 acres
Reese Davis ..	...	100 acres
Albert Mathis . . .		. 40 acres
Penn Taylor	. .	. . 75 acres
Lawrence Prince ...	.	. 30 acres
Schmutz Brothers	.	50 acres
George Prince .	. .	. 40 acres
L A. Pace	. ...	. 10 acses
Joseph Prince .		. 20 acres
Total	..	605 acres

Bishop Harvey A. Pace has a splendid tract of land, embracing 320 acres and extending along the main road into Harmony for a distance of three miles. About 100 acres of the tract is now broken up, forty acres of which is seeded to alfalfa, about 15 acres to corn, and a large acreage to small grains. The location and soil are ideal, and the traveler into Harmony is impressed with the appearance of the land and growing crops. It is situated on the south side of the road.

Among other extensive farmers might be mentioned Gottleib Schmutz, who added fifty acres this spring to his cultivated area, which has been planted to grain and corn.

Reese Davis has also planted 40 acres of corn this spring on newly broken land

A visitor to Harmony sees precious few idle men and boys. It is a community of hustlers and no one appears to have any time for street loafing. The people have an excellent reputation for paying their bills when due, and Harmony will yet be known as one of the most thrifty communities in the entire state.

Keep your eye on New Harmony.
—Iron County Record.

New Harmony, June 7.—The O. B B. club (Our Busy Bunch) have reorganized with an enrollment of 15 members. They have their by-laws made, but up to this time have not thought of a name by which it shall be called. They met at the home of Miss Cecil Taylor last week and report having had a very pleasant time.

J. G. Pace and family from Cedar are here visiting with relatives and friends. Mr. Pace speaks very highly of the canals that have been made here in the last year, he was surprised to see the nice crops of corn and small grain growing where a few years ago there was nothing but sage brush

Forest Rangers Moody and Harris were here last week counting the stock on the summer range, The stockmen were fairly successful in rounding their cattle up, however they will have another roundup soon to gather the remainder of their stock.

Joseph N. Prince has been confined to his room for two or three weeks past with pneumonia, at this writing he is on the way to recovery very nicely.

Last week Dan Barney met with a painful but not serious accident, at this time he is able to be at his regular work

Our farmers are waiting for the weather to settle so they can get to cutting their hay.

We have had some very nice rains which is encouraging to the dry farmer.

Maeser Dalley is here surveying a canal for the townspeople.

New Harmony, June 15 —Dr. Leonard was called to Harmony last week and brought Dr. Wilkinson with him; the results of their call were a nice baby boy and a nice little girl left at the home of Mrs. James L Taylor. At this writing mother and babes are getting along very nicely

President Day of the stake presidency was here last Sunday. His remarks were timely and highly appreciated by an attentive audience. Mr. Day left Parowan at 8 a. m. and got here in time for Sunday school.

A committee has been put in to arrange for a celebration on the 4th The program was read in church last Sunday

New Harmony, June 20 —Orren H Snow and wife, Vilo Redd Snow, have been here visiting friends and relatives Mrs Snow was born here and grew to womanhood in our little town   There was a dancing party and picnic given by the towns-people in their honor, a very pleas-ant and enjoyable time being had

Henry A. Pace and wife have re-turned from Parowan where they have been to attend the quarterly conference; the bishop reports a very pleasant time

A rabbit hunt is to come off here the 1st and 2nd of July, the los-ing side to give a dance and serve ice cream

The farmers are very busy with their 1st crop of alfalfa. The crop is about an average of past years

Mr, Andrew Schmutz and Miss Cecil Taylor will be married at Parowan on June 25

New Harmony, June 27 —Last week a bevy of young ladies and young married woman surprised Miss Cecil Taylor a day or two before she was married; they gave her a bundle shower, then followed a party after which cake and ice cream were served Before they went home they took Miss Cecil put her on a hayrake and rode her through the streets All expressed themselves as having had a nice time. Miss Taylor and Mr. Andrew Schmutz were married in Parowan on the 25th day of June; Elder Wilford Day of the Parowan Stake presidency performed the ceremony which unites them together for this life They have a host of friends wishing them a pleasant and prosperous journey through life

Ranger J M Moody was here last week doing business with the stock men, he says the feed on the summer range is fine and the stock are looking well

We are preparing to have a nice celebration on the 4th The various committees have everything fixed so that we will have a very pleasant time.

Our farmers quit hauling hay a few days last week on account of high winds from the south but at this time we have very fine haying weather

Donald Schmutz has returned from Kansas City where he has been with a few car loads of goats, he reports having had a very pleasant trip

J. W. Earnast from Los Angeles is here superintending the clearing and plowing of his farm just east of town

A rabbit hunt will come off this week, some of our boys went to Kanarra today to get guns for the hunt.

New Harmony, July 5 —We think we are not being treated just right in having the mail discontinued from here to Toquerville To transact any business with the county seat a letter must travel about 200 miles to reach St George a distance of about 42 miles Not very pleasant to have to take so much time to get a letter to and from St George, when we had the mail go south from here we could hear from the county seat in two days; now it will take nearly a week What is the matter with our postal service we wonder

The Fourth was celebrated in a fitting manner, a very good meeting in the forenoon, the afternoon was spent in sports of various kinds for both old and young, a ball game in the evening, at night a dance for the children and adults finished up the day's amusements, everybody seemed to have had a very pleasant time People from Cedar, Pine Valley, Kanaria and other surrounding towns came to spend the day with us Everything passed off without a hitch or accident to mar our pleasure.

On the 2nd of July the wedding reception of Mr. and Mrs Andrew Schmutz was given at the home of the bride's grandparents A very enjoyable time was spent by the townspeople The bride received many nice and useful presents

Last week the rabbit hunt came off. The hunt lasted one day and a half and 1492 rabbits were killed The losing side is to put up a dance and ice cream

The following is the precipitation for the six months ending June 30, 1914 Jan 7.86, Feb 4 39, Mar, 3 25, April 3 30 May 0 00, June 1 31in.

We had a few showers the latter part of June which did much good to our dry land corn.

Our dry land corn is looking very good.

New Harmony, July 14.—The committee for the 24th has met and arranged a nice program for the celebration of Pioneer day We look forward to a grand time on that day.

Mrs. Francis Prince has returned from Price, Utah, where she has been to visit a while with her son, John, and other relatives and friends Mrs Prince is feeling and looking well after her trip

No doubt this letter will reach you too late for this week's issue, we overlooked the fact the distance it has to go to reach St George

Maesor Dalley has returned home to Cedar city. Mr. Dalley has been here two or three weeks surveying for the townspeople.

Our school election passed off quietly. Gottheb Schmutz was elected to succeed himself for the ensuing three years

Quite a number of our townspeople have the grip.

New Harmony, July 19 —Mr. Alders, from Kanarra is here with his header harvesting the dry land grain J. Thomas Kerr is busy grubbing and plowing, he is having a little difficulty in getting fuel to run the engine but he is expecting a carload of fuel this week from Los Angeles This will be a busy week harvesting grain

Last week the Sunday school gave a dance and sold ice cream to raise money to buy books for the Sunday school. Everything went off fine and those present had a very pleasant time.

Samuel Kelsey from Mesa, Ariz, is here visiting with relatives and friends, he will send some of his children to the B A C. at Cedar City the coming school year.

New Harmony, July 26 —The late showers cause the farmers to be encouraged; on the dry land farms the corn crop has never been better than it is this season, so they look forward to a bounteous harvest in the fall

Mrs. Susan Pace and her granddaughter, Miss Laverna Taylor, have gone to Uinta to visit with Mrs Pace's parents, Mr. and Mrs Thomas Keel. they expect to be gone about a month.

The flock masters of our town report the sheep on the summer range as in fine condition and things look prosperous for a good sale of sheep this fall

Maesar Dalley, who has been surveying a canal for the Harmony people, came into town Friday last, and reports everything progressing nicely at that place   He says that when the canal he has just finished surveying is completed, it will carry sufficient water on the east bench to irrigate every foot of land there Mr Dalley states that never in the history of Harmony has there been so much land under cultivation, and that the crops this year are excellent, especially those of the "dry landers," some of them going as high as 40 bushels to the acre — Cedar City Observer.

The precipitation at New Harmony for the month of July was 2 95 inches, as shown by the local observer

New Harmony, Aug. 7. — The harvesting of small grain is a thing of the past for this season; the crop is a little above the average this year. The threshing machine will start soon if the weather will give the grain a chance to get dry. Mr Fawcett of St George has been here repairing the machine. It is estimated that the late rains have spoiled about 100 tons of hay in our neighborhood and still it showers every once in a while

The Harmony Pipe Line Co is going to have a cement tank put in to hold the water instead of the wooden one they now have Mr. Millet of Cedar is going to do the work.

Some of our flock masters are preparing to start soon to ship their sheep to the eastern or western maket; they report their sheep in fine shape

New Harmony, Aug 14 —The O H E club, formerly the O B B, club, had the entertainment of the season at the home of Bishop Henry A Pace Supper was served at 8 o0 on the lawn The tables were highly decorated with bouquets of various kinds of flowers, and groaned under their burden of loaded platters of chicken and delicaces that tempted the appetites of all the participants, after which the guests retired to the parlor where the evening was spent in music and games All left for their homes feeling it is good to get together and have a jolly time

Reese Davis and family have gone to Kanarra to attend the funeral of Mrs Davis' mother, "Aunt Polly " Mrs Davis has lived as she died, a faithful member in the church

The prospects for a good yield in the potato crop is not very bright, the early potatoes were almost an entire failure

Miss Mary Knell from New Castle has been here for two or three weeks for her health, she is much improved

Archibald Gale, from New Castle has been here visiting friends a day or two this week

Mr Fawcett from St George will start the threshing machine here next week

Washington County News
August 28, 1914

New Harmony, Aug 28.—The threshing machine has been doing a good business up to this date They have it all done but two more settings this morning The machine was running all right when a blaze of fire rushed out of the tail end of it The cause is hard to ascertain The straw was burned and the separator, but the stacks of grain were saved by the heroic efforts of the hands around the machine They hooked on to the separator while it was burning and pulled it away from the stack One bad feature about the fire was the lack of water, all the boys had being some in barrels taken out to water the stock at noon The machine was threshing for Bishop H A Pace on his farm a mile or two from town

Reed Prince the son of James L Prince was kicked the other day by a large horse, the horse was rough shod and had the boy been close to him no doubt it would have killed him

Miss Minnie Pace who has been visiting with friends in New Castle returned home today; she reports having had a very pleasant time

James O Tweedie from Cedar is here visiting with friends

Washington County News
September 4, 1914

New Harmony, Sept. 4.—Our farmers are very busy hauling corn. This season has been the best for dry land corn, the crop being fine this fall and far ahead of any corn crop in the past years

Part of the family of Ed. Whipple of Pine Valley has moved back. Mr. Whipple expects to have the whole family here in time to start the children in school.

Miss Velva Prince, daughter of Joseph W. and Vivian Prince, has been sick for two weeks, she has quite a high fever.

Wm. H Pace of Price has been on a short visit to see his grandfather, H. A. Pace. and other relatives and friends.

Miss Minnie Pace will teach school in Kanarra

New Harmony, Sept. 18 —The visitors to the fruit festival at St George have returned all well. They speak very highly of the hospitable treatment of the St. George people

Misses Mildred Pace and Rosalia Schmutz have gone to attend the Dixie academy. Some of our other young people are preparing to go to Cedar to the B A. C

Dr Leonard is in town today to see Miss Velva Prince It is reported that she is not getting along as well as was hoped for.

Our cowboys have gone to round up their stock and get them where they can handle them for the fall and winter.

Our district school will start the fore part of October Miss Verna Leavitt will teach here this school year.

The farmers are busy with the third crop of alfalfa

New Harmony, Sept 24.—The Commercial club of Cedar has extended us an invitation to attend the Iron county fair and compete for prizes the same as if we were in Iron conuty. We appreciate the invitation inasmuch as it is more convenient to attend the fair at Cedar than it is to go to St. George. Our townspeople would like to have the county lines changed so we could be in Iron county. If the good people of Washington county will give us their vote for the change it will be so much more convenient for us to attend our business in Iron county than it is in St George. What do you think about it, you Washington county people? An automobile load of men from Cedar has been to see us in the interest of the coming fair which will be held in Cedar this week, among them was a representative from the commercial club at Cedar and the editor of the Observer of Cedar City.

Miss Gladys Grant and Jesse Whipple from Pine Valley were married at the home of the bride's parents, last Friday night Sept. 18 We wish the young couple a pleasant and prosperous journey through life.

S. A. Gholeon from southern Arizona' is busy clearing land for some of our townspeople

New Harmony, Oct. 2 —The fair visitors were highly pleased with the sports, etc   The exhibit was a surprise to all; the dry land display was the best ever put out   All the dry land farmers are encouraged wonderfully.

Most of the able bodied men are out on a deer hunt   Several men and their families from surrounding settlements are with us for the purpose of hunting deer.

Bp Henry A Pace with his carpenters are very busy getting a roof on his new barn before it storms

Andrew Schmutz has just returned from Kanab where he has been to get some blooded goats

The political pot is beginning to simmer a little with our people.

The sheep men have their flocks from the summer range.

Coal hauling is the order of the day with us

New Harmony, Oct 27 —The fall work is nearly finished, but we have done no fall plowing to amount to much on account of the long dry spell we have had We have had no heavy freezing weather up to this time Some of our people have fresh tomatoes and green bean vines

Joseph N Prince while returning from Bellevue with his family the other day, met an automobile on one of the sharp turnes on the ledge How a collision was averted is almost a miracle but as it was the driver of the auto, Warren Cox, did not loose his head so none were hurt Mrs Prince's nervous system had a severe shock, but at this time she is much improved

Our school has started for this school year, the trustee had some repairing to do on the house having it cemented on the outside and a hard finish on the in Now it is done, it is a credit to the town

The threshing is finished at last, the two or three jobs left when the machine was burned in the summer, are finished without any more trouble

Frank Staheli left his threshing machine here for the winter, he has threshed a good quantity of grain this fall

Miss Verna Knell, of New Castle paid a short visit to her friends here. She has returned home

Miss Minnie Pace, who is teaching in Kanarra was home on a visit last Friday.

Hew Harmony, Nov 1 —President Marsden and former President Jones were the speakers in the sacramental meeting this afternoon Their remarks were timely and highly appreciated by the audience We had ward conference, all parties were unanimously sustained in their various callings

The O H E club gave a Hallowe'en party on Saturday. After the ghosts and goblins finished their part of the work The people enjoyed themselves in the dance. The entertainment was a success from beginning to finish.

The students attending high school write home that they are attending the right school, some at Cedar some at St George, all seem pleased with the school and the people with whom they associate

Robert F. Mathis made a trip to St George last week in his new automobile Mr. Mathis had some business with the county treasurer and to take his cousin, Mr Bochardt, late from Switzerland

We received word this evening that Uncle George Williams of Kanarra passed away after a lingering sickness Some of our townspeople will go over to the funeral

Claude Knell of New Castle came over to visit with friends and take in the Hallowe en party Some of the Kanarra young people came over to join us in the party

Last week the Democratic party reorganized L A Pace was elected chairman and Robert A Kirker secy

The sheep men are busy getting their flocks on the road to the winter ranges

New Harmony, Nov 15 —Last Sunday Elders Claude Knell and Robert Platt from New Castle were here as home missionaries, their talk was timely and highly appreciated by the audience

The young ladies have started their meeting for the winter; they gave an entertainment before starting to which all were invited and a very pleasant time was spent

Antone Prince and Evelyn Prince have gone to St George to take the winter course given at the Academy

Elmer Taylor has gone to Lund with turkeys, they will be shipped to Ogden for the Thanksgiving trade

Rangers Moody and McAllister were here a few days last week doing business with the townspeople

Our farmers are busy these fine days putting in their fall grain

Milton Herman and Floyd Grant of New Harmony, Washington county, walked half of the distance to this city, and enlisted in the navy Thursday afternoon, the former as an apprentice seaman, and the latter as hospital apprentice They left on the evening train for San Francisco.

New Harmony, Nov 22 —Our sheep men are anxious for storm. They can't move their flocks to the winter ranges until it rains or snows, they are just moving from place to place and patiently waiting

Bp Pace and counselors call on the town to turn out next Saturday and haul wood for the widows and the meeting house.

The entertaining committee has prepared a nice program for Thanksgiving so we look forward to a pleasant time

New Harmony, Nov 29 —Thanksgiving passed off very nicely here Family dinners were served and all had a very nice time. A dance for the children was given in the afternoon and one for adults at night.

Born, today, a daughter to Mr. and Mrs J L Prince; mother and babe getting along nicely.

Born, a daughter to Mrs Samuel A. Goulson; the babe lived only a short time

New Harmony, Dec 11 —Mrs. Julia Taylor widdow of the late Wm W. Taylor, was buried here. She had been living with her daughter, Mrs Samuel Roundy, at Mapleton, for a number of years Mrs Taylor was 84 years old and the cause of death was general debility Two of her daughters, Mrs DeLong and Mrs Roundy, and a son accompanied the corpse here for interment Mrs Taylor was a faithful member of the church, she crossed the plains with the hand cart company when she was a young girl

The ward entertaining committee is preparing to give the youngsters a good time Christmas eve The entertainment will consist of songs recitations speaches, etc ,after which there will be a Christmas tree and dancing

At last the drouth is broken, we have this morning about six inches of snow, and looks like more will come

The sheep men are rejoicing over the storm, they are now on their way to the winter ranges.

New Harmony, Dec 20 —Our townspeople are looking forward to a good time during the holidays School is closed for two weeks so the children will have quite a rest from their books

We have had some wintry weather with about 8 or 10 inches of snow, the coldest morning the thermometer registered zero, warm sunny days now

The county sheriffs of Iron and Beaver counties were here today trying to get trace of the convict who left camp without any ceremony.

Wm Chinn was surprised the other morning when he went to the barn to find one of his valuable work horses dead in its stall

The students from their various schools are home for the holidays and are all looking and feeling well.

Ranger J M. Moody is here doing business with the stockmen

New Harmony, Dec. 27. — On Saturday the 26th inst , Mr. and Mrs Francis Prince gave their golden wedding reception. A very good time was had, more than a hundred people sitting down to the tables which were loaded with the good things of life. Mr. and Mrs Prince gave a grand ball in the evening which was enjoyed by a crowded house

In last week's letter an error was made   The sheriffs from Iron and Beaver counties were after an optician, not the escaped convict

Our holidays are passing pleasantly.   Quite a number from the outside settlements are here; it is pleasant to have them come

John H Pace and John W. Prince of Price are here visiting their parents and other relatives and friends

A happy and prosperous New Year to you.

New Harmony, Jan 3 — The holidays are a thing of the past   All of our townspeople as well as the visitors express themselves as having had a jolly good time   The committee gave a prize dance which was fine, the prize winners were Lawrence Prince and Rose Schmutz, first, and John Whipple and his sister, Ruth Whipple Prince, second.

We are having an epidemic of the grip among the children, some quite severe but not of a serious nature

We have had some cold weather, the thermometer ranging from 20 to 12 below the freezing point.

Elmer Taylor is suffering with an attack of appendicitis and is in much pain.

Miss Mildred Pace of New Harmony who has been attending school here it quite ill with scarletina.

New Harmony, Jan 10 —We have two or three cases of scarlatina here, the patients are getting along very well, how, when or where we got the exposure is a mystery, the first one to take it is a little two or three year old girl of Mr. and Mrs Wm P Taylor

Have had some storm the last week but not more than 2 or 3 inches of snow

Mrs Flora Brown is having lumber hauled for her new house

New Harmony, Jan. 24 —The New Harmony Reservoir and Canal Co held their annual meeting the first Monday in this month and elected a vice-president and two directors for the ensuing two years. The company put a force of men to work to make a new canal to increase the stream but a cold wave has stopped the work. Yesterday the thermometer registered four degrees above zero.

Our dry farmers are quite concerned about the farming next summer as up to the present time there is not enough snow in the mountains to cause the creeks to rise On the 11 of Dec we had from 6 to 8 inches of snow and a little has fallen since

John Whipple is considering moving his saw mill from Pine Valley to this place He has gone to St George to see if he can get assistance to make a road to the timber.

Rov Grant and John Page made a trip to Parowan to get some full-blood Durham bulls All of our stockmen are going in for improving their stock

Miss LaVerne Taylor has returned from a trip to St George where she went to visit the schools

Andrew Schmutz was kicked by a horse and very painfully but not seriously hurt.

Washington County News
January 31, 1915

New Harmony, Jan 31 —We had a good storm; from Thursday to Saturday noon, 2 26 inches of rainfall Friday night a very heavy snow broke shade trees down and the telephone wire was broken in six or eight places by the heavy snow on the line, the line is in repair again. We have about 3 or 4 inches of water in the ground and it is covered with about 8 inches of snow, so we have some slush walking The mail had to be carried on horseback.

We are about through with the scarlet fever; the quarantine at the home of L A Pace has been raised and that of Wm. Taylor will be raised this week; these are the only two houses that have been under quarantine

We are very much disappointed to learn that we are going to have our mail cut down to a tri-weekly, we are petitioning the postal officers to have it at least six times a week

John Adams has been buying cattle here, he is having quite a time to get them rounded up to move them away.

Reese Davis and James E. Taylor are on their way from Lund loaded with goods; teams will go out to meet them

Some of our young men went out Saturday and rounded up about 100 rabbits.

Bp Henry A Pace has gone to Hurricane valley to look after his sheep

It is reported the snow is three feet deep on the Goddard ranch.

Washington County News
February 7, 1915

New Harmony, Feb 7—A petition has been signed to have our mail services continued six times a week instead of three times We think the mail matter that comes in and goes out of our town justifies a mail at least six times a week There are from sixteen to twenty daily papers taken here and to have to stop them and have a weekly or semi weekly instead is not just right

Last Tuesday the 2nd we had a downpour of rain, the precipitation for the day was 1 85 in on top of 6 in of snow.

Dr. Leonard was called to see the little babe of Mr. and Mrs G Lawrence Prince who has pneumonia.

New Harmony, Feb. 14 — Last week we have had 3 13 inches of rain, reported by the postmaster, who looks after the precipitation here The rain was not a downpour but a steady rain for about two days and put on two or three inches of snow to top on. At this time the snow is gone and we are having springlike weather.

Quite a number of our townspeople attended the round up at Cedar. They report having had a pleasant and profitable time They also say the roads are almost impassable between here and Cedar.

The little girl of Mr. and Mrs G. Lawrence Prince, who has pneumonia, is much better and will soon be well again if she continues to improve as she is at this time

All the children that had scarlet fever are well and will be permitted to attend school and other public gatherings again.

Born, a daughter to Mr. and Mrs Orson Hammond last week; all concerned doing nicely.

New Harmony, Feb 28 — We are having our share of rain and snow this month, up to this time we have had 5 91 inches

Elders Durham and Esplin have been doing missionary work here the past two or three weeks, holding cottage meetings and visiting and talking with the people The cottage meetings were well attended and appreciated by the people.

Born, a son at the home of Mrs Emma Grant Neilson Feb 25, a daughter at the home of Mrs Gladys Grant Whipple Feb 26 The mothers are sisters and the babies were born only 28 hours apart

A few bids have been put in for carrying the mail from here to Kanarra We feel that we are not treated right every time we think of our mail being cut down to three times a week.

Mrs Eliza Kelsey has been sick the past week or two, but her illness is not considered very serious

We had as nice a time as the weather would permit on Washington's birthday.

The roads are dry enough now for the mail to be carried in a buggy once more.

Mrs Cecil Taylor Schmutz is ill with stomach and kidney trouble

New Harmony, Mar. 7.—The people here have started to make a canal to take the high water out to cover nearly all the land in this valley. It is quite an undertaking but when finished it will be a big thing for Harmony. The water that goes by here in the spring will be spread out on the fertile land that now grows sage brush luxuriantly. The cost will be somewhere between six and ten thousand dollars. The principal part of the work can be done with teams and scrapers. The stock is taken and already work has begun.

The young men and young ladies gave a dance last week to raise money to carry on their associations. The officers are highly pleased with the way everything went off. The young ladies are preparing an entertainment in the near future in order to get books, etc., for their association

Jos W. Prince and Bp Henry A Price have returned from Hurricane valley where they have been looking after their sheep; they are pleased with the condition the sheep are in and the prospects for a good price for wool in the spring

The South Bench Canal Co will start this week on their new canal, they expect to have the water out on their farms this spring

New Harmony, Mar 14 —Joseph W Prince and others that attended the Round-Up at St George are highly pleased with the good talk they heard there. They feel well paid for the time spent

Spring has come at last, or at least the farmers think so, they are all busy plowing, working canals and other form work

The people that attended the quarterly conference at Cedar report having had a very good time.

Washington County News
March 21, 1915

New Harmony, Mai 21.— On Saturday, Mar. 20th, many friends of Mrs L. A. Pace were invited to attend her 50th birthday. A general good time was had. After spending the greater part of the afternoon in songs, recitations, etc , ice cream and cake were served.

Ranger J. M Moody was here last week doing business with the stockmen and blazing trees that will be necessary to remove in making some of the canals that are being made.

This morning Mr and Mrs E C Grant, Sid C Goddard and James Russell left to attend the fair Mr Russell will consult a doctor before he returns

Elders Hunter and Webster from Cedar were the speakers in the afternoon services, being here as home missionaries

George F, Prince and his father, Francis Prince, have just returned from a business trip to St George

Washington County News
April 4, 1915

New Harmony, April 4 —The young people have enjoyed Easter Sunday. All the youngsters went for a picnic in the afternoon. Some on Lawson hill, some to the Lone Pine, some to the Springs

Dr Macfarlane was called last week to see Mrs John A Condie Mrs Condie is suffering with an abscess on the face

John Whipple thinks the prospects bright to move their saw mill from Pine Valley over here this summer.

J. G Pace and wife are here visiting with their relatives and friends

New Harmony, Apr 18 —Ranger J. M. Moody has been here doing business with the stockmen. He called a meeting and showed them the advantage in forming a stock association. The men interested were favorably impressed and appointed two men to take the matter up with Supervisor Raphael and get what information they could in regard to the matter.

James Russell has returned from Los Angeles where he went to be treated for a cancer in the nose. He says he is feeling better than for twelve years.

Mr. and Mrs E. C. Grant and Sid C. Goddard have returned from the exposition and feel well paid for the time and money spent.

The eighth grade students have taken the examination and will wait anxiously to know whether or not they passed.

Mrs James L. Prince has gone to Cedar to be treated by Dr. Leonard for an abscess in the face and neck.

Joseph W. Prince is on the way to Iron Springs with his sheep to shear.

Bp Henry A Pace is shearing his sheep at home this spring

New Harmony, April 25 —Professors Sharp and Eldridge (Uncle Ben) lectured here last week on "The Dairy Cow". The lectures were highly appreciated.

The M I Assns closed their year's work last Monday night. The closing exercises consisted of songs, recitations, games, etc

Farmers, stockmen and others are rejoicing over the nice rain that fell here. It has done an immense amount of good.

A meeting was held last week and a petition for a precinct fence law election sent to the county commissioners

The men working on the state road come up to visit Harmony on Sundays and to get supplies

COUNTY 8 GRADE GRADUATES

ST. GEORGE

Alice Cannon
Aieta Cox
Afton McNeil
Annie Sullivan
Ellen Seegmiller
Florence Woodbury
Josephine Savage
Viola Fawcett
Elizabeth Smith
Fern Bryner
Nellie Pymin
Mattie Pendleton
Clara McAllister
Hazel Atkin
Marion Gates
John E. Keate
Milton Cottum
Edward Miles
Karl Pace
Clarence Cottam
Philip Foremaster
Henry Miles
Mary Blake
Glenn Snow
Glenn Webb
Andfew Baker
LeRoi Bentley
Vere Whipple
Julius Herman

Arthur L Riding
Delmar Blair
George E Miller

HURRICANE

Lois Bradshaw
Stella Wright
Hulda Sanders
Bessie Christensen
Maude Wright
Carrie Isom
Ruby Hall
Kate Spendlove
Burr Bradshaw
Whitney Spendlove
Clinton Hall
Samuel Wright
Herbert Isom
Thomas Eagar
Golden Langston
Clarence Cripps

ENTERPRISE

Milda Holt
Lela Simpkins
Netina Alger
Hazel Hall
Gertrude Hall
Arthur Crawford
Verneth Barnum

WASHINGTON

Irene Neilson
Verna Schlappy
Lena Jolley
Ella Tobler
Ellen Hall
Thelma Thayne
Nancy Prince
James Keate

SANTA CLARA

Ezra Tobler
Clement Gubler
Leona Stucki

PINE VALLEY

Mamie Gardner
Lizzie Snow

PINTO

Leone Eldridge

NEW HARMONY

George Schmutz
William Orren Taylor

TOQUERVILLE

Loren Higbee
Charles Bringhurst
Myrtle Klienman
William Dodge
Augustus Slack

LA VERKIN

Amelia Sanders
Joseph Hinton
Ovando Gubler
Walter Segler

LEEDS

Wilford Leany
Glen B Olsen
Willard McMullin
Delbert Sterling

GUNLOCK

Beatrice Hunt
Blanche Leavitt

ROCKVILLE

Melvin Petty
Warren Hirschi

VIRGIN

Alma Flanigan
Ada Beames

GRAFTON

Lenora Ballard
Edna Russell

New Harmony, May 1.—We have had a good rain and snow storm this week In twelve hours there was 1.28 inches of rainfall We have had more than two inches of rain in 24 hours. Trees have been broken and some fences broken down. The precipitation for April was 3 74 inches

Miss Minnie Pace has returned from Kanarra, where she has been teaching school the last school year. She reports a very pleasant entertainment at the close of school The Kanarra trustees wanted her to teach next year but she was engaged elsewhere

Quite a number of our townspeople have their wagons ready to haul wool but they have been delayed a week or more on account of the storm.

It is reported that some of our sheep men are having some loss among their flocks after shearing The storm is also causing some loss.

Mrs Ballard has been to Salt Lake to meet her sister, who lives in Thatcher, Ariz They came in yesterday from the north.

Last week after the storm cleared up some of our young men went out and killed 150 rabits in the afternoon

Frank P Kelsey has gone to Grafton to get his wife; he took his wife's mother and her sister with him.

Mrs. Flora Brown is moving in to her new home, a very neat little cottage.

The water in Ash creek is reported to be very high.

The school will not close here for two weeks.

Iron County Record
May 7, 1915

MRS. MARY C. GODDARD DEAD.

News was received here last Tuesday of the death at Leeds of Mrs. Mary A. Goddard, mother of G. C. and Sidney Goddard of this place and Harmony, the day previous. Her two sons at once set out to attend the funeral, but on account of the delay in getting the word, and the extremely stormy condition of the weather, with resultant muddy roads and swollen mountain streams intervening, were unable to get through by the appointed time, and were obliged to return home. Interment took place in the Harrisburg cemetery, where deceased has a daughter buried.

Deceased came to southern Utah in 1850, and has resided for the most part at New Harmony. She was the first white girl married in Payson, Utah, which town was named after her father, "Jimmie" Pace.

Three sons and one daughter survive her, a son and a daughter have gone before. The living children, in addition to those already mentioned, are William P. Goddard, residing in Mexico, and Mrs. Hannah Jolley of Washington, Utah.

Washington County News
May 23, 1915

New Harmony, May 23 —Some of our stock men are having a little hard run the last two or three weeks; they are loosing quite a number of cows and calves with a disease of some kind; we don't know what it is, but we do know that some of our full blood stock is dying of it

The farmer is pleased to get back on the farm again. Last week was too wet to do anything on the farm It looks now that we will not get as much corn in as we figured on

The sheep men are disappointed, some of them have five or six inches of snow on their lambing ground, but the last two or three days has helped to move the snow away

Some of the people of the town are in favor of a precinct fence law, so in the near future we will have an election in the matter

Miss Minnie Pace has gone to Salt Lake to take a course in sewing known as the Keister course

John Whipple has a case of blood poisoning in his hand, he is getting along fairly well

Our school is closed, some of the little ones thought it lasted too long.

Supervisor Raphael is here doing business with the cow boys

New Harmony, May 30 —John W. Prince has gone to Salt Lake City to undergo a very serious operation for tumor, cancer or something of that nature in the tube of the stomach, his wife went with him

The cattle men sent a wire this morning to Mr. Young, the state veterinarian, about so many of our cattle dying of poisoning or some other disease of which we know nothing

Supervisor Raphael and Ringer Moody were here two or three days last week surveying homesteads on the forest reserve for James D. Neilson and George A. Grant

June the 1st is the day set to cut our mail from six times a week to three times a week; that means 19 daily papers to be cut down to a semi-weekly

Primary conference was held here today, everything went off very nicely with the little ones

Election will be held here on Tuesday, 1st, to vote on a fence law.

Decoration day was observed here Sunday

New Harmony, June 6 —Last Friday and Saturday were "clean-up" days The men folks turned out and made our little town look like we had some pride in it, the ladies did their part, too, by preparing cake and lemonade for the workers

State Veterinarian Young sent Dr McGary here to investigate the cause of so many cattle dying He talked like it was because the stock had too much wood with their browse Said he would send some medicine, but it has not come

Word received from Jos. W Prince, who is in the hospital at Salt Lake City, is that he had a diseased gall which was removed and he is now doing nicely

We have had two or three nice showers the past week, 52 inches of precipitation

Farmers are cutting their first crop of hay, they expect two more good crops

The election for fence law carried, so we will have to fence our farms.

Born, a son to Mr. and Mrs Roy Grant, June 4.

Elder L. A. Pace Called to His Reward

[Special to the News]

New Harmony, Utah, June 13 — On Sunday morning Elder L A. Pace died at his home in New Harmony. His death has been one of the saddest hours, not only to the bereaved family but to everyone in our village

Not in years past has there been such a sudden shock to our citizens and such a gloom cast over our community.

Elder L A Pace was the second son of the late Bishop Wilson D Pace and Ann M Redd Pace of New Harmony, Utah He married Susan A Clark in the St George temple Dec 26, 1884 Of this union nine children were born, seven of whom survive him. The living children are Mrs Laurene P Taylor, Minnie, Ashby W., Mildred, Clark, Max, Merle, all of whom are residents of New Harmony. He is also survived by two brothers, W W Pace of Thatcher, Arizona, John G Pace of Cedar City, Utah, two sisters, Mrs Icinda Rance and Ireminda Blackburn of Salt Lake City, and two grandchildren, Claude V and Beula Taylor.

He fulfilled a mission of two years in the Eastern states faithfully in 1900 1902 On returning home he continued his mercantile business and farming He had always been a faithful member and worker in the church, well respected by all who knew him

Funeral services will be held at the Ward meeting house at 1 30 p m., June the 15th

Iron County Record
June 25, 1915

L. A. PACE GOES TO HIS LAST REST

Succumbs to Heart Failure June 13, and Funeral was Held Tuesday, the 15th, at 1 O'clock.

A tardy report of the death and funeral of the late L. A. Pace of New Harmony, who departed this life on the morning of Sunday, June 13, is just available. Heart failure is given as the cause of his death. Mrs. Pace arose on the morning mentioned and when breakfast was nearly ready went to Mr. Pace's room to call him. She found him lying upon the floor, apparently having been dead for a number of hours. Deceased had been in poor health for a number of years, and while he had complained a little the day previous, no alarm was felt over his condition, so that his death was a complete surprise and a severe shock to his family.

The funeral services were held in the Harmony meeting house Tuesday, June 15th, and there was a large attendance, not only of the people of Harmony, but also from Kanarra, Cedar City, New Castle and Lund. The speakers were Elders Jos. D. Cox of New Castle, W. W. Lunt of Cedar City, Reese J. Williams of Kanarra, and Albert F. Mathis of Harmony.

All spoke highly of the deceased, particularly commending him for his public spirit, devotion to family, home and town.

L. A. Pace was born April 19, 1859, in Spanish Fork, Utah, and moved to Harmony with his parents while still a small child. With the exception of about five years spent in Nutrioso, Apache county, Arizona, where he met and married Susan A. Clark, he has lived there ever since. The period spent in Arizona was from 1880 to 1885. He returned to Harmony with his wife and two children, and the remainder of his nine children were born in Harmony. They are: Loreen, (now Mrs. Will Taylor) Minnie, Josephine, Ashby, LaMond, Mildred, Clark, Max and Merle. LaMond and Josephine preceded him to the other shore, but the remainder survive him.

Mr. Pace was educated in the local schools and spent one winter at the B. Y. Academy at Provo. He taught school a year or two in Arizona and a number of years at Harmony.

For a number of years he served as school trustee in Harmony, and has held other positions of trust.

He was a prominent and useful citizen of Harmony and will be greatly missed by the people of that place.

Francis Prince and son, Geo F Prince, highly respected residents of New Harmony, were here Wednesday on land business. The latter reports crops looking good in his section, though not quite so good as last year owing to cold backward weather. There will be good crops of potatoes, squash, dry land corn and grain.

New Harmony, July 26 —The twenty-fourth passed off rather quietly; however, we had a number of visitors from outside places which helped to make the celebration a success

Mr and Mrs John Hall of———— and daughters Thelma and Ora were here visiting relatives and friends on the 24th

Mrs. Jos. W. Prince is confined to her bed with a serious condition of collar bone, but is improving.

Mr. and Mrs Jolley of———— were guests of Mr. and Mrs Harvey Pace the latter part of the week

Miss Verna Taylor has returned home from Logan where she has been attending summer school

Andrew Schmutz who has been ill for some time with quinsy is now able to be about

The forest rangers have been here for the past few days surveying boundary lines

Mrs Vilate Cottam of St. George is spending a few days here.

New Harmony, August 2 —A meeting was held yesterday to get the sentiments of the people in regard to an amusement hall. They voted for one and it will be open for bids in the near future

Dr. Paden and Rev Rice were here and held a meeting last night A large crowd was in attendance and they speak very highly of the remarks.

J L Prince, Elmer Taylor and Evelyn Prince have returned from the desert where they have been heading grain

J G. Pace of Cedar City was in town Thursday and Friday on business and visiting relatives

A number of people went to Kanarra Saturday evening to attend a theatre

The binders and headers are very busy now harvesting grain

Mrs Jos W Prince is now able to be about again.

New Harmony, Aug 10 —Born, a son to Mr and Mrs Andrew Schmutz, Aug 5, a daughter to Mr and Mrs Geo F Prince Aug 6, all concerned are doing nicely

The dry land corn is suffering for rain, there seems to be some concern about it maturing unless it receives some rain in the near future.

Donald Schmutz is with us again after an absence of some weeks in the mountains looking after his goats

The threshing machine is now under preparation and will begin threshing today or tomorrow

Alex Taylor of this place took a trip to Leeds Saturday and returned Monday

Alfred and Will Stucki of Santa Clara were visitors here Sunday

Grant Hale of Kanarra was here visiting friends Sunday

Francis Prince has just purchased a new "Ford" auto

Washington County News
August 29, 1915

New Harmony, Aug 29 —Principal and Mrs Woodward and Prof. and Mrs Nicholes of the Dixie Academy were here last Sunday and held a meeting in the interest of that school.

Mis L Grant and Mrs Gladys Whipple have returned from the ranch where they have been the greater part of the summer

Randall L Jones and Walter Mitchel were here Saturday on business pertaining to the new amusement hall

Some four townspeople who attended Elberta day at Hurricane report having had a splendid time.

Pres Marsden and Elders Lyman and Day were visitors at our Sacramental meeting last Sunday.

James L Prince, Geo L Prince and Elmer Taylor have gone out on the desert to get their grain

A daughter was born to Mr and Mrs Gus Permenter Aug. 25; all concerned doing well

Threshing is finished here for this season, there being a yield of over 5,000 bushels

Orson Hammond took a grist to the Washington mill the latter part of the week

Bp Henry A. Pace and Albert F Mathis went to Cedar City Saturday on business

Mason Rencher and Clare Gardner of Grass valley were visitors here recently

Washington County News
September 6, 1915

New Harmony, Sept 6 — The drouth was broken by a nice rain Wednesday and Thursday nights The amount of moisture was 66 in

Milfor Pace and his daughter, Neta, and Miss Reese of Loa were guests of Mr and Mrs Harvey A Pace, Sunday Mr Pace is taking his daughter to St George to attend the Dixie Academy

Miss Mary Knell of New Castle and Afton Allred of Fountain Green were guests of Miss Minnie Pace the latter part of the week

Mrs Flora Brown has returned home after having spent a few days at the Meadows and New Castle.

John Whipple and Miss Nela Whipple of Pine Valley were here Sunday and returned today

Mr and Mrs Wm Chinn have returned home from a visit to the Meadows and New Castle

Donald Schmutz left Thursday for Vernal where he expects to teach school.

Claude Knell was here visiting friends Sunday

New Harmony, Sept 13 —The following students have gone to St George to attend the Dixie Academy Miss La Verna Taylor and Rosellia Schmutz, Elmer Taylor, Antone Prince and Evelyn Prince

Mr. and Mrs Jos Prince, their daughter Velia and Miss Belle Williams went to St George to attend the "Fruit Festival " They report having had a splendid time

The Stake Mutual officers met with the local officers yesterday and filled some vacances preparatory to commencement of Mutual work for the season

The young people indulged in an oyster supper Sunday evening A very plesant time was had.

Grant Platt of Kanarra spent Sunday here visiting friends

Alex Taylor went to Leeds Sunday to visit friends

E C Grant is home for a few days

New Harmony, Sept. 21.—Wilford Pace of Loa is here visiting after attending the fruit festival at St George. He is on his way home

Mr. and Mrs Ray Grant have gone to Panguitch to visit the latter's mother, Mrs Page They expect to be gone about a week.

Mr. and Mrs A F. Mathis and Mrs Eliza Kelsey have gone to Price to spend a few days They went in Mr. Mathis' car.

Sidney Goddard was down from the ranch the latter part of the week visiting with his uncle, Wilford Pace

Mr and J. G. Pace and family of Cedar City were here visiting friends and relatives Sunday.

Prof Miller gave a lecture and picture show here Friday evening, all seemed to enjoy them.

Francis Prince, who has been feeling quite poorly for the past few days, is on the improve

Mrs Frank Kelsey is at Rockville visiting her mother, Mrs Ballard

Washington County News
October 4, 1915

New Harmony, Oct 4 —The six months old baby of Mrs Gladys Whipple died Wednesday, Sept. 29, of what is known as telescoping of the bowels The little one took ill very suddenly Monday afternoon and continued to grow worse until Tuesday evening when Dr Macfarlane of Cedar City was sent for The Dr ordered the baby taken to Cedar to the hospital where he and Dr. Leonard performed an operation, that being the only chance of saving its life. The baby died in a few hours after the operation.

Mr. and Mrs. Albert Mathis have returned from Price after a short visit there with Mr Mathis' father and relatives

Mr. and Mrs Berry Williams of Kanarra are here visiting Mrs Williams' mother, Mrs Sarah Davis

Bishop Henry A Pace has returned from Panguitch where he has been on business

E J. Whipple of Pine Valley is here hauling his corn and doing other fall work.

A crowd of young people went to Thorley's farm recently to attend a dancing party.

Miss Mae Williams of Kanarra was a guest of Miss Minnie Pace very recently.

Mrs Eliza Kelsey has returned from Price where she has been on a short visit.

Jesse Whipple was called home on account of the death of his baby.

Ashby Pace spent Sunday in New Castle visiting friends.

School began today with a good attendance

Washington County News
October 18, 1915

New Harmony, Oct 18 —Elmer Taylor, Evlyn Prince, Antone Prince, Lee Cox and Melvin Cox were here Saturday and Sunday from St George They spent the two days in the mountains hunting and report great success They returned with three fine deer

Francis Prince, Eliza Kelsey, Reese Davis, Ashby Pace and Frank Kelsey made a trip to Cedar the latter part of the week in Mr Prince's auto The road was so muddy that it made traveling diffic u't

Albert F. Mathis, Reuben Whipple and Mrs Ruth Prince went to Cedar City Friday on business

Miss Rosalia Schmutz who is attending the Dixie Academy spent Saturday and Sunday home

Mrs Vivian Prince has returned from Cedar where she has been having her teeth fixed

Ashby Pace and Frank Kelsey went to Parowan on business Friday

LeRoy Grant was down from the ranch on business Sunday

Forest Ranger, J. M Moody is here on business.

Washington County News
October 26, 1915

New Harmony, Oct 26 —Mr. Ashby Pace and Miss Verna Knell were married last Wednesday, Oct 20th, in the St. George temple They returned home Sunday by way of New Castle where they spent a few days. They have the best wishes of the community for a life of health, happiness and prosperity

Mr. and Mrs Lawrence Prince, Misses Minnie and Mildred Pace and Clark Pace went to New Castle last Friday to attend the wedding reception of Mr. and. Mrs. Ashby Pace.

W. O. Bentley, secretary of the school board of Washington county, was a visitor at school Monday and Tuesday. He was looking after the interests of the school.

A company of men from Cedar City held a meeting here last night in the interest of a railroad. The citizens voted to sustain the movement.

Mrs. L. A. Pace entertained at a family wedding dinner last evening in honor of her son, Ashby W. Pace, and wife

A number of men are on the roundup trip. They are bringing in the cattle to sell.

Washington County News
November 1, 1915

New Harmony, Nov 1.—The past few days have been spent in anxiety over the forest fire which is now burning on Pine Valley mountain Forest Ranger Moody was notified and immediately ordered a number of men to do what they could to extinguish it, but it was soon learned that it would take a large force to make any headway at all There are now seventeen men working with it and it is thought that they will soon have it under control

Mrs Frank Kelsey has returned from Cedar City whe e she has been to have her throat lanced She has been suffering from quinsy.

James G. Knell of New Castle was here Sunday visiting his daughter, Mrs Verna K Pace

Miss Belle Williams of Kanarra is here visiting Mrs Jos W. Prince

Some of the boys have gone to Modena to drive cattle

New Harmony, Utah, Nov. 1, 1915.

Jim Knell of New Castle was a visitor here yesterday.

* * *

Some time last week a fire broke out in the mountains southwest of here. Forest Rangers Moody and Mc-Allister, with a party of town men, are up there trying to keep the fire from spreading.

* * *

Reese Davis came in from Lund today with a load of freight.

* * *

Mrs. J. D. Neilson, who spent the summer here, has returned to her home in Monroe.

* * *

Mrs. Frank Kelsey and baby, who have been ill, are now on the improve.

* * *

E. R. Higbee of Toquerville, was here last week buying cattle.

* * *

James E. Taylor brought in a big deer last night.

New Harmony, Utah, Nov. 9, 1915.

Dr. M. J. Macfarlane was called down last week to see Jos. W. Prince, who is suffering from stomach trouble.

* * *

Mrs. Gladys G. Whipple has returned from Cedar City. where she has been to have some dental work done.

* * *

Miss Belle Willliams, who is here visiting Mrs. Vivian Prince, is quite ill with bronchitis.

* * *

Bp. Henry A. Pace has a new Ford car. We are proud to say that we have three of them in town and hope there will be more in the near future.

* * *

The small daughter of Mr. and Mrs. O. Hammond has been quite ill, but is now on the improve.

New Harmony, Nov 8 —The long drouth was broken Saturday by a nice rain, the amount of precipitation being .88 inches.

The Primary was reorganized yesterday with Mrs Emma Neilson president and Cecil Schmutz and Melissa Hammond councilers

Jos W. Prince, who has been suffering from an acute attack of stomach trouble, is now able to be out again.

Frank Kelsey, Alex Taylor and George Schmutz returned from Modena where they have been with cattle

Wm. P. Taylor, Orren Taylor and J. L Prince returned from Parowan Saturday with lumber.

Mrs. Ruth Whipple is in Pine Valley visiting her parents, Mr. and Mrs J E. Whipple

Mrs. Lottie Kelsey who has been quite ill for the past few weeks is recovering.

Bishop H. A Pace has just purchased a Ford car.

Washington County News
November 11, 1915

Mr. and Mrs Jeremiah Leavitt have gone to Harmony by way of St. George where they will visit friends and relatives

New Harmony, Nov 22 —The barns of Albert F Matthis and Wm. P Taylor are now nearing completion. These gentlemen with Bishop Pace have taken a splendid step in moving their barns back from the street, and if a number more would follow their example our town would be much improved.

Bishop Pace, who had the misfortune to have a horse fall with him and roll on his foot, is now able to wear his shoe

Miss Belle Williams, a guest of Mrs. Jos W. Prince, is slowly recovering from a severe attack of bronchitis.

Some of the young people (?) went to Kanarra Friday night to attend a dance; a pleasant time is reported.

E C Grant underwent an operation last Tuesday, and is still in a rather serious condition

Attorneys Lund and Pickett of St. George were in town today on business

Ira McMullin of Leeds is here repairing the house of Ashby W. Pace.

New Harmony, Utah, Nov. 30, 1915.

Thanksgiving passed off very quietly here, the principal attractions being a children's dance in the afternoon and one for adults in the evening.

* * *

E. C. Grant, who has been ill for some time is now on the road to recovery.

* * *

Mary Knell and Walter Spencer of New Castle spent Thanksgiving here. Mrs. Ashby Pace returned home with them Saturday to visit relatives at New Castle.

* * *

Antone Prince of this place and Vilate Cottam of St. George were married on Thanksgiving Day. We all wish them a long life of wedded happiness.

* * *

Dr. A. N. Leonard was in town yesterday seeing some of his patients.

Washington County News
December 6, 1915

New Harmony, Dec 6 — We have had a nice storm It rained all night Friday night and continued all the following day until evening when it turned to a snow storm, about an inch of snow falling

Our town's people enjoyed a rare musical treat Friday evening Mr and Mrs Willard Andelin give a concert that was well attended.

Miss Mildred Pace has returned from Cedar City where she has been for several days visiting relatives

Mrs Lottie Kelsey, who has been to Cedar City getting some dental work done, has returned home

A committee has been put in for the Christmas holidays and a rousing good time is anticipated.

The stake presidency was here Sunday to attend ward conference

Washington County News
December 13, 1915

New Harmony, Dec 13 — Bishop Henry A. Pace, Mrs Harvey A Pace, Mr. and Mrs Gottlieb Schmutz and Golda Prince went to attend conference yesterday at Parowan.

Mrs. Lottie Kelsey has been very ill for the past few days with a touch of pneumonia; she is somewhat improved.

Jos. W. Prince has returned home from Salt Lake City where he has been on business.

E J. Whipple of Pine Valley is here looking after his interests in this section

Mrs. Laurence Prince is able to be about again after a severe attack of the grip

Mrs Ashby W. Pace has returned from a visit to New Castle.

Iron County Record
December 14, 1915

New Harmony, Utah, Dec. 14, 1915.

Committees have been appointed and they have arranged a program for Christmas Day and for the week following. We are anticipating a good time.

* * *

Mr. and Mrs. Berry Williams and family of Kanarra are here visiting Mrs. Williams' mother, Mrs. Reese Davis.

* * *

We are having an epidemic of la grippe among the children and some of the grown folks as well. Mrs. Frank Kelsey has been quite ill. It monia, but she is now getting better.

* * *

Joseph W. Prince is home from Salt Lake, where he has been on business.

Claud Knell of New Castle was a visitor here Sunday. Claud comes over quite often.

* * *

Mason Rencher was here again last week. He is also a frequent visitor.

* * *

Mrs. Vivian Prince is in Cedar city, having her ear treated. The trouble is not known to your correspondent.

Bishop Pace and mother, Mrs. Harvey Pace, and Mr. and Mrs. Gotleib Schmutz went to Parowan for conference Sunday.

Iron County Record
December 28, 1915

New Harmony, Utah, Dec. 28, 1915.

Anna Bell Schmutz and Mason Rencher have gone to St. George to spend New Years. It is reported that they will be married before they return home.

* * *

The Old Folk's party last night was a complete success. Thanks to the committee and the men with autos, everyone had a free ride to the hall.

* * *

Antone Prince will give a wedding dance here tonight.

* * *

Grant Batty is here from Twin Falls, Idaho, visiting with Mr. and Mrs. James L. Prince. He is Mrs. Prince's brother.

* * *

Grant Hale of Kanarra is spending the holidays here.

Washington County News
December 29, 1915

Mr and Mrs Antone Prince went to New Harmony Saturday to spend Christmas holidays with relatives.

Washington County News
January 3, 1916

New Harmony, Jan 3 —The Old Folks party given last Monday was one of the very best things of the season. The old people being taken to the hall in autos, were seated to a hot dinner at five, after which a short program was given and a dance followed. All seemed to enjoy the evening in a really sociable manner.

Wm. P. Taylor has gone to Cedar City where he will receive his appointment as a home missionary, his labor will doubtless keep him three weeks or a month in some sections of the stake.

The students who came home to spend the Christmas vacation have had some little difficulty in returning to their work on account of the storm

Miss Anna Belle Schmutz and Mason Rancher who were married in St. George, Jan. 1st, receive the best wishes of this community.

We have had a great deal of storm of late, the amount of snow fall being twenty inches.

Mr. and Mrs Ashby Pace spent the holidays in New Castle with Mrs Pace's relatives.

Jas. W. Prince left yesterday morning for Salt Lake City on business

Mr. and Mrs Antone Prince returned to St George today.

Mrs. Sadie Grant has moved down from the ranch

The holidays passed very pleasantly and, in spite of the heavy storms, the dances were carried on successfully.

New Year's evening was spent in a Leap Year ball The participants were taken to the hall in sleighs.

Washington County News
January 17, 1916

New Harmony Jan 17 — We had a great deal 1st rm since January came in there has been scarcely a day since the first without storm

A F Matthis returned home last week from a trip east with his sheep Soon after his arrival he left for Cedar City to fulfill a home mission

G Lawrence Prince reports nice weather in St George he seems to think it is a nice thing to see the ground once in a while

Mr and Mrs E C Grant and daughter Gladys have returned from St George where they have been on business

Mrs A F Matthis has been to St George on business also Mrs Amelia Schmntz

Mrs Lawrence Prince and little child are improving after a severe illness

Washington County News
January 24, 1916

New Harmony Jan 24 — The storm still continues the amount of precipitation being 5 42 inches

Mr and Mrs Frank Kelsey and Mrs A F Mathis went to Cedar Friday to attend the Book of Mormon' play given by the Walter s Co

Home missionaries Mathison and Dalley have gone to Hamiltons Fort to continue their labors

Bishop Henry A Pace has returned from Hurricane where he has been on business

Orren Kelsey who has been to St George on business returned home Sunday

Mrs Joseph Prince is slowly recovering after an illness of a week

New Harmony Jan 31 —The wind storm last Thursday night did considerable damage there were eight large trees uprooted the forest ranger's salt house blown over the door blown from a barn and the window glass blown from some of the houses also a number of stove pipes went tumbling to the ground

Mrs Olive Chinn was hostess at a supper party given for Miss Inez Duffin in honor of her birthday last Wednesday evening at the home of her grandmother Mrs Delta Hammond

Mr and Mrs A W Pace entertained at a birthday dinner Sunday evening in honor of Lurene P Taylor

Born a son to Mr and Mrs G Albert Grant January 25th

\

New Harmony Feb 14 —Our town's people participated in a dance Saturday evening given in honor of Lincoln's birthday

Mrs Jas W Prince who has been quite ill for the past two weeks is improving nicely

Mrs Flora Brown has returned from Lund after an absence of about three months

Bishop Henry A Pace has gone to Hurricane valley to see about his sheep

Mrs Wm P Taylor has gone to Cedar City to have dental work done

John and Reuben Whipple of Pine Valley are spending a few days here

Eugene Leavitt of Gunlock is here visiting friends and relatives

Iron County Record
February 22, 1916

New Harmony, Utah, Feb. 22, 1916.
James D. Knell and daughter Mary of New Castle came this way from Cedar City, where they had been to attend the Round-up, and spent Sunday with Mr. and Mrs. Ashby W. Pace. Mrs. Pace was formerly Miss Verna Knell.

* * *

Albert F. Mathis, who was at the Round-up, reports having had a fine time. He says we that were not there missed something worth while.

* * *

Elders R. G. Williams and W. C. Reeves of Kanarra were home missionaries here Sunday.

* * *

The minstrel show that was here on the 15th was——, well, like all the rest. If you have been to one, you have been to them all.

* * *

The good weather that we have had has enabled the farmers to do a little work on their land.

Washington County News
February 22, 1916

New Harmony Feb 22 —A F Mathis and Reece Davis who attended the Round up at Cedar City report having ha l a splendid time and fell well paid for the time tl ey spent there

James G Knell and his daughter Mary returned to tl eir home at New Castle to day They have been spending a few days visiting relatives and friends

Elders R G William and W C Reeves of Kanarra occupied the time in sacrament meeting Sunday

The children were treated to a dance this afternoon the occasion being Washington s b rth lay

New Harmony Feb 28 —W O
Bentley county school supervisor
visited our school last Wedesday.
He also held a meeting with the
citizens explaining the r ew school
system His remarks were much
appreciated and we invite him to
come again

An ice cream party was given at
the home of Mrs Sadie Grant last
Friday evening Tho e attending
report having had a very enjoyable
time

Bp Henry Pace has returned
from Hurricane valley where he has
been to look after his sheep

Mrs Sad e Grant and Mrs Em
m a Neilson entertaine l at a social
on Washington s birthday

Reece Davis has just returned
fr m I und with a load f frei ht

New Harmony Mar 6 —Gotthei Schmutz met with a seri us acci der Friday while he w s in the field feeding cattle Among the cattle was an animal that woul l fight it started for him an l havin, a pitch f irk in his han l he trie l to protect himself with it b it the an in al was t o str ng for him it knock ed him down and butted l im sev eral times breal ing six ribs Dr McFarl ine was sent for and states that it will be some time l efore Mr Schmutz will be able to get around again However he feels somewhat improved

A benefit entertainment for church organ was given Friday even ing in the meeting house It was a complete success and much praise is due the ones taking part and thanks is given the officers who spent their time to help make it a success

Leslie Anderson of Lehi is here helping Bp Pace with his spring w irk

Jos W Prince has just complet ed a new fence around his premises

John Whipple of Pine Valley is here doing some of his spring work

A new fer ce is being completed in front of E C Grant s residence

New Harmony March 13 —G Schmutz who was severely injured by a bull some time ago is slowly recovering

Mr and Mrs Mason Rencher of Grass Valley are spending a few days here with Mrs Rencher s parents Mr and Mrs Gottlieb Schmutz

Some of the boys went to Kanarra Friday evening to attend a play given by the Kanarra mutual dra matic club

The teacher took the school for an outing up in the pastures Friday The trip was thoroughly enjoyed

Miss Belle Williams has returned from Cedar where she had been to have some dental work done

Ashby Pace and Reuben Whipple have returned from St George with seed grain

Some of our people went to Paro wan to attend conference yesterday

B F Anderson of Echo Farm was here on business Wednesday

Alex Taylor went to Leeds Satur day returning Monday

Iron County Record
March 13, 1916

New Harmony, Utah, Mar. 13.

Ex-Bishop Gotleib Schmutz, who was injured by a bull some weeks ago, is not getting along as well as we would like. We hope for improvement soon.

* * *

Mrs. Frank Kelsey, who has been to Grafton to visit her parents, returned home yesterday bringing her mother, Mrs. Ballard, with her.

* * *

Those who attended conference at Parowan from this place were: Mr. and Mrs. Joseph Prince, A. F. Mathis, William Faught and Mr. Boshart. They returned home this morning.

* * *

Bishop Pace and mother, Susan E. Pace, made a flying trip to Cedar City today.

Mr. and Mrs. Mason Rencher of Pine Valley came over Saturday to visit Mrs. Rencher's parents. Mrs. Rencher was formerly Miss Anna Bell Schmutz.

* * *

Leslie Anderson of Lehi is here working with Bishop Pace.

* * *

Ashby Pace and James L. Prince have been down to St. George on business.

* * *

The Relief Society will give an entertainment on the 17th and after it a dance and oyster supper.

Washington County News
March 16, 1916

Mr and Mrs Antone Prince went to New Harmony Monday where they intend making their home

Washington County News
March 27, 1916

New Harmony March 27 —The Y J M I A adjourned last evening till fall The meetings have been splendid this season and the girls expressed themselves as being sorry to have them discontinue

The young married people participated in a chicken supper last Wednesday night at the home of Mr and Mrs Ashby W Pace A splendid time is reported

The time in sacramental meeting yesterday was occupied by Elders Don Forsythe and John Tullis of New Castle The remarks were timely and good

The storm last week put the farmers back in their spring work but after the two or three days of sunshine they are all busy again

Andrew Schmutz who has finished shearing his goats expects to leave in the morning for Lund with wool

Iron County Record
March 27, 1916

New Harmony, Utah, Mar. 27, 1916.

Gottlieb Schmutz who has been very ill for a few weeks from an injury received, is now improving slowly.

* * *

The snow storm that visited us last week, or the frost that followed in its wake, killed the apricots, but the rest of the fruit is not injured as yet.

* * *

Elders John Tullis and Donald Forsyth of Newcastle visited us yesterday as home missionaries.

* * *

The young married people were entertained Wednesday evening by Mr. and Mrs. Ashby Pace at their home. Mrs. Pace is a charming hostess and every one enjoyed themselves.

* * *

The people are beginning to clean up around their homes and some of them are building new fences, which makes the town look better and fresher.

Washington County News
April 3, 1916

New Harmony April 3 —G tt
ieb Schmutz is slowly recovering
fr m the injuries he received some
time ago but he is still confined to
his bed

Mr and Mrs Joseph W Prince
and daughter Velva and Mrs Vilate
C Prince made a trip to St George
Saturday returning Sunday

A birthday party was given at the
home of Miss Merle Pace Saturday
evening the participants report a
splendid time

Eugene and Blanche Leavitt of
Gunlock were here during the latter
part of the week visiting relatives
and friends

Mr and Mrs Frank Kelsey en
tertained at an ice cream party last
Wednesday A lively time was had

R A Kirker is in Parowan on
business

New Harmony   April 17 —The school observed Arbor day by cleaning the school house and premises At 2 30 a program was given and a tree planted in the school garden the teacher and each of the children removed a shovel full of soil and planted a poplar tree presented to the school by Francis Prince

An ice cream party was given at the home of Mr and Mrs Lawrence Prince last night   Such a splendid time was indulged in that the participants are planning another soon, of a different character however

A number of the Relief society members went to St George last Wednesday and did two days work in the temple

Elmer Taylor and Evlyn Prince have returned home after spending the winter in St George attending the Academy

Stake Pres Marsden and councilor Lyman and sister Lyman occupied the time in church Sunday

After several weeks of illness G Schmutz is able to walk about in the house

New Harmony, Utah, April 24, 1916. A short time ago Elder George Spilsbury of Toquerville expressed a desire to visit the Harmony Sunday School once more, and it being his birthday on the 21st inst, the superintendent of our Sunday School sent an invitation for him to visit us on Easter Sunday. He and his son David came, and the members of the Sunday School and others met at the meeting house at nine-thirty and were taken in autos to a beautiful green spot, which the superintendent and his aids had prepared. When all were assembled, Sunday School was held, Brother Spilsbury and his son taking up most of the time in talking to the children. They then had a delicious lunch and returned to town for the sacramental meeting. Bro. Spilsbury is 98 years old and is in perfect health.

* * *

Grant Hale and Josephine Kelsey will be married in the St. George temple Wednesday, April 26. They have the congratulations of their many friends.

* * *

Those from this place who attended the opera presented by the Dixie Academy at Cedar City say that it was something grand.

Washington County News
May 4, 1916

Miss Evelyn Thurston left Monday for New Harmony, where she intends teaching piano music this summer.

Iron County Record
May 8, 1916

New Harmony, Utah, May 8, 1916.
The young folks, married and single, were entertained at the home of Mr. and Mrs. Frank Kelsey last night. Ice cream and crackers were served. Everyone had an enjoyable time.

*   *   *

Mrs. William Chinn is in Gunlock visiting her parents. She also attended the wedding reception of her brother, Eugene Leavitt, of Gunlock, and Vilate Barney of this place, who were married in the St. George temple May 2nd.

*   *   *

There has been some illness among the babies of this place the past week, but all are a little better at this writing.

*   *   *

Henry Mathis, an old resident of Harmony, is here from Price visiting his son Albert. The old friends of Brother Mathis are pleased to have him among them again.

*   *   *

There is a very nice line of ladies' hats at the Co-op. Store.

*   *   *

Laverna Taylor, Eldon and Rosalia Schmutz, are home again after attending school at St. George the past winter.

*   *   *

Mrs. Antone Prince is visiting relatives and friends at St. George.
Miss Evelyn Thurston of St. George will spend the summer here giving music lessons.

Washington County News
May 9, 1916

Gunlock May 9 —Eugene Leavitt of Gunlock and Vilate Barney of New Harmony were married in the St George temple May 2 1916 The bride is the charming daughter of Mr and Mrs Joseph Barney the groom is a son of Mr and Mrs Jeremiah Leavitt a well respected young man They have the best wishes of the community at large A reception was given at the home of the groom s parents there were 62 people present There was a dance given at night and a very nice time was had The young couple have moved to their new home at Cactus flatt

Mr and Mrs Dan Barney and Mrs Joseph Barney Nora and Luella Barney and Mrs Gladys Whipple from New Harmony were here to attend the wedding of Mr and Mrs Eugene Leavitt Mr Barney came over to play for the dance his music being enjoyed very much Mr and Mrs Woodruff Tullis Mr and Mrs Robert Platt and Mr and Mrs Joseph Platt of New Castle and Mr and Mrs Thomas Leavitt of Enterprise were also here to attend the wedding of Mr and Mrs Eugene Leavitt

Iron County Record
May 15, 1916

New Harmony, Utah, May 15, 1916. Born.—To Bishop and Mrs. Henry A. Pace May 8. Mother and babe are doing nicely.

*   *   *

Mrs. William Chinn, who has been visiting friends and relatives at Gunlock, Utah, returned home last week.

*   *   *

Donald Schmutz returned home last night from Price, Utah, where he has been teaching school the past winter. He brought a wife home with him. Mrs. Schmutz was formerly Miss Timothy. We wish them all kinds of happiness.

*   *   *

William P. Taylor is quite ill at this writing. Dr. Leonard was called down to see him Saturday.

*   *

Mr. and Mrs. Berry Williams were over from Kanarra Sunday to the birthday dinner of Mrs. Williams' mother, Mrs. Sarah P. Davis.

*   *   *

Mrs. Francis Prince started to Carey, Idaho, this morning to visit her grand-daughter, Mrs. Florence Phippen.

Washington County News
May 18, 1916

Anton B Prince left Tuesday for his home at New Harmony after spending a few days here

Iron County Record
May 20, 1916

New Harmony, Utah, May 20, 1916.
James Russell is quite ill at this writing.

* * *

Primary conference was held here last Sunday. There was a good program rendered by the teachers and children, every one seeming to enjoy it. Mrs. Jennie Hunter and Miss Janet Rollo of the Stake Board were our visitors. The "busy hour" which was given by Mrs. Hunter was greatly appreciated by all present.

* * *

The heavy frost we had last Wednesday killed nearly all of the garden stuff, such as tomatoes, melons, beans, cucumbers, early potatoes, etc.

* * *

Bishop Pace went to St. George last Thursday, taking Emma Neilson to do temple work. They report things looking a little "frostie" down there.

* * *

Mr. Dan Barney and family have moved to St. Thomas, Nev.

Iron County Record
June 5, 1916

New Harmony, Utah, June 5.
Mrs. Amelia Schmutz and Sadie Grant, members of the Relief Society, also went to St. George recently to do ordinance work in the temple.
(The above two names were inadvertantly omitted from an item sent with last week's correspondence.—Ed. Record.)

* * *

James Russell is reported to be better the past few days.

* * *

Mr. and Mrs. M. O. Woolsey were over from their ranch and spent Sunday wth Mr. and Mrs. O. Hammond.

* * *

The men and boys have most of their crops in and are doing some improvement work on the pipe line.

Washington County News
July 6, 1916

Mr and Mrs Antone Prince of
New Harmony are here visiting at
the home of the latter s parents
Mr and Mrs Geo F Cottam

Washington County News
August 8, 1916

Jos Prince of New Harmony was
in town on business Wednesday

Iron County Record
August 15, 1916

New Harmony, Utah, Aug. 15.
William Chinn has gone to Panguitch to haul lumber.
* * *
Ashby Pace went to New Castle
Saturday after his wife, who has been
visiting there.
* * *
Miss Irene Rhoner of Salt Lake City
is here visiting relatives and friends.
* * *
Mr. and Mrs. Oren Kelsey have returned from Fairview, Utah, where
they have been to visit their daughter and family.
* * *
Quite a number of our young people
are going to St. George to attend
school this winter. Mr. and Mrs. J.
W. Prince will also spend the winter
in St. George, while their daughter
Velva will continue her music lssons
under Miss Evelyn Thurston, who has
been giving lessons here the past four
months.

Washington County News
August 17, 1916

NOTICE TO WATER USERS
State Engineer s Office
Salt Lake City Utah July 28 1916

Notice is hereby gi en that Joseph W
Prince whose post office address is New
Harmony Utah has made application in
accoidance with the requirements of the
Compiled Laws of Utah 1907 as amended by
the Session Laws of Utah 1909 1911 and 1915
to approp iate three 8 cubic feet of ate
per second from Cohmance Canyo 1 Creek
Washington County Utah Said ater v i l
be diverted at a point which bears south 46
deg ees 15 minutes east 2500 feet f o 1 the
northwest corner of Section 21 Township 38
south Range 18 west Salt Lake base and
1 1eridian and conveyed by means of a ditch
for a distance of 875 feet a d there used from
January 1 to Dece nbe1 81 inclusive of each
year to irrigate 16) acres of land emb aced
in the northeast q arter of Section 21 to n
ship and range aforesaid This application
is designated in the State Engineer s office
as No 6 59

All p otests against the granting of said
application stating the ressons therefor
must be 1 1de by affidavit in duplicate ac
co 1panied by a fee of $ 50 and filed in this
office v ithin thii ty (30 days after the com
pletion of the publication of this notice
W D BEERS
State Engineer
Date of first publicatio 1 Aug s1 10 19 6 date
of comp etion of publication September 9
1916

Iron County Record
August 21, 1916

New Harmony, Utah, Aug. 21.
Threshing began here yesterday.
* * *
Mrs. William Chinn has gone to
Gunlock to see her parents.
* * *
Elder Claude Knell was a home
missionary here Sunday. He gave us
some good things to think about.
* * *
Donald Schmutz and William Tay-
lor of this place were home mission-
aries at Cedar City Sunday. Mrs.
Schmutz, Mrs. Taylor, and Rosalia
Schmutz went with them.
* * *
Vera and Legrand Pace of Cedar
City and Iva Knell of Newcastle, were
visiting relatives and friends here Sat-
urday and Sunday. Minnie Pace and
Irene Rhoner returned to Cedar with
them Sunday evening. Miss Rhoner
will go from there to her home in Salt
Lake

County Teachers

Springdale, C Water Cottam
          Florence Gifford
Rockville Marvin Terry
          Bessie MacDonald
Grafton, Christene MacDonald
Virgin Clinton R Burt
          Winnie Midgley
La Verkin Emil J Graf
          Linda Fletcher
Toquerville, Sherman Cooper
  "   Vera Bringhurst
  '   Mary Starr
Hurricane, Irvin Harmon
          Chauncey Sandberg
  "   La Verna Taylor
  "   Lula Romney
          Josephine Spendlove
Leeds Chas F Hansen
          Margaret Olsen
Washington Willard Nisson
          H R Bentley
  '   Leila Phillips
  "   Emily Sandberg
St George John T Woodbury, Jr
  '   Wm E Woodbury

  "   Fred Fawcett
  '   Guy Hafen
  "   Karl Snow
  "   Lena Nelson
  "   Annie Atkin
  "   Mishie Seegmiller
  '   Emma McAllister
  "   Metta C Morris
  '   Idna Wadsworth
  '   Marie Clark Art
  "   J W McAllister, Music
Bloomington Pearl Larson
Santa Clara, Val Hafen
          Rhoda R Oviatt
  '   Ruth Westover
Gunlock, Lula Wilson
Central Olive F Woolley
Pine Valley, G Delos Hyatt
New Harmony, Minnie Pace
Enterprise, Wm Staheli
          Birney K Farnsworth
  "   Tillie Winsor
  "   Lucile Wood
Glencove James F Cottam

Iron County Record
September 4, 1916

New Harmony, Utah, Sept. 4, 1916.
Mr. and Mrs. J. G. Pace of Cedar
City were in town yesterday.

* * *

President Marsden and Elder Wm.
Palmer were speakers at our Sacra-
mental meeting yesterday. We were
also favored with a visit from the
Stake officers of the Y. M. and Y. L.
M. I. A.

* * *

Elmer Taylor, Golda Prince, Mildred Pace and Rosalia Schmutz are
going to St. George Wednesday, and
will attend school there the coming
winter. Quite a number of our townspeople are going to the festival at St.
George.

* * *

Bishop Pace and family returned
home yesterday from their trip thru
the northern part of the state. The
Bp. attended the Sheep and Wool
Growers convention at Salt Lake while
Mrs. Pace and children visited her
sister at Provo.

Washington County News
September 14, 1916

Mrs Antone Prince returned to
her home at New Harmony Wed
nesday after spending a few days
here

New Harmony, Utah, Sept. 19, 1916.

A baby girl arrived at the home of Mr. and Mrs. James L. Prince Saturday, the 16th. All concerned doing nicely.

* * *

Eldon and George Schmutz have gone to St. George, where they will attend school this winter.

* * *

Our school started on the 11th, with Miss Minnie Pace as teacher.

* * *

Those attending the Iron County fair from this place were, Mr. and Mrs. George F. Prince, Mr. and Mrs. Francis Prince, Mr. and Mrs. Reese Davis, Mr. S. C. Goddard, Mr. and Mrs. Frank Kelsey, George A. Grant, Flora Brown, Wm. Brown, Irving Prince, Mrs. Gladys Grant, Mrs. E. C. Grant, Mr. and Mrs. Orson Hammond, Bp. and Mrs. Henry A. Pace, Mrs. Delta Hammond, Mrs. Susan E. Pace, Alex Taylor and Mr. and Mrs. Lawrence Prince. We would be pleased to see half that number at conference.

Mrs. Batty of Twin Falls, Idaho, is here visiting her daughter, Mrs. Jas. L. Prince.

* * *

Mr. and Mrs. J. W. Imlay and Mr. and Mrs. John Hall of Hurricane were visitors here last week.

* * *

Mr. and Mrs. Bert Morris spent Sunday and Monday here visiting friends.

* * *

Laverna Taylor has gone to Hurricane to teach school this winter.

* * *

Mrs. Mason Rencher who has been here putting up fruit the past week, returned home Saturday.

* * *

James Adair, who has been here the past three months, has gone to Price.

New Harmony, Utah, Oct. 2, 1916

The Sunday School at this place was reorganized yesterday, with Donald Schmutz as superintendent and Andrew Schmutz and Antone Prince as assistants; Gladys Grant as secretary. Wm. P. Taylor was sustained as second counsellor to Bp. Pace, Joseph W. Prince having resigned that position when he moved away.

* * *

Mrs. Flora Brown has gone to St. George to work in the hotel.

* * *

Mr. and Mrs. Leroy Grant have returned home from Panguitch, where they have been to visit Mrs. Grant's mother and sister.

* * *

A. F. Mathis went to St. George last week to represent the republicans of this place at the county convention.

* * *

Joseph Barney has sold his effects here and will move away soon.

New Harmony Oct 3 —We are having some very stormy and cold weather everything is frosted and the tops of our mountians are white with snow   Albert Mathis grain bin was struck with lightning and an old bed that stood out at the end of Guss Permenter s house was also struck and the shock numbed Mrs Permenter for about three hours

J W Prince has gone to lund to sell his sheep

Mrs Lottie Kelsey has gone to Grafton to visit her mother

Great Rainfall

The weather bureau observer at New Harmony has sent in card giving observations for week ending Oct 7th which shows that 1 40 inches of rain fell at that place on Oc 3 and 3 22 on Oct 6 a total of 4 62 inches   That must have been a great rain on the 6th and it is no wonder that the mail service was demoralized   The reporter s name is not signed to the card

New Harmony Oct 17—The deer season is raising some excitement here every man and boy ten g out trying their luck but at this date there have been but two killed

Mrs L A Pace was washing when her wash house caught fire and burned to the gr und before they could save a thing

Mrs I A Pace Ashby Pace Frank Kelsey and Wm P Taylor made a trip to St George last week on land business

The stockmen are busy gathering their cattle and getting ready for a sale which will be in a few days

Mr and Mrs Frank Petty of Cedar City are here visiting Mrs Antone Prince,

Iron County Record
October 17, 1916

New Harmony, Utah, Oct. 17, 1916.

Born—a girl to Mr. and Mrs. J. D. Neilson, Oct. 16. Dr. Macfarlane in attendance.

* * *

Elmer Taylor, Evelyn Prince, Eldon Schmutz, George Schmutz, Melvin Cox and Paul Thurston came up from St. George Saturday to hunt deer. They hunted two days, but being unsuccessful, returned to school this morning.

* * *

Quite an excitement was caused yesterday when the wash house of Mrs. L. A. Pace caught fire. They were unable to extinguish the flames, as they had gained such headway before being discovered. The loss is estimated at $200.00.

* * *

There is considerable sickness among the children and a number of the grown folks are also complaining.

* * *

John Condie, who has been sick for two or three weeks, is slowly recovering.

* * *

Two deer have thus far been brought in since the season opened, Bert Grant and Grant Hale being the fortunate hunters.

Washington County News
October 31, 1916

New Harmony Oct 31 —The deer season ends to day There has been quite a number from Cedar St George and other places here during the hunting season but few of them got deer there have been but ten killed

Miss Mary Knell of Newcastle has returned home she has been here visiting her sister Mrs A W Pace

Born a daughter to Mr and Mrs Albert Mathis Oct 19 all concerned doing nicely

Miss Minnie Pace entertained a crowd of friends at her home Sunday night

County Supervisor Bentley is here visiting the school

New Harmony Nov 7 —Miss Minnie Pace and Mrs A W Pace gave a Halloween party Saturday evening all present report having had the time of their life

Arthur Paxman Herman Stucki Leo A Snow and James Judd held a Democratic rally Friday night

Robt Kirker is here from Parowan

Orson Hammond has gone to work for Tom Thorley for the winter

New Harmony Nov 20 —Frank Kelsey George Prince Ashby Pace and Lawrence Prince left Sunday morning for the big plain to get pasture for their cattle during the winter

Pres Day and Elder Mathison of Parowan were here to visit our Sunday afternoon meeting they gave us some very good talk

Mrs Sadie Grant has returned to her home at——after spending a few days here visiting

Mr and Mrs Joseph W Prince were in town last week from St George on business

John Condie who has been under the doctor s care for some time is slowly improving

New Harmony Nov 28 —Grant the little son of Mr and Mrs John Condie is very ill

Reese Davis has just returned from Lund he brought a new piano for his children

John Whipple is here from Pine Valley looking after his cattle and other property

Sid Goddard has returned to his ranch after spending a few days here

Mrs Bert Grant has gone to Payson to spend the winter with her folks

The farmers are busy plowing and putting in fall grain

Jeremiah Leavitt and wife has gone to New Harmony to spend Thanksgiving with their daughter Mrs Will Chinn

New Harmony Dec 4—Frank Kelsey Ashby Pace Lawrence Prince R y Grant J D Neilson Ingrand Pace and Frank Middleton left today with cattle taking them out to the Big Plain pasture for the winter

Ashby Pace and Vernice Brown have returned from Grass valley where they had been alter horses,

Born a son to Mr and Mrs William Chinn Dec 2 mother and babe doing nicely

Miss Minnie Pace the school teacher entertained the parents last Wedne day afternoon

Mr and Mrs Mason Rancher are here fr m Grass valley visiting rel atives and friends

The general committee gave a dance last Friday night all present had a fine time

The town and county are grading ur road over to the c unty line

John Hall of Hurricane is here on business

Washington County News
December 11, 1916

New Harmony Dec 11—There
was a traveling picture show came
through here the latter part f the
week a large crowd attended and
enjoyed it

Reese Davis and a number of men
left Sunday for Lund to bring the
new thresher home they have just
bought

Roy Grant has just returned t
his home at Gottards ranch after
spending a few days here

Mr and Mrs Cox are here from
Hinckley visiting Mr and Mrs
Orin Kelsey

Miss Minnie Pace has gone to St
George to attend the teachers con
vention

Washington County News
December 19, 1916

New Harmony Dec 19 —Wil
liam Faught who has been here
working for Albert Mathis and
othes for the last two years was cal
led home Saturday on account of
his mother being very ill

Mrs Reese Davis entertained the
Sunday scho l officers last Wednes
day night Ice cream was served
and a good time was had by all
present

The town has just got a new
threshing machine which is thresh
ing lucern seed for Wm Chinn and
Reece Davis

Vera Leavitt has returned home
after spending a few weeks here
with her sister Mrs Olive Chinn

Miss Minnie Pace left this morn
ing for Salt Lake City to attend the
teachers institute.

Antone Prince is home again
after spending a few weeks in St
George

J W Prince of St George was
here last week to visit his father and
mother

Bishop H A Pace left yesterday
for his sheep herd in Hurricane
valley

Miss Gladys Grant has gone to
St George f r her health

Earl Jackson of Toquerville is a
business visitor here

Washington County News
December 26, 1916

New Harmony, Dec 26 —We have 16 inches of snow and looks very favorable for getting more

Elmer Taylor Evelyn Prince Golda Prince Mildred Pace Eldon Schmutz George Schmutz and Rose Schmutz are home from St George for the holidays

Miss Minnie Pace and Verna Taylor have returned from Salt Lake where they went to attend teachers convention

Bishop Henry Pace has just returned from Hurricane Valley where he has been to see about his sheep

Ray Pace and John Pace and wife are here from Price to see their father, Harvey A Pace

Mr and Mrs Roy Grant have moved down from their ranch to town for the winter

Reese Davis has just returned from Lund where he has been after goods for his store

Gottlieb Schmutz has returned from Washington where he has been to the mill

Andrew Schmutz has been hauling hay out to his goats as they are snowed in

M O Woolsey is here building him a new house he has it nearly done

Christmas was very quiet not many stirring as it snowed all day

Washington County News
January 9, 1917

New Harmony Jan 9 —Mrs Ant Prin is just in from St G here spending a few weeks with her parents

M O Woolsey has just completed his new home and moved his family into it

Ashby Pace has returned from Newcastle where he has been visiting friends for a few days

Washington County News
January 11, 1917

Mrs Antone Prince returned to her home at New Harmony Monday after spending some time here visiting relatives and friends

New Harmony, Utah, Jan. 15, 1917.

Mrs. A. B. Prince has returned home from St. George, where she has been visiting her parents. She brings back a baby girl with her, which was born at St. George Dec. 8, 1916.

* * *

A. F. Mathis has gone to Cedar City to have some dental work done.

* * *

Mrs. Clara Woodard has moved to this place from the ranch in order to send her children to school.

* * *

A. F. Mathis is having some work done on a spring about a mile above his farm. He is working to increase the stream of water that he has piped onto his farm. J. D. Nielson and Wm. Brown are doing the work.

* * *

Our town is building up with the balance of the country, as evidence the erection of a number of new barns recently and the construction of a new home by M. O. Woolsey, which is almost completed.

* * *

Mrs. John Condie is quite ill at this writing.

* * *

J. G. Prince has commenced digging a well on his dry farm east of town.

* * *

New Harmony, Jan. 16 —Lawrence Prince is digging a well out on his dry farm; if he gets water he expects to move his family out

We are having some of the coldest weather now that we have had this winter. Quite a number are laid up with bad colds.

Mr and Mrs Reese Davis went to Kanarra Sunday to visit their daughter, Mrs Berry Williams

Some of our young people went to Kanarra Friday to a theater and report a very good time

Albert Mathis is having some work done out on his water claim north of his farm

Mrs Delta Hammond has gone to Provo to spend a few months with her daughter.

Mrs John Condie is very ill.

New Harmony, Jan 23 —Last Thursday Antone Prince went down to the field to feed his cattle, when he was attacked by two coyotes They chased his dog around his horse which he was riding He tried to scare them away but they showed fight and refused to go, so Antone came home for a gun The animals followed him for about a quarter of a mile He got his gun and went back but was unable to get them.

M O Woolsey had just moved his family into their new home when it caught fire Help was near and the fire was put out without doing much damage.

Miss Flora Brown has just returned from St George where she has been for the past four months working for Mrs M. A Orton

Mrs. Wm Chinn and family have gone to Gunlock to spend a few days visiting relatives and friends

Born. a son to Mr. and Mrs Frank Kelsey. Jan 19, mother and babe doing nicely.

Mrs John Condie is very ill, it is reported that she has typhoid fever.

Iron County Record
January 28, 1917

New Harmony, Utah, Jan. 28, 1917.

Dr. M. J. Macfarlane was called down from Cedar Thursday night to see Mrs. John Condie, who has been ill some three or four weeks.

* * *

The stork visited the home of Mr. and Mrs. Frank Kelsey Friday, the 19th inst., leaving a baby boy. This is their second boy. Mother and babe doing nicely.

* * *

Mr. and Mrs. Walter Hall of Minersville are here visiting Mr. and Mrs. Francis Prince.

* * *

Mr. E. C. Grant was called home from Hurricane last week on account of the illness of his daughter, Mrs. John Condie.

* * *

Bro. Harvey A. Pace, who has been confined to the house with a bad cold, is able to be on the street again.

* * *

We are having plenty of snow and cold weather.

Washington County News
January 30, 1917

New Harmony, Jan. 30 —Mrs. John Condie who has been ill for some time is still confined to her bed and is in a very serious condition.

Miss Lenora Ballard and Eugene Russell of Grafton were in town Saturday visiting relatives and friends

E C Grant was called home on account of sickness; he has been working for J. W. Imlay at Hurricane.

Mr. and Mrs Walter Hall of Minersville are here visiting with Mr. and Mrs. Francis Prince.

The town is busy putting out poison for rabbits and coyotes

Washington County News
February 13, 1917

New Harmony, Feb 13 —The funeral of Mrs Nellie Grant Condie was held here last Thursday. She was the wife of John Condie and daughter of Mr and Mrs Eddie Grant. She leaves a family of four children, A number of friends and relatives from surrounding places came to be with the family in their trouble

Antone Prince and Frank Kelsey have been trapping for the past month They got a mountain lion last week They are having remarkably good success

Floyd Grant is here visiting his father and mother after a three years' absence

Ashby Pace has gone to Hurricane Valley to look after Bishop Pace's sheep camp.

Mrs. David Ballard of——is here visiting friends and relatives

Roy Grant is quite sick

New Harmony, Utah, Feb. 13.

Mrs. Eleanor Condie Called.

Eleanor Grant Condie departed this life Wednesday, February 7th, having succumbed to the dreaded disease—typhoid-pneumonia. Funeral services were held Friday in the Ward meeting house. Elders Oren Kelsey, Wm. P. Taylor, Albert Mathis, and Bishop Henry A. Pace were the speakers.

Eleanor (Nellie, as she was known to her friends) was born March 21, 1987, at this place. She leaves a husband, four children a father, mother, three brothers and two sisters to mourn her untimely demise.

She was the wife of Mr. John Condie of this place.

* * *

Dr. A. N. Leonard was seen on the streets yesterday, having come down to examine some of our townspeople who are taking out life insurance policies.

* * *

E. L. Grant is on the sicklist this week.

* * *

Mrs. David Ballard of Grafton is visiting her daughter, Mrs. Frank Kelsey.

New Harmony, Utah, Feb. 27, 1917.

Mrs. Bert Grant returned home to-day from Spanish Fork, where she has spent the greater part of the winter with her parents, Mr. and Mrs. John Farr.

* * *

Ashby Pace is home from Hurricane Valley, where he has been looking after Bp. Paces' sheep for a few weeks.

* * *

We have had spring weather the last two days and every one feels better.

* * *

E. C. Grant has returned to his work at Hurricane.

* * *

Mrs. Clara Woddard is at Bingham visiting Mr. Woodard, who has employment there.

Washington County News
February 27, 1917

New Harmony, Feb 27 —The town all turned out last week and had a rabbit hunt but the rabbits are not so plentiful as thay were, there was only 25 killed in a day's hunt with 16 men.

Roy Grant, Ashby Pace, Jim Prince and Frank Kelsey have gone to the Big Plain after their cattle that have been out there for the winter

We are enjoying some nice spring weather after wading in snow two feet deep for the last two months

Mrs Clara Grant is home again after spending the winter with her parents in Payson.

Born, a daughter to Mr. and Mrs Grant Hales, Feb. 19, all concerned doing nicely

Donald Schmutz is home again after spending the winter at the goat herd

Jos. W. Prince of St George was a business visitor here last week.

Gardner brothers are here from Pine Valley looking after cattle

Antone Prince has gone to St George with a load of grain

Washington County News
March 6, 1917

New Harmony, March 6 —Reese Davis and Antone Prince have gone to Lund after lumber to build a house for Antone Prince

Mrs Florence Phippen of Carey, Idaho, is here visiting friends and relatives

Leslie Anderson of American Fork is here working for Bishop Pace.

The county assessor is here looking over property.

New Harmony, March 12 — Mrs Abbie Pace had a rag bee Friday and served a delicious lunch and ice cream A good time was had.

Mr. and Mrs Batty have returned to their home in Idaho after spending some time here visiting their daughter, Mrs J L Prince

Elders Adams and Durham of Parowan visited our meeting Sunday and gave us some very good instructions

Donald Schmutz has just returned home from Grapevine where he has been herding goats

We have three inches of snow and some very cold weather for this time of the year.

New Harmony, Utah, Mar. 13, 1917.

Mr. and Mrs. Grant Hale have returned home from Cedar City, where they have been spending a few weeks with Mr. and Mrs. Jesse Ford.

* * *

Roy Grant, Ashby Pace, Frank Kelsey, James I. Prince and George L. Prince have gone to the Big Plains near Hurricane to get their cattle, which have been wintering there.

* * *

Ward Conference was held here Sunday afternoon, with Elder Hugh L. Adams of the Stake Presidency, in charge. We were also honored with the presence of Bro. Durham of the Stake Sunday School Board.

* * *

Mrs. Florence K. Phippen of Carey, Idaho, is here visiting her mother, Mrs. Eliza Kelsey, and her grandparents, Mr. and Mrs. Francis Prince.

NEW HARMONY.

(Crowded out last issue.)

New Marmony, Utah, Mar. 20, 1917.
Born—a son to Mr. and Mrs. Donald Schmutz Sunday, Mar. 18. Dr. Macfarlane in attendance. All concerned doing nicely.

* * *

Forest Supervisor and Ranger McAllister held a meeting here yesterday with the cattle men.

* * *

The Relief Society social that was given here last night was a decided success. The program consisted of songs, recitations, sentiments and games, and a delicious luncheon of ice cream and cake was served. Every one seemed to enjoy themselves. The decorations were of green and white.

J. F. Woodard is here visiting his family.

* * *

Bert Grant has returned to his work for Bishop Pace at Hurricane Valley, with the sheep.

New Harmony, April 3 —Dr. Fisher was in town Sunday inviting everyone to attend his lecture at Cedar City Sunday evening Sixteen went from this place and report it being fine

Spring has come at last and the fields are beginning to look green The farmers are busy cleaning ditches and putting in their spring grain.

Mrs Clifton and her hired men are here doing some work on Maser Dalley's homestead, which she has rented for the summer.

Donald Schmutz has a long smile on his face now as he has become the proud father of a fine son.

Martin McAllister, the forest ranger, is here counting cattle on the spring range

Jed Woodard is here again after an absence of three years,

E A Mitchell of Parowan is here buying cattle

New Harmony, Utah, April 11. The short drama "Rube and His Ma," was played to an appreciative audience last Wednesday night, by the S. S. officers. The parts were well taken by all the performers. After the play the Relief Society gave a dance and sold ice cream, the proceeds from which were turned over to the bishop of the ward for the purpose of buying an individual Sacramental service set.

* * *

Our cowboys have gone to Dixie again to look after some of their cattle, which they were unable to find when down last.

* * *

Those who attended the Schildkrest concert at Cedar City last week, from this place, speak of it as being something worth while. Those attending were: Bishop and Mrs. Henry A. Pace, Mr. and Mrs. Albert F. Mathis, Mr. and Mrs. George F. Prince, Mr. and Mrs. J. D. Neilson and Mr. Frank Kelsey.

* * *

Mrs. Frank Kelsey is visiting her mother at Grafton at present.

* * *

Mr. and Mrs. Berry Williams and Mr. and Mrs. Raymond Williams of Kanarra were visitors here last Sunday.

* * *

It is feared that the infant daughter of Mr. and Mrs. Grant Halle has measles. Hopes are entertained, however, that it is nothing more than an infant rash. A physician has not been called yet.

* * *

Jed F. Woodard has gone to Gould's to shear sheep.

Washington County News
April 17, 1917

New Harmony, Apr 17—We are
having a very nice rain which will
do the world of good as our crops
were suffering

Leroy Grant, Ashby Pace and
Frank Kelsey have returned from
the big plain where they have been
looking after their cattle.

Henry A Pace and Francis Prince
have returned from St George
where they had been on business.

The state land inspector was here
last week looking over some homesteads and other property.

Antone Prince has returned from
Lund where he has been for material for his new home.

J D Neilson has bought Flora
Brown out and intends making this
his future home.

Claud Knell of Newcastle is here
visiting friends and relatives.

Washington County News
April 19, 1917

Evelyn Prince of New Harmony,
who has been attending school here
returned to his home Tuesday.

In the district court last Friday
before Judge Morris, Fred Swenson
was acquitted by a jury on a charge
of drunkenness brought by this
city. Will Roundy of New Harmony was acquitted by a jury on a
charge of throwing down fences

Washington County News
May 3, 1917

Miss Minnie Pace of New Har
mony is spending this week here
visiting with relatives

Mrs Antone Prince of New Harmony arrived here Saturday to
spend some time visiting her parents, Mr and Mrs George T Cottam.

Iron County Record
May 8, 1917

New Harmony, Utah, May 8, 1917.
Evelyn Prince, who has been confined to her room for a short time with measles, is now able to be about again.

Our students have returned home from St. George, where they have attended the "Dixie" this winter. Their names are Mildred Pace, Elmer Taylor, Evelyn Prince, Eldon Schmutz, George Schmutz, Golda Prince and Rosella Schmutz. The latter has now gone to Grass Valley to visit her sister, Mrs. Mason Rencher.

It is reported that S. C. Goddard is very ill.

Quite a number of our people went to St. George last week for the school exercises. Among them were Mrs. Minnie Pace, Oren and Rulon Taylor, Clark Pace, Miss Gladys Grant, Mrs. Cecil Schmutz and Susan E. Pace.

Washington County News
May 10, 1917

Miss Rose Schmutz of New Harmony who spent the past winter here left Monday for Pine Valley to visit relatives there.

Miss Golda Prince and Mildred Pace who have been attending school here the past winter left for their home at New Harmony, Saturday Miss Mary Lund accompanied them to visit

Washington County News
May 17, 1917

Mrs Hannah Jolley left Friday for Cedar City upon receiving word of the serious illness of her brother, Sidney Goddard of New Harmony.

County Military Census is Completed

Co Assessor Herman W. Stucki has completed the census of all males of Washington county between the ages of 18 and 45 which shows a total of 1028, 220 of whom are between 18 and 22 years of age, and 808 between 23 and 45.

From the list the Co Assessor has kindly sent the News, we are unable to give the number that will be liable for service under the selective draft for the big army to be raised which takes in all males between 21 and 30 inclusive

The numbers shown in the various towns follows: Virgin, 28, La-Verkin 30, Rockville 29, Enterprise 111, Leeds 81, Pine Valley and Central 34, New Harmony 29, Springdale 34, Gunlock 16, Hurricane 135, Washington 86, St. George 333, Santa Clara 59 Toquerville 7, Pinto 5 Total 1028.

Washington County News
May 22, 1917

New Harmony, May 22 —Sid Goddard who underwent an operation two weeks ago is improving and is coming home before long Miss Gladys Grant who also underwent an operation is improving nicely.

Independence Taylor who fell from a tree last week and broke two of his ribs is improving nicely

We are having some very nice spring rains The farmers are very busy planting corn.

James L Prince who was kicked by a horse last week is now able to be around again

Donald Schmutz has returned from St George where he has been on business

A W Pace has gone to Newcastle to visit friend and relatives.

Evlyn Prince has gone to Marysvale for the summer, to work

Grant Hales has gone to herd sheep for the summer.

Bert Grant has gone to Cedar to work this summer.

Antone Prince is busy building his new home.

Bishop Pace has just bought a new Buick car.

Marion Prince is quite sick with measles

NEW HARMONY

New Harmony, Utah, May 23,
Mr. A. W. Pace went to Newcastle
Monday for seed potatoes.

❖ ❖

Mrs. Maria Page and daughter Mrs.
Alex Ireland of Panguitch, spent a
few days here, with Mrs. LeRoy
Grant last week. They were on their
way home from Long Beach, California, where they have been enjoying
life for the past six months, out of
the snow.

❖ ❖

The small son of Mr. and Mrs. Geo.
F. Prince is confined to his room with
measles.

❖ ❖

Mrs. Verna Pace is in Cedar City
visiting her sister, Miss Mary Knell,
of Newcastle, who was operated on
for appendicitis last week at the Macfarlane Hospital.

❖ ❖

Mrs. Amelia Schmutz is in Saint
George visiting relatives and working
in the temple.

❖ ❖

Mr. and Mrs. Mason Rencher came
over from Grass Valley Monday to
bring Miss Rosalia Schmutz, who has
been visiting there a short time.

❖ ❖

Miss Gladys Grant, who was operated for appendicitis at the Macfarlane Hospital, is doing nicely and will
be able to come home the latter part
of this week.

❖ ❖

Bishop Pace has purchased a new
Buick car, which is a great improvement over the jitney he has been driving heretofore.

❖ ❖

Mr. Evlyn Prince has gone to
Frisco on business.

New Harmony, June 4—The cattle men are very busy gathering their cattle on the range and putting them on the reserve; quite a number are dying with some disease

Mrs Palmer and Mrs Lunt, both of Cedar City, held a Primary conference here Sunday; they gave some very good instructions.

Miss Gladys Grant is home from Cedar City again after an operation for appendicitis; she is getting along nicely.

Sid Goddard who underwent a very serious operation at the Cedar City hospital is now able to come home.

Lesley Anderson has gone to American Fork and expects to move his family here for the summer

Mrs Jesperson, an aged lady 82 years old was thrown from a wagon and was quite badly bruised.

Orson Hammond is home from the sheep herd to spend the summer.

Bishop Pace returned home a few days ago with a new Buick car.

New Harmony, June 11—Prof. Tollestrup visited our Sunday afternoon meeting. He wants to organize a band and give music lessons once a week to our choir

Mr and Mrs Charles Petty of Hurricane were visitors here Wednesday. Mrs Anton Prince returned home with them

Mr and Mrs Jeslie Anderson arrived here Sunday from American Fork. They expect to spend the summer here

Mrs Delta Hammond returned home yesterday after spending the winter at Provo visiting her daughter.

Mr and Mrs J W Prince have returned home after spending the winter in St George

Mr. and Mrs Reere Davis spent Sunday at Kanarra visiting relatives and friends,

New Harmony, Utah, June 20, 1917.

Mr. and Mrs. J. Leavitt of Gunlock are visiting relatives here.

※ ※

Mr. and Mrs. W. Tullis of Newcastle were visitors here Sunday.

※ ※

Miss Iva Knell of Newcastle was a visitor here Sunday.

※ ※

Mr. Ed. Tulls was seen on the streets Monday.

※ ※

The farmers here are busy getting up their first crop of hay.

※ ※

Mrs. Susan A. Pace is in Cedar with her daughter Minnie.

※ ※

Mrs. Bert Grant is visiting Mrs. Leroy Grant at the Goddard and Grant ranch.

※ ※

Miss Vera and Mr. Legrand Pace and Claud Blackburn were visitors here Sunday.

※ ※

Bishop and Mrs. Henry A. Pace, Mr. and Mrs. Donald Schmutz and Wm. P. Taylor went to conference Sunday.

Mr. Gotleib Schmutz has gone to Salt Lake to be treated for spinal trouble.

※ ※

Mrs. Amelia Schmutz returned home from Grass Valley Sunday. She had been visiting her daughter, Mrs. Mason Rencher.

※ ※

Mrs. Cecil Schmutz was operated upon yesterday at the Macfarlane hospital for appendicitis and gall stones; Miss Minnie Pace for appendicitis. Both are from this place.

Washington County News
July 9, 1917

New Harmony, July 9 —We had a very nice time on the 4th. The day was well spent in running races and other sports and on the 5th Kanarrah joined us in all kinds of sports. There were parties here from Cedar City, Pine Valley, American Fork, Kanarrah and Grafton All had a very nice time and we envite them to join us again on the 24th

Mrs David Ballard of Grafton who has been here visiting her daughter has gone to Cedar City to be operated on for gall stones

The Cottam boys of St. George who have been here plastering have returned home for a while.

Mrs Mason Rancher of Grass valley is here visiting her mother

Iron County Record
July 11. 1917

New Harmony, Utah, July 11, 1917.
We are anticipating a good time on Pioneer Day.

❁ ❁

Mr. George F. Prince has been having his home replastered.

❁ ❁

The new home of Mr. and Mrs. Antone Prince is almost completed.

❁ ❁

Mrs. G. F. Prince, Mrs. A. F. Mathis and thir children are in Pine Valley visiting relatives.

❁ ❁

Miss Gladys Grant is visiting Mrs. Leroy Grant at Page's ranch, where Godard and Grant are puting up hay.

❁ ❁

The Kanarra people came over on the 5th and joined us in our sports. All had a good time and we invite them to come again.

❁ ❁

Mrs. Orson Hammond and children and mother, Mrs. M. O. Woolsey, returned home Sunday from Kenilsworth, Carbon County, where they have been visiting Mrs. Albert Taylor, daughter of Mrs. Woolsey.

Harmony, Utah, Aug. 1, 1917.

Andrew Schmutz has returned home from the goat head.

＊ ＊

Painter and Paperhanger. T. F. Brady.

＊ ＊

The Shmutz brothers have been buying a bunch of blooded goats.

＊ ＊

T. F. Brady, Painter and Paper-hanger.

＊ ＊

The farmers have begun hauling their grain and they will soon be threshing.

＊ ＊

Get me? If not, drop me a card. T. F. Brady, Painter and Paper-hanger.

＊ ＊

John Condie and children have returned from Cache Valley where they have been visiting realitives.

J. W. Prince brought his car home from Cedar to-day where it has been in the garage being re-paird.

＊ ＊

Dr. Gower has finished his work here and has gone to Kanarra, where he will stay a few days do-ing dental work.

＊ ＊

Mr. and Mrs. J. D. Nielson and children have gone to the Goddard and Grant ranch, where Mr. Niel-son will help put up the hay.

＊ ＊

A shower was given monday evening, to Mr. and Mrs. Clarence Inglestead who were married July 20. Mrs. Inglestead was formerly Laverna Taylor of this place.

Washington County News
September 6, 1917

Mr. and Mrs Jos W Prince have moved here from New Harmony and intend making this city their permanent home. Mr. Prince is a prosperous sheep man who is highly spoken of by those acquainted with him and we welcome him and his family to this city.

Iron County Record
September 10, 1917

New Harmony, Utah, Sept. 12, 1917.

J. W. Imlay of Hurricane was a visitor here Sunday.

* *

A. F. Mathis returned home Sunday from St. George, where he was called as one of the jurymen for this term of court.

* *

Bp. Gotleib Schmutz returned home Monday from Salt Lake City, where he has been under the care of a doctor nearly all summer.

* *

J. W. Prince was in town this week, having come to take his daughter Velva home to St. George. She has been visiting friends and relatives here a few days.

* *

Monday night Prof. McAllister, Mr. Nichols and Mr. Bleak, with two young ladies, (names not known) from the Dixie Normal College, gave a concert at the home of Bp. Pace. Every one present enjoyed the music and the readings very much.

* *

Principal Homer of the B. A. C. at Cedar City, with Messrs. Lewis and Roylance and Miss Gardner, visited our Sacramental meeting Sunday and gave some good talks and rendered some beautiful music, which was greatly appreciated by those present.

* *

Quite a number of our people have gone to St. George for the Fruit Festival. Among them are Mr. and Mrs. Donald Schmutz, Mr. and Mrs. Francis Prince, Mr. and Mrs. Frank Kelsey, Mrs. E. C. Grant, Miss Gladys Grant, Miss Rose Schmutz and Mr. Eldon Schmutz.

New Harmony, Sept 10 —Miss Golda Prince underwent an operation at Cedar City for appendicis and is getting along nicely.

Several of the B A. C. teachers visited our meeting Sunday and give us some very good talk and also some fine music

Mr and Mrs Donald Schmutz have moved to their new home, just bought from J. W. Prince

Several of our boys will leave for Dixie in a few days where they will attend school this winter.

Mr and Mrs Bennett and family are here from Logan visiting Mrs Sarah Davis.

Netta Davis has returned home after spending a week in St. George.

New Harmony, Sept 17 —Gottlieb Schmutz has returned home after an absence of about four months in Salt Lake under a doctor's care He is very much improved

A number of our people attended the fruit festival at St George and all reported having a fine time

Mrs Johnson from Minersville is here visiting Mr. and Mrs. Francis Prince.

Mrs Clara Grant has gone to spend the winter at Spanish Fork,

New Harmony, Sept. 25.—The farmers are all busy hauling corn We have had quite a heavy frost during the past week.

Mrs Marvin Terry of Rockville spent a short time here visiting her sister, Mrs. Donald Schmutz

Mrs. Minerva Johnson has returned to Minersville after spending some time here visiting

Mr. and Mrs. Frank Petty of Cedar City spent Sunday here visiting.

Our school started last Monday with Miss Minnie Pace as teacher.

Mr. and Mrs Mart Woolsey have returned to their ranch at————

David Gourley, Co. Field Agt , held a meeting here last night.

J. W. Prince was here from St George on business Sunday.

The people are talking of building a new schoolhouse

New Harmony, Utah, Oct. 3, 1917.

Mrs. Frank Kelsey has gone to Grafton to put up fruit.

＊　＊

Mr. and Mrs. Wm. Chinn made a business trip to Cedar City Saturday.

＊　＊

Bishop Pace and A. F. Mathis went to Lund today to deliver a bunch of sheep which they are selling.

＊　＊

Mr. and Mrs. J. G. Pace and their son, Legrande, and Claud Blackburn were here to the social last evening.

＊　＊

Bishop Bennett and family who have been visiting friends and relatives here for a few weeks will return to their home in the morning.

＊　＊

Mr. and Mrs. Mason Rencher came over from Grass Valley Monday to visit relatives and see Mrs. Rencher's brother before he left for the training camps.

＊　＊

George F. Prince went to St. George last week with his daughter, Golda, who will attend school this winter at the Dixie Normal College. Others from this place who are going to school at St. George are Oren Taylor, Clark Pace, Irving Prince, Alex Taylor and George Schmutz.

＊　＊

Our school has been moved from the school house on the hill to the meeting house until the school board can erect a new building. The old house is unsafe for school purposes.

A dance and social was given last night in honor of Eldon Schmutz, our one recruit, who left this morning for the training camps. His mother, brother and two sisters with a number of our townspeople accompanied him as far as Lund. The cars were beautifully decorated and draped with "Old Glory" and the National colors. The best wishes and prayers of the community will be with Eldon while he is away.

Iron County Record
October 17, 1917

New Harmony, Utah, Oct. 17, 1917.

The farmers are threshing their alfalfa seed now.

* *

The Y. L. M. I. A. commenced their winter's work last Sunday night.

* *

Albert F. Mathis has traded in his old Ford car on a new one of the same make.

* *

Born.—A girl to Mr. and Mrs. Wm. P. Taylor Oct. 16. Mother and babe doing nicely.

* *

Mr. and Mrs. George E. Slade of Breen, Colorado, are here visiting relatives. Mrs. Slade is a sister to Mrs. E. C. Grant of this place. The sisters had not met for twenty years.

Iron County Record
October 30, 1917

New Harmony, Utah, Oct. 30, 1917

E. C. Grant is home again after an absence of several months at the sheep herd.

* *

Wm. P. Taylor, Gus Permenter and J. D. Neilson are hauling their winter supply of coal from the Cedar mines.

* *

Mrs. Francis Prince has returned home from Panguitch, where she has been visiting relatives and old time friends.

* *

The Stake Board of the Y. M. and Y. L. M. I. A. met with the young ladies and young men in their meeting Sunday afternoon.

* *

Mrs. W. D. Watts, Vaughn Watts, and Mrs. Mont McDonald of Cedar City, are visiting friends and buying apples and potatoes here.

New Harmony, Nov. 1.—The social given at the home of Mrs If A Pace on Halloween was a huge success Some of tho more nervous ones, however, were glad to return to the house after having gone through goblin land and witnessing some very weird and ghostly sights

The Y M M I. A. and Y. L. M I. A. officers were here Sunday and gave the preliminary program in mutual. A splendid number was a talk given by Mrs. John Fuller on "Activity Work."

A Halloween party was given at the home of Mr. and Mrs William Chinn on Wednesday evening The participants report a splendid time

Mrs W. D Watts, her daughter, Mrs McDonald, and son, Vann, of Cedar City spent a few days here visiting friends and getting fruit.

Claud P Blackburn is here spending a few days with Mrs L A Pace and family before returning to his home at Salt Lake City.

The farmers are making well of the splended weather we are having after a few days of freezing weather.

Jas E Taylor is confined to his bed as a result of a disease of the leg

E C Grant is home from the sheep herd to spend a short time

New Harmony, Nov. 12 —Wallace Duffin left here last Friday to go to Provo to take the winter course at the B Y. U   He was accompanied that far by Claude P Blackburn who will go on to his home at Salt Lake City.

W O Bentley, Co School Supr., spent Friday here visiting the school and looking after the general welfare of the school

Mrs Verna K Pace has gone to Newcastle to spend a few days visiting relatives and friends.

Mr and Mrs LeRoy Grant are receiving congratulations over the arrival of their first son

Mrs Frank P. Kelsey has returned home after a visit of a few weeks' duration at Grafton

Mrs Elizabeth Prince who has been visiting in Panguitch a few days has returned home.

Chas Sullivan of St George was here the latter part of the week buying cattle.

Delbert Woolsey of Woolsey's ranch was in town Friday on business.

Mason Rencher of Grass Valley was here Saturday on business.

New Harmony, Nov 19 —Elder Wm Palmer of Cedar City and Elders Hollihock and L N Marsden and sister Marsden of Parhwan were speakers at church Sunday.   Their particular messages were along the lines of Sunday School, Religion class and High Priest work

Dr. M. J. Macfarlane of Cedar City was called to attend Jas. E. Taylor who has been suffering a great deal from severe pain in the leg   The leg was put into a cast and the doctor thinks that after a while the bone will recover sufficient to prevent serious results

M. O. Woolsey is having his house plastered which will make an improvement in it and make it much more efficient for the coming of winter.

A number of our town's people went to Cedar City Monday evening to participate in an entertainment, a number of the school Lyceum course.

Jas. G Knell and his daughter, Mary, of Newcastle are here for a short visit with relatives and friends.

Mrs Verna K. Pace has returned home after a short visit at Newcastle

Iron County Record
November 20, 1917

New Harmony, Utah, Nov. 20.

M. O. Woolsey has been having some work done on his home.

❈ ❈

Miss Mary Knell of New Castle is visiting relatives and friends here.

❈ ❈

A number of people of this place attended the concert at Cedar City last evening.

❈ ❈

A Thanksgiving program will be given in the Mutual Improvement Association Sunday evening.

❈ ❈

Dr. M. J. Macfarlane came down Sunday to see James E. Taylor, who is suffering with a bad ankle.

❈ ❈

The infant son of Mr. and Mrs. Leroy Grant, who has been very weak since birth two weeks ago, is improving rapidly.

❈ ❈

President and Mrs. L. N. Marsden and Elder Holyoak of Parowan, and Elder Wm. R. Palmer of Cedar City were visitors at our Sabbath School and Sacramental meeting Sunday.

New Harmony, Nov. 26 —The Thanksgiving program Sunday evening was splendidly given and well attended. Some of the attendants expressed themselves as being anxious to attend something of the kind a little more often

The new house Bishop H. A. Pace is having erected on Cliff View farm is well under way. A num- of workmen are employed there.

Those participating in the chicken supper Friday evening at the home of Mr and Mrs Donald Schmutz report a lively time.

Mr and Mrs John Ballard and Mrs. Ballard's sister of Cedar City were here Sunday visiting Mr. and Mrs Frank P. Kelsey.

Evelyn Prince who has been in Idaho for the past six or seven months has returned home.

Mrs Verna T. Englestead went to Cedar Sunday on business.

LaGrand Pace of Cedar City was here on business Saturday.

New Harmony, Dec 3 —Mr. and Mrs Wm Chinn, Mr and Mrs. Ashby W. Pace, and Mrs Amber Schmutz went to spend Thanksgiving at Newcastle They report a splendid time

Thanksgiving passed off rather quietly. There was no public celebration but several family dinners

Harvey A. Pace is feeling rather poorly and has been confined to his bed for a day or two

All of our students attending school at St. George came home to spend Thanksgiving.

David Gourley, the county agent, held a meeting with the farmers Wednesday evening

Miss Mary Knell has returned to her home at Newcastle.

Mr. and Mrs Andrew Sorensen left Thursday for New Harmony to attend the funeral of Harvey A. Pace.

Mrs Antone Prince returned to her home at New Harmony after spending Thanksgiving here with her parents

Misses Mary Lund and Golda Prince spent Thanksgiving at New Harmony; they returned home Friday, Evelyn Prince accompanied them. He returned to his home Monday.

New Harmony, Dec 10 —The people of our town were very much surprised and shocked to learn of the sudden death of Elder Harvey A Pace last Tuesday morning. He had been ailing for a day or two but was much better and able to be outside walking about on Monday That night he was quite hearty and went to bed feeling apparently as well as usual During the night he made a slight gasp and instantly his wife was at his side but to no avail as he was gone before she could call for help There was a large funeral, people coming from Leeds, St George, Hurricane and Kanarra to pay their last respects The speakers at the services were Elders John W Platt of Kanarra and H. E Duffin of this place All of his children, James F.,John, Levi B. and Maggie Pace of Price were here, also his grandsons, Elmer Taylor who is attending school at the U of U. and Alex Tayler who is attending school at St George

Elders Lyman and Adams of the stake presidency and sisters Lyman and Adams, Stake Relief Society workers, visited our wards Sunday and held meetings urging the Saints to do their duty.

Those attending the social at Mr. and Mrs. Frank O. Kelsey's report a fine time

Draft Register Notice

All persons registered preparatory to military service, except those who have been drafted will receive a questionnaire which must be filled out and returned within seven days from date of mailing Any person entitled to receive one who fails to comply with the above will be guilty of a misdemeanor punishable by fine or one year's imprisonment. The The questionnaires will be sent out as follows 5% on each day for 20 days beginning Dec 15, 1917, and on each of said days the men holding numbers given on the respective dates should hold themselves in readiness to receive and immediately fill out and return the same to the local board

Date		Order No
Dec	15	1 to 44
"	16	45 to 83
"	17	84 to 115
"	18	116 to 146
"	19	147 to 171
"	20	172 to 196
"	21	197 to 221
"	22	222 to 246
"	23	247 to 271
"	24	272 to 296
"	25	297 to 321
"	26	322 to 346
"	27	347 to 371
"	28	372 to 396
"	29	397 to 421
"	30	422 to 446
"	31	447 to 471
Jan.	1	472 to 496
"	2	497 to 521
"	3	522 to 543

Any registrant desiring assistance or advice in filling out the questionnaire can obtain the same by calling on either of the following named persons who will be authorized to administer the necessary oaths

David H. Morris, St George
Leo A. Snow, St. George
George R Lund, St George
Chas G Y Higgins, St George
Jos S Snow, St George
Albert H. Pike, St George
D. Clark Watson, St George
David Hirschi, Rockville
Sylvester Earl, Virgin
Emil Graff, La Verkin
Chas B Petty, Hurricane
James Judd, Hurricane
Ellis J. Pickett, Hurricane
Martin Anderson, Toquerville
W. H Slack, Toquerville
Albert Matthis, New Harmony
Chas Hanson, Leeds
A A Paxman, Washington
W. O. Nisson, Washington
Israel Neilson, jr., Washington
Herman Stucki, Santa Clara
A Alma Nelson, Enterprise
Louis Lund, Enterprise
Antone Ivins, Enterprise
Mason Gardner Pine Valley
Clifford Empey, Central
J S P Bowler, Gunlock

Mr and Mrs Antone Prince arrived here Friday from New Harmony to visit with friends and relatives.

HARVEY A. PACE

Funeral services for Harvey A. Pace were held at the ward meeting house in New Harmony, Dec. 7, 1917. Albert F. Mathis, first councilor to Bishop Henry A. Pace, presiding Appropriate music was furnished by the ward choir, which rendered "Resting Now from Care and Sorrow," "Sweet Hour of Prayer," favorite selections of the deceased. and "I've Heard of a Beautiful City," solo by Elder Joseph W Prince, assisted by the choir Timely remarks were made by Elders John W. Platt of Kanarra and Hesikiah Duffin of New Harmony, who eulogized the life of the departed Services opened by Elder Orren Kelsey and closed by Elder William P Taylor, the grave being dedicated by Elder Albert F Mathis

The subject of this sketch was born near Murfreesboro, Tenn., Oct. 12, 18 38, being the third son of William Pace and Margaret Nichols As a lad of fifteen he crossed the plains, with his parents, in Brigham Young's company, driving stock the entire distance He located at Provo from which town he moved to Spanish Fork, in 1851

His early manhood was spent in these two towns which afterward develped into populous cities Here he was constantly engaged in developing Spanish Fork, assisting immigrants to Utah and protecting the resident citizens against the depredations of the Indians led by Walker and others He married Ann Elizabeth Redd in Spanish Fork, Aug 28, 1853, by whom he had ten children, four of whom survive him In 1861 he with his family moved to Southern Utah, settling in New Harmony, Washington Co Here also he met Susan E. Keel, whom he married in Salt Lake City, July 11, 1870, by whom he had four children, two of whom survive him.

His life was ever and always a monument of inspiration to those with whom he came in contact or who had the pleasure of associating with him. Quiet and unassuming in his ways yet commanding respect from all, generous beyond a doubt, his entire life was devoted to the uplifting of his home community.

He held many positions of trust, both civil and ecclesiastical. He acted for many years as councilor to the bishop of the ward and as superintendent of the Sunday school of New Harmony

He is survived by a numerous posterity who will idolize his memory and rise up and call him blessed. Besides his wife, his descendents consist of fourteen children of whom only six are living, who are as follows. John, James, Margaret A., Levi B., Nancy E, and Henry A His grandchildren total fifty-nine and his great grandchildren thirty eight.

Iron County Record
December 26, 1917

NEW HARMONY.

—'18—

New Harmony, Utah, Dec. 26, 1917.

—'18—

Mr. and Mrs. William Chinn are in Gunlock visiting Mr. and Mrs. J. Leavitt, Mrs. Chinn's parents.

—'18—

Velva Prince of St. George spent Xmas here with relatives and friends, returning home this morning.

—'18—

Our students of the Dixie Normal College at St. George are home for a week's vacation.

—'18—

Mr. and Mrs. Mason Rencher are here spending the holidays with Mrs. Rencher's parents.

—'18—

Mr. and Mrs. Leroy Grant went to Toquerville today to visit a few days with Mr. and Mrs. E. R. Higbee.

—'18—

Mr. and Mrs. Donald Schmutz are visiting in St. George.

The county clerk has issued marriage licenses as follows: Dec 22, to Mr Sterling Russell of Virgin and Miss Lila Farnsworth of St. George, Mr Frederick Samuel Chadburn of Central and Miss Harriet Beacham of St George, Dec 23, to Mr. Joseph Millard Allen and Miss Ethel Cox, both of Cane Beds, Ariz ; Dec 26, to Mr. George Evlyn Prince of New Harmony and Miss Mary Lund of St. George.

Mr. Evlyn Prince and Miss Mary Lund were married here December 27th by Pres Geo F. Whitehead

The bride is a daughter of Mrs. Mame Seegmiller and the late Miles Lund, an amiable and very highly respected young lady who has a very large circle of friends. The groom is a son of Mr and Mrs George Prince of New Harmony, and is a young man of excellent qualities who is well spoken of by all acquainted with him

Handsome cards announced a reception the same evening in Andrew Price's amusement hall, where a large number of friends of young couple had a delightful time

New Harmony, Jan 7 — Jas. D Taylor, who has been suffering from a disease of the leg, is improving nicely and is able to be about on crutches

Mrs Frank P. Kelsey, in company with her sister Nora, has returned home after a short visit at Grafton with relatives and friends

We are hoping for better results from our telephone system since there has been some repairing done on the line

Mr and Mrs LeRoy Grant have returned home after spending a week in Toquerville visiting friends

Mr and Mrs. Ashby W Pace have returned from Newcastle where they spent a part of the holidays

Mrs Amber T Schmutz has returned home after spending the holiday vacation at St. George

Arch Ballard of——is here visiting with his sister, Mrs Lottie B Kelsey

Wm P. Taylor has gone to St. George with a load of potatoes

Afton Ballard of——was here for a short time the past week

New Harmony, Jan. 21.—Jas E. Taylor is improving nicely now; his leg has improved enough that he is able to stand a part of his weight on it without the aid of his crutch.

Mrs Reese Davis has returned home from Kanarra where she has been for several days nursing her daughter, Mrs Berry Williams, who is the happy mother of a new girl

Bishop Pace's new home at Cliff View farm is completed and ready for occupancy. The workmen returned to their homes in Cedar Monday.

The little son of Mr and Mrs Frank P. Kelsey, who has been suffering from an attack of scarlet fever, is recovering splendidly

Donald Schmutz has returned home after spending a few days in Dixie looking after the interests of his goats.

Henry A Pace has returned from a trip to Dixie where he has been looking after his sheep interests

A. F. Mathis has gone to Salt Lake City to attend the Wool Growers' convention.

Mr. and Mrs M. O Woolsey of ———were in town Sunday.

NEW HARMONY.

(Received too late for last issue.)

New Harmony, Utah, Jan. 30, 1918. George Wood of Cedar City and Roy Armstrong of Enoch were visitors here yesterday.

* * *

Mr. and Mrs. Evelyn Prince of St. George are visiting Mr. Prince's parents, Mr. and Mrs. Geo. F. Prince.

* * *

Mr. A. F. Mathis returned last night from Enterprise, where he has been in the interest of his sheep.

* * *

Mrs. Della Hammond is quite ill at this writing.

* * *

There is quite an epidemic of la grippe among the children of this place at present.

* * *

Leslie Anderson and family have moved into the new home that Bp. Pace has built on his farm.

New Harmony, Feb 4 —Iron County Agent, Esplin and Dr Leonard, in company with Miss Bernella Gardner and Miss Luke of the B A. C , accupied the time in church Sunday in interest of the Round-up which is being held this week at the B A C.

For the past week A F. Matthis has had several men employed on his farm repairing and adding pipe to the old system. These changes will make it much more convenient for him

Joseph Duffin of Provo is here visiting his daughter, Mrs Myrtle Anderson Mr Duffin is returning from attending his brother's funeral at Toquerville

Mrs Delta Hammond is recovering from an attack of influenza and a severe pain under her shoulder

Andrew Schmutz is home again after several weeks duration in Dixie looking after his goats.

The infant son of Mr and Mrs Donald Schmutz is recovering from an attack of bronchitis

Several of our town's people are attending the Round up in Cedar City this week

Mr and Mrs Evlyn Prince of St George are spending a few days here

Washington County News
February 18, 1918

New Harmony, Feb 18 —Born, a son to Mr and Mrs Andrew Schmutz, Feb 14, the infant lived but a very short time A daughter to Mr and Mrs. Orson Hammond, Feb 16

Mr. and Mrs Wm Chinn have gone to Gunlock to attend the funeral of Mrs Chinn's sister, Miss Vera Leavitt.

Mrs. Bert Grant has returned from Payson where she has been spending the winter with her parents

Our town is in deep sympathy with Mr. and Mrs. Jerry Leavitt over the loss of their daughter Miss Vera.

S S Smith, the U. S. farm loan agent, was doing business here Sunday with the business men of the town.

H. E Price, the government land inspector, was here Sunday and spent some time going over the land

The ice cream party at the home of Mr. and Mrs. Lawrence Prince Saturday evening was a huge success

A doctor was called from Cedar City today to attend Mrs E C. Grant, who hurt herself lifting.

The south wind brought us our first snow storm, containing enough moisture to settle the dust

Orson Hammond is home from the sheep herd where he has been all winter.

Iron County Record
February 19, 1918

New Harmony, Utah, Feb. 19, 1918.
Born, to Mr. and Mrs. Orson Hammond, a girl.

* * *

George Smith of Provo is a business visitor here this week.

Everyone is rejocing over the little snow storm we are having yesterday and today.

* * *

Born, to Mr. and Mrs. Andrew Schmutz, a boy. The baby died at birth. Mother doing nicely.

* * *

Miss Golda Prince is home from St. George where she has been attending school this winter.

* * *

Dr. Macfarlane was called down to see Mrs. E. C. Grant yesterday, who is suffering from an attack of heart trouble.

* * *

Bishop Pace returned home this week from the Hurricane country where he has been looking after his sheep.

* * *

Mr. and Mrs. William Chinn have gone to Gunlock to attend the funeral of Vera Leavitt, sister to Mrs. Chinn.

New Harmony, Feb 25 —Everyone is wearing a broad smile as a result of the welcome rain storm, which started last Thursday night and continued off and on up till Sunday evening

A crowd of our young people went to Kanarra last Thursday evening to attend the double wedding dance of Mr and Mrs B. F. Anderson and Mr. and Mrs King

Messrs Albert F. Mathis, Jas. L Prince, Wm P Taylor, John E Whipple and Antone B. Prince went to St. George Friday on land business

Mrs Jas E Taylor is quite ill but is somewhat better at this writing

Mrs. Lottie B Kelsey has gone to Grafton to attend her father who is ill.

W Mitchell was here the latter part of the week buying cattle.

Mrs A W. Pace is in Cedar City having some dental work done.

Wilford Andreason of Lehi is here working for Henry A Pace

Miss Rose Schmutz spent the end of the week in Cedar City.

Donald Schmutz went to Cedar Sunday on business.

New Harmony, Mar 4 —The school made a marked improvement during the month of February in the purchasing of Thrift Stamps The report shows $32 as compared with $13 the previous month Several of the children have exchanged their Thrift cards for War Saving Stamps

Alex Taylor who has been attending school at St George this winter returned home Sunday, to put in his spring crop

Those participating in the social at Mr and Mrs Leslie Anderson's Sunday evening report a splendid time.

County Agt David Gourley and Mr. Winder held a meeting here Thursday evening with the farmers

Francis Prince who has been feeling somewhat indisposed for the past week is feeling much improved

LeGrand Pace of Cedar City was here the latter part of the week visiting relatives and friends

Irving Prince is home again after spending the winter in St George attending school.

Mason Rencher af Grass valley spent a few days here last week

Iron County Record
March 5, 1918

New Harmony, Utah, Mar. 5, 1918.

Mrs. Grant Hale spent Sunday at Kanarra with relatives.

* * *

A committee has been appointed to arrange a social for the anniversary of the Relief Society.

* * *

Mr. and Mrs. Leslie Anderson entertained the young people at their home Sunday evening.

* * *

The Sunday School is rehearsing and will present to the public in the near future the play, "The Arrival of Kitty."

* * *

Mrs. James E. Taylor and Mrs. Jas. L. Prince, who have been on the sick-list the past few weeks, are much improved at this writing

* * *

Mr. and Mrs. Jos. W. Prince, Dr and Mrs. McCall and Mis. Belle W l liams of St. George are the guests of Mr. and Mrs. Francis Prince of this Mr. and Mrs. Francis Prince of this place.

Washington County News
March 18, 1918

New Harmony, Mar 18 —"The Arrival of Kitty" presented by the school last Friday evening was a huge success Much credit is due those taking part

Mason Rencher, of Grass Valley came over last Saturday for his wife who has been here visiting with her parents, Mr and Mrs. Gottlieb Schmutz for some time

The young people participated in a chicken supper at the home of Mr and Mrs. Leslie Andreason Sunday evening and an exceptionally fine time is reported.

Miss Gladys Grant left Saturday for the northern part of the state to visit friends and relatives.

The Sunday school staged "The Arrival of Kitty" at Kanarra Saturday evening.

Mr. and Mrs Evlyn Prince returned to St. George last Sunday

Levi Gardner of Grass Valley spent Saturday and Sunday here.

Iron County Record
March 20, 1918

New Harmony, Utah, Mar. 20.

Mr. J. L. Prince is able to be out again after an illness of a few weeks.

* * *

Miss Gladys Grant has gone to Salt Lake and Murray to visit relatives and friends.

* * *

Messrs. Mason Rencher and Levi Gardner of Grass Valley were visitors here Sunday.

* * *

The Red Cross members made ten suits of pajamas last week and returned them to St. George.

* * *

An interesting program was rendered by the Relief Society Sunday evening at the ward meeting house.

* * *

Mr. John Condie was down from Cedar City Sunday to visit his children. His brother Dave was with him.

* * *

The "Arrival of Kitty" was presented to a large and appreciative audience Friday evening. The proceeds will be used for the benefit of the Sunday School.

* * *

Mrs. Mason Rencher, who has been spending the winter here with her parents, Mr. and Mrs. Gottleib Schmutz, returned to her home at Grass Valley Monday.

New Harmony, Mar. 25 —The Sunday school dramatic club, presented "The Arrival of Kitty" Saturday evening in Enoch, the proceeds to go to the Red Cross Much credit is due them for their spirit and loyalty

H E Duffin of Provo was here last week and sold out his possessions. He has bought land in Idaho and expects to leave soon for that locality

Frank P Kelsey has gone to Grafton for his wife who has been there for some time visiting relatives and friends

Leslie Andreason who has been very ill with grippe is improving and is able to be at work again

Mrs G Lawrence Prince has gone to Overton to visit with her parents, Mr. and Mrs E J Whipple

The amount of precipitation since February 22nd is eleven and eighty-seven hundredths inches

Dr and Mrs Frank Petty of Cedar City were guests of Mr and Mrs. Antone Prince Sunday

Mrs Francis Prince has gone to Overton to spend some time visiting relatives and friends,

Arch Ballard has returned to his home in Grafton

New Harmony, April 1 —Wm P Taylor returned from Lund last Saturday where he has been for freight While there he received a close call to death by lightning He was on his wagon and a mile or two this side of Lund when he received the shock, he was dazed for a short time. His horses became frightened at the clap of thunder that followed immediately and for some time he was unable to handle the lines sufficiently to control his team, but fortunately there was nothing really serious

The friends of Eldon Schmutz, who is in the lumber division of the Camp Lewis quarters, will be pleased to note that he is able to be at work again after a three weeks lay off, due to an accident he received while cutting down trees It seemed that the axe glanced and severed his foot through the tissue of the bone thus causing a bad wound

Last Tuesday Antone B Prince killed a coyote, the following day he located the den and was successful in capturing nine small ones

John E Whipple, who has been ill for the past week with a severe pain in his side, is able to be at work again

Ruben Whipple has returned home from St. George where he has been attending school the past winter

Miss Gladys Grant is home again after a visit of a few days duration in the northern part of the state

J. Claud Knell of Newcastle was here Saturday and Sunday visiting relatives and friends

A number of our town's people went to Cedar City Sunday to attend the M. I A. contest

W O. Bentley, Jr., and Miss McAllister of St George were visiting school last week

Washington County News
April 8, 1918

New Harmony, April 8 — Mrs Francis Prince has returned home from Overton, Nev, where she has been visiting relatives and friends

Those attending conference in Salt Lake City are Carl Boshard, John E Whipple, Mrs Delta Hammond and Mrs. Leslie Anderson

Mr and Mrs G L Eldridge of Newcastle were here last Friday to purchase seed corn

Mrs Lawrence Prince has returned home, after a two weeks visit in Logan, Nev

Bishop Henry A Pace made a business trip to Washington, Saturday.

The snow storm we had last Wednesday, amounted to 5½ inches

Mrs Donald Schmutz is in St George doing temple work.

Washington County News
April 15, 1918

New Harmony, Apr 15 — Geo F Whitehead and Elson Morris of St George were here Sunday, talking on Liberty Bonds.

Mrs Delta Hammond and Mrs Leslie Anderson are home again, after spending two weeks in the northern part of the state.

Clark Pace and George Schmutz have returned home, after attending school the past winter at the D. N C

Carl Boshard and John Whipple returned home the fore part of the week from Salt Lake City

Elders Armstrong and Esplin, of Enoch, were home missionaries here Sunday

Mr and Mrs A. F. Mathis made a business trip to Cedar City Thursday.

Mrs Ashby W Pace is visiting relatives and friends in Newcastle

Mrs Donald Schmutz has returned home from St George.

New Harmony, April 23 —District Forester L F. Kneipp, Chief of Grazing Homer Fenn, and W M. Mace, forest supervisor and M L McAllister, forest ranger, were here Tuesday, discussing grazing matters with the forest users

Marion, the 11-year old son of Mr and Mrs Geo F Prince, underwent an operation for appendicitis Saturday.

Born, a son to Mr and Mrs Englestead, April 15. Mr Englestead is in training at Camp Lewis.

Rose Schmutz is at the Macfarlane hospital, where she has undergone an operation for appendicitis

Orren Taylor has returned home after spending the past winter at the D N. C

Mr and Mrs Henry A. Pace made a business trip to Cedar City, Saturday.

Stewart Thorley, of Cedar City, was here Monday on business

Mrs Ashby W. Pace has returned home from Newcastle.

NEW HARMONY.

New Harmony, Utah, Apr. 24, 1918.
Mrs. Ashby Pace is visiting relatives at Newcastle.

* * *

Miss Rose Schmutz was operated on Saturday for appendicitis at the Macfarlane hospital.

Mrs. Delta Hammond and Mrs. Leslie Anderson returned home from American Fork where they have been visiting relatives.

* * *

Mrs. Donald Schmutz returned home last week from St. George where she has been visiting relatives and doing work in the temple.

* * *

April 15th, Dr. Macfarlane attended the birth of a son at the home of Mr. and Mrs. Clarence Inglestead. Mr. Inglestead is in training at Camp Lewis.

George Schmutz and Clark Pace returned home Saturday from St. George where they attended school the past winter.

Iron County Record
April 30, 1918

New Harmony, Utah, April 30, 1918.

Our school closed for the summer vacation last week.

* * *

Elwin Ballard of Grafton is here visiting his sister, Mrs. Frank Kelsey.

* * *

Orrin Taylor has an attack of the mumps, contracted at St. George before he left school.

* * *

George F. and George L. Prince are shearing sheep for Berry Williams, back of the Kanarra fields.

* * *

Mr. A. F. Mathis, John Whipple and Mr. and Mrs. James L. Prince went to St. George Sunday on business.

* * *

Clinton and Vivian Milne of Saint George are doing some painting and plastering here this week for various people.

* * *

Rose Schmutz and Marion Prince came home Sunday from the Macfarlane Hospital and are recovering in good shape from their operations for appendicitis.

Soldier Boys Leave

The drafted boys left last Saturday morning for Camp Lewis, Wash. There were 10 of them, eight from this county and two, Ernest Yett and Jonathan D. Waring, from Arizona. The boys from this county were: Henry Melvin Gibson, George Spendlove, David Thatcher Ballard and Joseph Harvey Wright, all of Hurricane, David Leslie Spilsbury of Toquerville, Karl Alfred McMullin of Leeds, Lawrence Leavitt of Gunlock, and John R Pearson of New Harmony.

Washington County News
May 7, 1918

New Harmony, May, 7 — Bp Henry A Pace has purchased a shearing plant and is shearing now at Cliff View farm.

Mrs C J. Whipple and Mrs Jesse Whipple of Logan, Nev , are here visiting relatives and friends

Elmer Taylor has returned home from Salt Lake, where he has been attending the U of U

Mary Knell of New Castle is here visiting her sister, Mrs A. W. Pace

Mrs Malissa Hammond is in St George visiting.

Orren Taylor is confined to his bed with the mumps

Washington County News
May 9, 1918

Leave Tomorrow

The two drafted boys, Sheridan Ballard of Grafton and Edward Staheli of New Harmony will leave tomorrow morning for Fort McDowell, Calif

Washington County News
May 14, 1918

New Harmony, May 14 — R D Garver and W H Mohler of Ogden have been here the past week surveying the U S forest reserve

Clarence Englestead has returned home He has been honorably discharged from training at Camp Lewis, Wash

Ashby Pace and Reuben Whipple have returned home from Modena where they have been shearing sheep

Claude Knell from Newcastle was here Tuesday visiting relatives and friends.

Nora Ballard of Grafton is here visiting her sister, Mrs Frank Kelsey.

Lillie Knell of Cedar City was a visitor here Tuesday

Washington County News
May 20, 1918

New Harmony, May 20 —The Red Cross gave a social last Friday night. Refreshments were served and a very enjoyable time was had

Minnie, Mildred and Clark Pace and Rose Schmutz went to Newcastle last Saturday to attend the wedding of Mr and Mrs. Walter M Spencer.

Mrs A W. Pace has been confined to her room for a few days with lagrippe but is on the improve now.

Orson Hammond has returned home after spending the winter at sheep herd.

Ashby Pace and Reese Davis have gone to Harrisburg to shear sheep

There are a number of cases of mumps in town

New Harmony, Utah, May 22, 1918.

Mr. and Mrs. James E. Taylor have five children very ill with the mumps.

* * *

Mr. and Mrs. Berry Williams were here from Kanarra yesterday visiting relatives.

* * *

Mr. and Mrs. Jerry Levitt of Gunlock were here last week visiting their daughter, Mrs. Wm. Chinn.

* * *

Mrs. LeRoy Grant will go to San Francisco the last of this week to visit her mother and sister, Mrs. Moria Pace and Mrs. Nora Ireland.

* * *

Mr. Durham and Mrs. Nicholas of the Sunday School board were visitors here yesterday. Mr. Durham occupied the time at afternoon meeting giving some very valuable instructions *

* * *

* * *

The members of the Red Cross gave a social at the Ward meeting house Friday night. Cake and lemonade was served and everyone enjoyed themselves playing games.

* * *

Mrs. Hannah Williams has a new Buick car to do her traveling in. Two other cars have been ordered to be delivered to parties at Kanarra in June.

* * *

Misses Minnie and Mildred Pace, Rose Schmutz and Clark Pace went to Newcastle last week to attend the wedding reception of Mr. and Mrs. Walter Spencer. Mrs. Spencer was formerly Miss Mary Knell. Her friends of this place wish them a long life of wedded happiness.

Elmer Taylor of New Harmony was a business visitor here Wednesday

Mr and Mrs Evlyn Prince left last Thursday for their home at New Harmony after visiting for some time here.

Miss Golda Prince of New Harmony came down Wednesday to visit friends and relatives for a few days. ·

Still Boosting For The Arrowhead Trail

Mr and Mrs. Charles H Bigelow left Tuesday for New Harmony and other points north after spending several days here, guests of the Hotel Dixie, Mr Bigelow on business connected with the Arrowhead Trail, to which he devotes greatly of his time and means

Mr. Bigelow is seeking to arouse sentiment in favor of improvment of this highway, of which he is the "father," and is leaving nothing undone that he can do toward this end. He forsees that it will become the main transcontinental highway, if it is pushed, and will be the main factor in the upbuilding of this section of the country through which it passes Its importance is emphasized just now on account of the war, which is likely to make passenger travel and produce shipments on the railroads almost prohibitory.

We hope Mr. Bigelow can succeed in interesting the northern people in the Arrowhead Trail, which means as much to them as it does to us And we al-o hope that Mr. Bigelow can see his way clear to stay with the proposition to which he has devoted so much of his time, money and energy He deserves to see success crown his efforts

Iron County Record
June 11, 1918

NEW HARMONY.

New Harmony, Utah, June 11.

Granville Pace of Cedar City was a business visitor here the first of the week.

* * *

Arthur and Gus Slack and Leland Bringhurst of Toquerville were here today looking for work.

* * *

Mrs. Francis Prince has returned home from St. George, where she has been visiting her son Joseph W. Prince and family.

* * *

Mrs. Donald Schmutz has gone to Vernal, Uintah county, to spend part of the summer with her father and family.

* * *

Mr. and Mrs. J. Leavitt of Gunlock and their daughter, Mrs. Wood Tullis, passed through here en route home from Panguitch, where they had been visiting relatives.

Washington County News
June 20, 1918

Stake President Wilford Day, and counselors Lyman and Adams of Parowan were here Sunday. They gave some very good talk in the afternoon meeting

The Primary officers entertained the Primary children at a lawn party last Friday. Refreshments were served and a very nice time was had

Charles Burke and daughters Jennie and Vella of Virgin were visitors here Sunday.

Mr and Mrs Jesse Ford of Kanarra were here Wednesday visiting relatives and friends

Donald Schmutz has gone to Kansas City, Mo., to sell his goats

M. O Woolsey of Woolsey's ranch was here on business Saturday.

Washington County News
June 24, 1918

New Harmony, June 24 —Ardeth, the three year old daughter of Mr, and Mrs Leslie Anderson, has been very ill, but is on the improve now.

Mason Rancher of Grass valley was here Wednesday and returned home Friday accompanied by Miss Ethel Schmutz

Mrs. G. Prementer has returned home after spending several days visiting friends in St George.

A number of town people attended conference in Cedar City, Saturday and Sunday.

Elmer Taylor has returned home after spending the past two months at the sheep herd

Ora Workman of Hurricane is here visiting relatives and friends

Carl Boshart is in Cedar City visiting relatives and friends

Le Grande Pace of Cedar City was a visitor here Sunday

The first cutting of hay is now up

Iron County record
June 25, 1918

NEW HARMONY.

New Harmony, Utah, June 25.
Martin McAllister of St. George is
a busines visitor here today.

* * *

Evelyn Prince and Grant Hale
started to Marysvale this morning to
hunt work.

* * *

Mrs. Grant Hale has gone to Kanarra to spend a short time with relatives.

* * *

Legrand Pace of Cedar City was
visiting relatives and friends here
Sunday.

* * *

Donald Schmutz has gone to Kansas City with a bunch of goats which
the Schmutz Brothers are selling.

* * *

Mrs. Evelyn Prince, who has been
visiting here for a short time, returned this morning.

* * *

Mrs. Bessie Permenter returned
home Friday from St. George, where
she had been visiting Mr. and Mrs.
J. W. Prince.

* * *

A number of our people attended
conference at Cedar City Saturday
and Sunday. Among them were Bp.
and Mrs. Henry A. Pace, Mr. and Mrs.
A. F. Mathis, Mr. and Mrs. Orson
Hammond, William P. Taylor, John
Whipple, Carl Boshardt, Mrs. Leslie
Anderson and Mrs. Sarah Davis.

Washington County News
July 2, 1918

NEW HARMONY

Miss Minnie Pace has returned home after a five weeks' visit in California and Arizona. She reports a delightful trip

Mrs G E Prince has returned to her home in St George, after spending the past month here

Forest Ranger, M L McAllister of Leeds was here a few days last week on business.

Jas E Taylor has the new contract for the mail between Harmony and Kanarra

A. F Mathis has purchased him a new Buick car

Evelyn Prince has gone to Marysvale to work

Mrs L A Pace is on the sick list

Mr. and Mrs J W Prince and daughter, Miss Velva, left Wednesday for New Harmony to spend a few days visiting.

Iron County Record
July 26, 1918

Word was received here yesterday of the death of Mrs. Joseph Prince, of St. George, following an operation of a serious nature. The Princes were until a year or two ago residents of New Harmony, and have many relatives here and at that place. J. G. Pace and wife of Cedar City will leave today to attend the funeral, going via New Harmony to pick up some more of the relatives and will be present at the funeral services.

New Harmony, July 30 — A gloom was cast over our town on learning of the sad death of Mrs Jos W Prince Mrs Prince was formerly a resident of this place A large number of our town's people went to St George to attend the funeral

Mrs Eliza P. Kelsey was called to Idaho a few days ago to be in attendence at an operation on her daughter, Mrs Florence Phippin The last report states that she is getting along nicely.

Several of our town's people spent the Twenty fourth in Kanarra where the two towns joined in celebrating Pioneer day A most enjoyable time was spent.

Mr and Mrs Williamson and family of Paragoonah spent the week here visiting Mrs Williamson's sister. Mrs J. L Prince.

Mrs L A Pace has returned home from Springville where she has been visiting her sister for the past two weeks

Jas G Knell, his daughter, Iva, and James Thornton of Newcastle have been here visiting relatives and friends

Born, a son to Mr and Mrs Grant Hale, July 11, a daughter to Mr and Mrs James D Neilson, July 25

Ashby W. Pace has received a notification to appear in St George Aug 3, for examination for service

Miss Fern Timothy of Vernal is here visiting with her sister, Mrs Donald Schmutz

A company of Government men are here surveying

TAYLOR-HIRSCHI

Mr Elmer Taylor and Miss Susie Hirschi were married here on Monday, July 29, by Pres D H Snow

The bride is a daughter of Bishop and Mrs David Hirschi of Rockville a most estimable and highly respected young lady whose friends are numbered by those who know her The groom is a grandson of Mrs Susan E Pace and the late Harvey A Pace of New Harmony, whose parents died while he was very young, he is a most exemplary young man a graduate of the Dixie Normal college where he was generally respected and loved by all for his many excellent qualities He is in class I of the 1918 draft

They have the best wishes of a host of friends for their future happiness

Vivian Pace Prince

wife of Jos W. Prince, was born in New Harmony, Utah, Aug 27, 1877, she lived in New Harmony with her parents until 1887 when they moved to Nutrioso, Arizona, her home until 1893 when she came back to New Harmony to live with her father's first wife by request of her father, she was in New Harmony until 1896 when she accepted a position as clerk from her uncle at Luna, New Mexico, where she remained until early in 1899 when she returned to meet her future husband, Jos W. Prince, whom she married in the St George temple Mar 1, 1900 Mrs Prince was a daughter of Wilson D. Pace, former Bishop of New Harmony, and Lizzie Lee Pace She was always a devoted and affectionate child and a most devoted and loving wife She has been a patient sufferer and has never been a well woman, though she always looked at the future with a smile and never complained She was the mother of six children, five boys and one girl, she is survived by but one child and her husband All through life she was a lover of childdren and a lover of the Gospel, in all her sickness and operations she could always see joy, satisfaction and comfort in the Gospel She lived and died with the Gospel burning within her, full of hope for the future Her greatest pleasure was found in helping those in distress

Funeral services were held in the St George tabernacle Friday afternoon under direction of the East Ward bishopric The stand was decorated with a profusion of roses and other flowers, also the casket There was a very large attendance, many coming from New Harmony, Cedar City,, Hurricane and other places The hyms sung by the choir were 'Farewell all Earthly Honors' and 'I Need Thee Every Hour" The following solos were rendered "I Have Read of A Beautiful City," by Mrs Metta Morris, 'When The Mists Have Rolled Away," byMrs W. O. Bentley, jr , 'Rock of Ages," by Jos W McAllister, and 'O Dry Those Tears," by Mrs W R Pike The opening prayer was offered by Elder Arthur F. Miles, and benedction by Elder Jos T. Atkin

Elder Albert Mathis of New Harmony spoke of the self-sacrificing nature of the deceased sister, she lived for others and her greatest joy was in doing good for others, he had known her 20 years, and she was always cheerful and hopeful, and was of a very hospitable disposition Other speakers were Pres Geo F. Whitehead, Judge D H Morris and Bishop I C Macfarlane They all eulogized the many esteemable qualities of the deceased, her pleasant and cheerful manner while enduring much suffering and her thought and care for others—"she was one of God's noble women "

Interment was made in the city cemetary, the remains being followed by 18 autos The grave was covered with flowers, tributes to the worth of the departed by many friends who had known and loved her through her life time

Washington County News
August 6, 1918

New Harmony, Aug, 6 —A farewell party was given Mr. and Mrs Elmer Taylor last Saturday evening A large crowd was present and a most enjoyable time was had The Enoch orchestra furnished the music for the dance Some of the young people from Kanarra participated in the fun Mr and Mrs Elmer Taylor left Monday morning for Washington, D C, where Mr Taylor has accepted a government position as typewriter

Miss Ada Slack was taken to her home at Woolsey s ranch the latter part of the week, she was very ill, the doctor pronounced it typhoid fever.

Mr and Mrs John Schmutz and two daughters are here visiting Mr and Mrs Gottlieb Schmutz

Mrs E Grant and her daughter, Gladys, have gone to the ranch to spend the remainder of the summer

Mrs Anna Belle Rencher of Grass Valley is here visiting relatives and friends

Clarence Englestead is back from Kanab where he has been on business

The little shower we had this morning put new life into the crops

Mrs Myrtle Anderson returned to Lehi Monday

Washington County News
August 19, 1918

New Harmony, Aug 19 —The weather the past week has been very cool and very much like fall

Born, a son to Mr and Mrs Wm Chinn on the 13th inst, all concerned doing nicely.

Mason Rancher of Grass Valley spent a few days here the latter part of the week

Afton Ballard of Grafton is here visiting with his sister, Mrs Frank Kelsey

Bp H A Pace and wife have gone to Cedar City on business

Iron County Record
August 20, 1918

NEW HARMONY.

New Harmony, Utah, Aug. 20, 1918.
Threshing began here tdoay.

* * *

Mason Rencher of Pine Valley was a visitor here last week.

* * *

Afton Ballard of Grafton is here visiting his sister, Mrs. Frank Kelsey.

* * *

Born—a son to Mr. and Mrs. Wm. Chinn Wednesday the 14th. All concerned doing nicely.

* * *

Miss Jennie Burk, who has been visiting relatives here for some time returned to her home at Virgin last week.

Washington County News
August 26, 1918

New Harmony, Aug 26 —Annetta, the little daughter of Mr and Mrs Orson Hammond fell from a tree Saturday evening breaking her collar bone She is doing nicely .

Leslie Andreason left here today for Lehi where he will join his wife who left about three weeks ago

John Cottam road supervisor was here for a short time last week to see his sister, Mrs Antone Prince

To Leave For Camp Kearny Sept. 3rd to 6th

The following is the final quotas of the draft, to leave for Camp Kearny, Cal , Sept 3rd to 6th

Alma H Jacobson Pine Valley
Joseph Stirling, Leeds
Richard Henry Atkin, St George
Dilworth Beckstrom, Pine Valley
George A Lemmon, Virgin
Theodore Prince, New Harmony
Heber Hirschi Rockville
Edwin Stucki Santa Clara
Robert Louis Hinkson, St George
William Carter, St George
Junius J Duncan, St George
Neal Dee Keate, St George
Hyrum Ruesch, Springdale
Levi Atkin, St George
Wm, Zimmermann New Harmony
Henry W. Miller, St George
Clark Bryner, St George
Victor Angell, Leeds
Lorin Reber, Santa Clara
David George Thayne, Washington
Herbert Isom, Hurricane
William Malin Cox, Pine Valley
Arthur Herbert Olds, Toquerville
Afton Ballard, Grafton
Rodney Harrison Snow, P ne Valley
Thomas Stratton, Hurricane

David Burr Bradshaw, Hurricane
Raymond Leon Miller, Washington
Ernest E Stucki, Santa Clara
George Evlyn Prince, New Harmony
Lorin Church Miles, St George
Earl Worthen, St George
David Lester Canfield, Enterprise
Leland H Bringhurst, Toquerville
Arthur Terry, Rockville
Sherman Lamb, St George
Levi Empey, St George
Clarence Amos Jones, Gunlock
Walter P. Gubler, Santa Clara
Wilfred Henry Williams, Springdale
Floyd Spilsbury, Toquerville
Ashby W. Pace, New Harmony
Robert L Covington, Washington
Rolland N. Whitehead, St George
Lafayette J McConnel, Cedar City

NEW HARMONY

New Harmony, Utah, Sept. 3, 1918.

Born—A girl to Mr. and Mrs. Mason Reacher Friday, Aug. 30th.

* * *

Mr. and Mrs. Granville Pace and children were visitors here Sunday.

* * *

Mrs. Frank Kelsey has gone to Grafton to put up fruit.

* * *

G. A. Grant and G. L. Prince have gone on the "round-up" on Kanarra mountain.

* * *

A concert was given by members of the Dixie Normal College Sunday night. Everyone was out and enjoyed the numbers rendered.

* * *

Claud Knell, Iva Knell, Merle Thornton and Miss Cox were over from Newcastle to attend the dance Friday night.

* * *

Dr. Petty and Frank Wood of Cedar City were speakers at Sacramental meeting Sunday. Their subjects were the military training that will be given at the B. A. C. this winter.

* * *

Gotleib Schmutz and son George returned last week from Beaver, where they have been after their sheep, which have been rented for a few years.

* * *

An entertainment was given Friday night in honor of our soldier boys who will leave this week for Camp Kearney. Bp. Pace talked a short time, also Evelyn Prince, one of the Sammies. Miss Fern Tymothy sang a solo. Dancing was the main feature of the evening, which closed with a feast of melons.

Washington County News
September 5, 1918

Jos W. Prince and daughter, Miss
Velva -left Wednesday for New Harmony to be gone for a few days

Washington County News
September 10, 1918

New Harmony, Sept 10 —Evlyn
Prince and William Zimmerman left
for Camp Kearney Friday. A party
was given in their honor the Friday
before

Miss Mildred Pace has accepted a
position as clerk at the Petty mercantile at Hurricane for the coming
winter,

Born, a daughter to Mr and Mrs
Mason Rancher; all concerned doing
nicely,

Miss Minnie Pace has gone to Hurricane to teach school

Washington County News
September 16, 1918

New Harmony, Sept 16 —Mr and
Mrs Henry Pace, John Prince and
James Mathis returned to their home
in Price after visiting with relatives
and friends for a short time

Mr and Mrs William P Taylor
have gone to Hurricane on business

Mrs Hugo Price has returned to
her home in Provo after spending
several weeks here

School will not start here for some
time on account of not having a new
building

NEW HARMONY

New Harmony, Utah, Sept. 17.

Delbert Woolsey and family were visitors here last week.

* * *

Bishop Pace is on Kanara mountain looking after his sheep.

* * *

Mr. and Mrs. William Chinn have gone to Gunlock for fruit and to visit relatives.

* * *

Gladys Grant has gone to St. George to attend the Dixie Normal College this winter.

* * *

Mr. and Mrs. Henry Pace, John W. Prince and James Mathis of Price, Utah, were visiting relatives and friends here last week.

* * *

A number of our townspeople attended the Festival at St. George. Among them were Rose Schmutz, Mrs. E. C. Grant, Rulon and Oren Taylor, Clark Pace and James L. Prince.

New Harmony, Oct 1 —Mr and Mrs Albert Mathis went to Hurricane Friday after James Mathis who has been bathing in the hot springs for rheumatism He reports his health as very much improved

Mr and Mrs Antone Prince returned from Hurricane ysterday where they went after a load of fruit

Mr and Mrs H A Pace and Mr and Mrs Albert Mathis are visitors at the State fair this week

Mr and Mrs Frank Kelsey have gone to Salt Lake to attend the State fair

School opened yesterday with Miss Rosella Schmutz as teacher

Iron County Record
October 10, 1918

List of Names of Registrants of The Class of September, 1918

Whose Registration Cards are in Possession of the Local Board Published in the Order of Their Liability for Military Service—Numbers Given are the Registration Numbers.

FIRST HUNDRED NAMES

Reg. No.	NAME	Address.
322	Joseph Elvert Pierce	Lund.
438	Frank Leslie Gower	Cedar City.
20	Wallace Alma Flanigan	Cedar City.
535	Herbert Clarkson Davis	Sahara.
219	Chas. Allen Hollinghead	Parowan.
625	John R. Robinson, Jr.	Cedar City.
72	John Edward Westerhold	Cedar City
348	William Jewell Wilcock	Parowan.
4	Arthur Francis Louis	Cedar City.
134	James Bulloch	Cedar City.
395	Thomas Ward Bettridge	Parowan.
623	Lot Marion Pexton	Nephi, Utah.
228	George Henry Durham	Parowan.
413	Thornton Armstrong Jones	Enoch.
256	Parley Moyle	EnEnterprise.
399	Bruhn Dwain Decker	Parowan.
500	David James Edwards	Paragonah.
496	David A. Lamoreaux Jr.	Paragonah.
124	Joseph E. Haslam	Cedar City.
143	Geo. Clarence Goddard	Cedar City.
178	Benj. Raymor Lawrence	Summit.
64	John Henry Fife	Cedar City.
612	Clarence G. Paramore	Parowan.
456	Carl Ludwig Kittleson	Prout.
33	Horatio Owen Rice	Cedar City.
77	Israel Taylor Neilson	Cedar City.
82	Henry Aldridge Thorley	Cedar City.
108	Donald Parry Mackelprang	Cedar.
101	Adelbert Bywater	Cedar City.
628	Jose Villa	Cedar City.
130	John Cuttler Carpenter	Cedar City.
189	John Henry Dalley	Summit.
468	Edward James McGrath	Modena.
225	Hyrum Lester Fox	Parowan.
489	Edwin W. Williamson	Paragonah.
544	Bert Riason Frasure	Prout.
478	Jesse William Topham	Paragonah.
121	Frank Henry Petty	Cedar City.
590	Wm. Henry Fretwell	Cedar City.
276	Edward Ambrose Burton	Parowan.
330	John Willard Green	Salt Lake City.
162	Widdard Ernest Corry	Cedar City.
346	William Richards Adams	Parowan.
469	Lonie Elsworth Paddock	Modena.
354	William Martell Eyre	Minersville.
254	John Hardman Tullis	Newcastle.
249	John Geary Page	Little Pinto, Utah.

Reg. No.	NAME	Address.
534	Henry Terrel Griffin	Sahara.
1	Amos Fredrick Root	Cedar City.
473	Stephen Burrows Barton	Paragonah
205	Edward James Higbee	Cedar City.
113	Herbert Price Haight	Cedar City.
597	Erastus Bertleson Dalley	Cedar.
182	Christain Peterson	Summit.
115	Archie James Gale	Cedar City.
87	John Sixtus Haslam	Cedar City.
302	Ether Leroy Carter	Lund.
604	Geo. Albert Robinson	Paragonah.
631	Arthur Merrill Willis	Kanarra.
481	Archie M. Lamoreaux	Paragonah.
550	Thomas Gilbert Barton	Toquerville.
458	Melvin Dewitt Heist	Heist.
194	Thomas Henry Rowley	Parowan.
79	Wm. John Matheson	Cedar City.
176	Martin Frank Jacobson	Cedar City.
629	Clarence Lynd	Beryl, Utah.
369	George Smith Wimmer	Parowan.
160	Edward Horton Parry	Cedar City.
543	Nicholas Megia Chocen	Colton, Cal.
8	John Harvey Ballard	Cedar City.
46	Oscar Mayo Wills	Lund, Utah.
521	Ceylon Davis	Kanarra.
54	Alonzo Jones Higbee	Cedar City.
568	Ernest Webster	Cedar City.
30	James Ronald Urie	Cedar City.
541	Jones Preston Wiliams	Kanarra.
385	John Logan Lowder	Parowan.
359	Hans Jorgon Mortensen	Parowan.
32	Thomas Roy Urie	Cedar City.
242	Wm. Sylvester Benson	Parowan.
225	Frank King Gurr	Parowan.
144	Daniel Enoch Matheson	Enoch.
536	Charles Mart'n Magnussen	Sahara.
277	Edward Reeves Liston	Parowan.
185	John Ronald Lowe	Summit.
429	Wilford Dover	Cedar City.
325	Charles Warren Booth	Lund.
450	Carlos A. Castillo	Modena.
204	Lehi Aldridge Thorley	Cedar City.
384	Marcus L. Guymon, Jr.	Parowan.
485	Benj. Wm. Openshaw	Paragonah.
409	George Louis Burton	Parowan.
241	David Phillip Barton	Parowan.
273	John Arthur Evans	Parowan.
588	Chris Ashdown	Cedar City.
158	Fred Garfield Burkholder	Lund.
403	Peter Hanson Gurr	Parowan.

Reg. No.	NAME	Address.
84	Charles Edwin Adams	Parowan.
62	James McDonald Hamilton	Cedar.
545	Samuel Miner Alison	Prout.

SECOND HUNDRED NAMES

92—Wm. Chatterley Macfarlane, Cedar.
444—Ralph James Wilcock, Spry, Utah.
462—Thomas James Haycock, Parowan.
230—Andrew F. Neilson, Henrieville, Utah
626—Preston Swapp, Cedar City.
367—Julion Evans Rollins, Parowan.
449—Patricio Gutierres, Modena.
38—David Claud Urie, Cedar City.
375—Clifton Taylor, Parowan.
21—Thomas Chatterley Thorley, Cedar.
42—Thomas Oscar Stokes, Preston, Ida.
48—John Albert Loveless, Cedar City.
109—Erwin David Rhead, S. L. City.
        1384 S. 14th East St.
311—Domingo Lopez, Nada.
599—Carl Augustus Burkholder, Cedar.
398—Reuben Wesley Gould, Parowan.
151—James Darwin Nelson, Cedar City.
152—Francis Rollo, Cedar City.
405—David Albert Matheson, Parowan.
394—Frank Elwood Jensen, Parowan.
516—Lewis Merill Groves, Kanarra.
374—Wm. Henry Orton, Parowan.
204—Evelyn Connay Parry, Cedar City.
190—Oscar Jones Hulet, Summit.
418—Robert Mumford, Enoch.
696—J. William Walker, Cedar City.
622—Jonathan Davis Morrill, Modena.
424—Charles Franklin Stevens, Enoch.
117—Jas. Alexander Tweedie, Cedar City.
279—John Raymond Lee, Parowan.
147—Golden Haight, Cedar City.
155—Wm. Henry Clark, Cedar City.
141—Horton David Haight, Cedar City.
527—Albert Davis, Kanarra.
58—Menzies John Macfarlane, Cedar.
284—Chas. Augustus Orton, Parowan.
349—Clark Ward Lyman, Parowan.
262—Robert Platt, Newcastle.
295—Marion Andrew Simkins, Parowan.
86—Edwin Reid Cox, Hamilton's Fort.
452—Celestian Cruz, Modena.
454—Wm. Thomas Davenport, Paragonah.
260—Joseph Ernest Eldridge, Pinto, Utah.
165—Jedidiah Francis Woodard, Cedar.
283—John Melvin Ward, Parowan.
390—Junius Dewey Bentley, Parowan.
432—John Edward Dover, Cedar City.
116—Karl Wood, Cedar City
352—Joseph Richard Lister, Parowan.

209—John William Berry, Kanarra.
140—Geo. Webster Esplin, Enoch.
308—John Ray Brown, Lund, Utah.
240—Joseph Ervin Stevens, Parowan.
335—Geo. Rasmus Mickelson, Parowan.
247—Joseph Rasmussen, Parowan.
23—Robert Bauer, Cedar City.
571—John Moody Foster, Cedar City.
98—Joseph Adam Kopp, Cedar City.
434—Thomas Adams Bladen, Cedar City.
224—Frank Anderson Matheson, Parowan
135—Thomas Dix, Cedar City.
453—George Kiyomon Takai, Modena.
411—Lawrence Johnson, Parowan.
455—Sextus Johnson, Modena.
139—Jas. Whittaker Chatterley, Cedar.
414—Wm. Franklin Armstrong, Enoch.
216—Orian Burton Lyman, Parowan.
506—Von Willard Watts, Cedar City.
356—Joseph Rasmus Bentley, Parowan.
547—Jasper McPherson Sweeney, Beryl.
148—Carlos Lee Jones, Cedar City.
373—Jas. Corey Robinson, Jr., Parowan.
317—Job Franklin Hall, Lund.
613—John H. Williamson, Paragonah.
392—Ray Bentley, Parowan.
120—John Stephen Christenson, Cedar.
488—Thomas Alex. Edwards, Paragonah.
288—William Leech Adams, Parowan.

314—Peter Thompson Keillor, Nada.
508—Joseph S. Williams, Kanarra.
389—Herbert Harold Trimmer, Parowan.
191—Jesse Ernest Dalley, Summit.
586—Francis H. Middleton, Cedar City.
184—Niels Christian Madsen, Summit.
107—Guss Chatterley Pendleton, Cedar.
243—Garfield Merritt Clark, Parowan.
507—Lenda Glenn Williams, Kanarra.
480—Milton Luther Dailey, Paragonah.
585—Ralph F. Perry, Cedar City.
281—Eugene Meeks Dalton, Parowan.
552—Royal S. Gardner, Cedar City.
93—John Abner Adams, Cedar City.
529—Jesse Franklin Williams, Kanarra.
76—Joseph Smith Thompson, Cedar City.
391—George Leo Ence, Parowan.
343—Claud Charles Hollberg, Parowan.
55—Mitchell Monroe Smith, Cedar City.
591—Fred Barnson, Cedar City.
542—Lucio Axgona Duxascano, Beryl.

THIRD HUNDRED NAMES

Reg. No.	NAME	Address.
251	Jesse Turner Forsyth, Newcastle.	
47	Ora Alexander Martin, Cedar City.	
605	James William Barton, Paragonah.	
217	John William Taylor, Parowan.	
200	Wm. Francis Whitney, Parowan.	
383	Joseph Moroni Jensen, Parowan.	
350	George Chester Gunn, Parowan.	
470	Merlin June Topham, Parowan.	
91	Ellis Melbourne Colvin, Lund.	
567	William Henry Bess, Cedar City.	
253	Edmund Leroy Grant, New Harmony	
122	Millard Don Watson, Cedar City.	
504	John Henry Williams, Kanarra.	
446	Esperidion Flores, Modena.	
386	Ellis Threlkeld Orton, Parowan.	
592	James Wm. Middleton, Cedar City.	
467	Thomas John Dooley, Heist.	
12	William Arthur Condie, Cedar City.	
553	Arthur James Bryant, Cedar City.	
282	Willard Andrew Wood, Parowan.	
429	Lorenzo Matheson, Enoch.	
370	Delbert Ward Mortensen, Parowan.	
145	Andrew Nevan M. Rollo, Cedar City	
206	George Albert Lunt, Cedar City.	
448	Sabastian Enrriques, Modena.	
5	William Heyborne, Cedar City.	
126	James Corlett Parry, Cedar City.	

222—Archibald Benson, Parowan.
88—Thos. William Mumford, Cedar City.
299—Lawrence L. Davis, Parowan.
190—John B. Topham, Jr., Paragonah.
45—David Dunn Sherratt, Cedar City.
197—Eloyd Battenson Burton, Parowan.
236—Bart Ward Mortensen, Parowan.
50—John Aaron Batt, Cedar City.
323—Fred C. Waldschmidt, Lund.
2—Daniel Brown Clark, Cedar City.
96—Wm. Rees Palmer, Cedar City.
258—Neil Donald Forsyth, Newcastle.
181—Graham Brown McAllister, Summit.
297—John William Bentley, Parowan.
532—Harry Jay Patten, Sahara.
563—Chas. Christian Bowler, Cedar City.
65—George William Perry, Cedar City.
267—Heber Eldridge Harrison, Newcastle.
566—John Middleton, Cedar City.
167—Albert Urie Nelson, Cedar City.
10—Grant Parry, Cedar City.
449—Roger Harris, Cedar City.
406—John Henry Jensen, Parowan.
54—Frank Richard Lambeth, Cedar City.
546—Numinzo Fucarino, Enterprise.
179—John Farrow, Summit, Utah.
380—Joseph Bartlette Dalton, Parowan.
465—Frank Gilbert Webster, Prout.
15—Grant Rountree Hunter, Cedar City.
372—Thomas Davenport, Parowan.
232—Alvin Richard Benson, Parowan.
382—Blanchard Eli Whitney, Parowan.
511—William Andrew Berry, Kanarra.
400—Le Roy Myers, Parowan.
355—James Le Roy Hyatt, Parowan.
464—Harmel Jacob Bauer, Cedar City.
577—Archibald Walker, Summit.
138—Thomas Wendell Bayles, Parowan.
266—Roy Pack, Enterprise.
211—Peter Taylor Neilson, Cedar City.
99—James Mashburn, Cedar City.
393—William Delbert Smith, Parowan.
574—Thomas Lawrence, Cedar City.
231—John Horace Miller, Parowan.
237—Calvin Crane Connell, Parowan.
611—John Henry Prothero, Paragonah.
257—Thomas Bennett, Parowan.
169—Arnold Lamar Graff, Kanarra.
327—John H. Johnston, Lund.
512—Reese James Williams, Kanarra.
51—Henry Lunt Jones, Cedar City.
125—Randall Lunt Jones, Cedar City.

538—Michael Rilley, Sahara.
136—Hyrum Chandler Ford, Cedar City.
75—William Sherratt, Cedar City.
172—William L. Jones, Cedar City.
209—Ernest A. Walker, Mesquite, Nev.
530—Samuel Thomas Ford, Kanarra.
561—Horace Alvin Dover, Cedar City.
174—Fred Bywater, Cedar City.
110—Morgan Rollo, Cedar City.
332—George Frith, Jr., Parowan.
589—Cornelius Wanner, Cedar City.
408—George Ellis Bentley, Parowan.
104—Corydon Walker, Cedar City.
156—Jacob Nephi Smith, Cedar City.
560—David William Webster, Cedar City.
234—William Glenn Clark, Parowan.
520—Carl Putman Casad, Sahara.
11—Rex Perry, Cedar City.
627—Paul Sanford Pierson, Lund.
544—Norman Scott Beeler, Beryl.
593—Walter Murie, Cedar City.

Washington County News
October 14, 1918

New Harmony Oct 14—Mrs
Verna K Pace has returned from
Newcastle where she has been visit-
ing for the past week with her sister,
Mrs Walter Spencer from Colorado

Washington County News
October 21, 1918

New Harmony, Oct 21—Some
surveyors from Ogden were here last
week to survey a road through the
Harmony canyon Supervisor Mace
will be here to oversee the beginning
of the work which will commence
this week

Charles Cottam of St George has
taken the contract to build the school
house Work will commence on it
some time this week

We are proud to say that we have
gone ' over the top ' in our subscrip-
tion for the 4th Liberty Loan

Washington County News
October 28, 1918

New Harmony, Oct 28—There is
no influenza here yet Every pre-
caution is being taken to keep it from
here The town is under a strict
quarantine and there will be no public gatherings of any sort

Work will commence on the canyon road this week The new road
will be via the coal mine

Road Supervisor, John Cottam was
here last week to look over the canyon road project

Lumber is being brought from the
station, preparatory to starting the
school house

Washington County News
October 31, 1918

Miss Gladys Grant left Tuesday for
her home at New Harmony.

Iron County Record
November 8, 1918

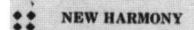

NEW HARMONY

Work will begin on the new road through Pace's canyon this week.

* * *

New Harmony went over the top in the Liberty Loan, every family subscribing.

* * *

Forest Superintendent Mace and Ranger McAllister, with two others, were here last week in the interests of the new road proposition.

* * *

Mr. and Mrs. Robert Bridge of Salt Lake and Mr. and Mrs. Lynn Imlay of Grantsville are visiting relatives here, Mr. and Mrs. Francis Prince.

Washington County News
November 11, 1918

New Harmony, Nov 11 —We are rejoicing today over the news we received of peace being restored We certainly hope it is so this time and we feel that it is

Most of our townsmen are working on the canyon road, the weather is favorable for such and everything is progressing nicely Eliza Kelsey and Golda Prince are cooking for the men

School started today after being closed for come time We thought it unnecessary to close things longer as there is no sickness whatever

There is no "Flu" here yet and we are trying hard to keep it out

New Harmony, Utah, Nov. 12, 1918

Miss Nora Ballard of Grafton is here visiting her sister, Mrs. Frank Kelsey.

* * *

The Misses Minnie and Mildred Pace are home on a "flu" vacation. Minnie has been teaching school at Hurricane and Mildred clerks in Petty's store at the same place.

* * *

Miss Fern Timothy has gone to Rockville to visit her sister, Mrs. Lamer Terry.

* * *

A number of our town boys are working on the road through the canyon.

* * *

Stewart Thorley of Cedar was a business visitor here Saturday. He didn't get out of his car on account of the town being quarantined.

* * *

We haven't had any "Flu's yet and do not want any.

———W.S.S.———

J. P'S & CONSTABLES LLECTED

Following are the justices of the peace and constables elected on the 5th inst , the justice of the peace being the first name shown at each place

Springdale, F D Gifford, John Ruesch Rockville, Marvin Terry, P. Jones Virgin, Thomas Maloney, E W. Young Toquerville, J Z Neagle, M W Bringhurst La Verkin, E J Graff, Roy Button Leeds, Ira S McMullin, Don Fuller Washington, John Tanner, W. A Westover St George, F L Daggett, C. R Worthen Bloomington L J. Larson, Wallace Blake Santa Clara, Adolph Hafen, Ernest Reber Gunlock, F. J Bowler, E S Jones Veyo, Jas Cottam, C R Leavitt Central, Ed Harper, W E Bracken Pine Valley, Mason Gardner, Bruce Snow New Harmony, John Whipple, Frank Kelsey, Pinto, W. J. Knell, LeRoy McLaughlin. Enterprise, Joseph Fish, Arthur Huntsman

New Harmony, Nov. 19 — We went ' over the top ' in our donations for the War Work fund We have never fallen short in any of our calls for donations yet and we want to keep up to the mark

Herbert Knell, Rulon Knell and Leon Eldridge of Pinto and Woodruff Tullis of Newcastle came over last week to work on the road.

Miss Fern Timothy returned from Rockville Friday where she had been to see her sister, Mrs Marvin Terry

Work has been postponed indefinitely on the schoolhouse on account of the influenza at St George.

Washington County News
November 28, 1918

Marion Gates left Wednesday morning for New Harmony expecting to be there for some time working on the road

Iron County News
December 3, 1918

New Harmony, Utah, Dec. 3, 1918.

The town of Harmony is quarantined against strangers.

* * *

Mrs. Lamar Terry of Rockfille is here visiting her sister, Mrs. Donald Schmutz.

* * *

Work began on our new school house Saturday. The Cottam Brothers of St. George have the contract.

* * *

Mr. and Mrs. Duane Leavitt of Gunlock are here visiting their sister, Mrs. Wm. Chinn.

* * *

James E. Taylor is able to be around again after being laid up with a lame leg for some time.

* * *

Messrs. Fern and Vila Davis are recovering from an attack of the mumps.

* * *

Veda, the small daughter of Mr. and Mrs. Wm. P. Taylor, who fell on a rock some two weeks ago and fractured her jaw, is on the improve.

Washington County News
December 5, 1918

Marion Gates returned home Sunday after spending two weeks at New Harmony

Washington County News
December 12, 1918

New Harmony, Dec 2 —Work
commenced on the school house today with a force af several men We
hope that the weather will be good
so that they can rush it to completion.

School has been going again for
two weeks but it has been deemed
unwise to hold any other public meetings yet for awhile.

Mr and Mrs, Marvin Terry of
Rockville were visitors of Mr. and
Mrs Donald Schmutz last week.
————— W S S.—————

Iron County Record
December 18, 1918

New Harmony, Utah, Dec. 18.
Claud Knell was a visitor here last
week.

Mrs. Amelia Schmutz is quite ill
at this writing.

Work has been discontinued on the
canyon road.

Dr. Macfarlane was called down to
attend James L. Prince Sunday. Mr.
Prince is suffering with asthma.

Mrs. John Farr and daughter of
Spanish Fork are here visiting their
daughter and sister, respectively, Mrs.
Bert Grant.

J. W. Prince of St. George was in
town today returning home this afternoon and taking James L. Prince with
him.

Gladys Grant and Juanita Davis
have returned from St. George, where
they have been attending the Dixie
College. The schools have been closed
again on acocunt of inuuenza.

Washington County News
December 23, 1918

New Harmony, Dec 23 —The new
schoolhouse is under headway but
will not be finished until after the
holidays For that reason there will
be no public celebrations

Two of our soldier boys have returned home, Eldon Schmutz and
Elmer Taylor, the former going a
year ago last Oct and the latter last
Aug We welcome them back

Lorenzo Prince has gone to St
George to stay an indefinite time for
his health

Claude Knell of Newcastle was in
town last week visiting friends and
relatives

There is no sickness here, just two
or thre cases of mumps,

Washington County News
January 2, 1919

WILL COMPLETE HARMONY CAN-
YON ROAD EARLY IN SPRING

On account of inclement weather,
construction work on the New Har-
mony-Page Ranch Road through
Pace's Canyon has been suspended
until spring This project requires
about three miles of new construction approximately two miles of
which is now completed The funds
for the road have been furnished by
the Forest Service with cooperation
of Iron and Washington Counties,
and citizens of New Harmony, Pinto
and Newcastle The work has been
done under the direction of the Forest Service with William F. Gates in
charge of the crew The road will
form an important link in the road
systems of both Washington and Iron
Counties furnishing a direct route
between the eastern end of Washington County and the settlements in the
western part as well as Iron County
towns The road when completed will
have a maximum grade of 10 per
cent and this grade will be necessary
for only a short distance at one or
two points The grade averages
about ten feet in width and is located on the south exposure and has a
bed of decayed granite which is excellent road material It is expected that the work will be resumed and
the road completed as early as possible in the spring

Washington County News
January 9, 1919

Orin Taylor arrived here Sunday from New Harmony to attend school at the D N C

Washington County News
January 13, 1919

New Harmony, Jan 13 —A welcome home party was given Friday night in honor of the soldier boys, Eldon Schmutz and Elmer Taylor. Refreshments were served and an enjoyable time was had

Holidays passed off quietly with several house parties and four dances. The school house was finished enough for dancing purposes by the last of December.

Orin Taylor, Elmer Taylor and Will Prince have gone to St George to attend the D. N. C.

Iva Knell of Newcastle returned home today after spending the holidays here.

LeGrande and Vera Pace of Cedar City were town visitors yesterday and today.

Washington County News
January 27, 1919

New Harmony, Jan. 27.—Charles Cottam and son C W. Cottam and Able Riding have returned home after being here for some time working on the new school house. The painting is being done by Clinton and Herbert Milne.

Frank Kelsey returned from Grafton yesterday where he had been to see his wife. He was accompanied back by Clarence Inglestead who has been south for some time

Evlyn Prince, another of our soldier boys returned home last week after an absence of several months

Bp. H A Pace went to Hurricane today on business

Iron County Record
January 28, 1919

New Harmony, Utah, Jan. 28, 1919.

William Reeves and Sons of Kanarra are here baling hay.

* * *

Mr. and Mrs. Donald Fuller of Leeds were visitors here Sunday.

* * *

Clifton and Herbert Milne of St. George are here doing some painting and papering.

* * *

Charles Cottam and Son, of Saint George have completed the school house, for which they had the contract, and have returned home.

Washington County News
February 3, 1919

New Harmony, Feb 3 —Last Thursday and Friday our townsmen turned out in a rabbit hunt, the losing side to give a dance   The two sides tallied about even, altogethei about 100 rabbits being killed   It is not known definitely when the dance will be yet

We are rejoicing over the snow that fell last week   This is the first real snow storm we have had

Mr. and Mrs Mason Rencher of Grass valley were town visitors last week,

Albert Mathis went to Newcastle yesterday on business.

Evlyn Prince returned Tuesday night from New Harmony where he has been working for some time

New Harmony, Utah, Feb. 4, 1919.

Clinton and Herbert Milne returned to their home at St. George ytsterday after working some two weeks here at their trade of painting and paperhanging.

* * *

Something like a thousand rabbits were killed last Thursday and Friday in the big rabbit hunt. Since the snow came the men and boys are hunting them with dogs and clubs.

* * *

Mr. and Mrs. Mason Rencher of Grass Valley were visiting relatives here last week.

* * *

Mrs. Leroy Grant came down from the ranch for a few days' visit last week.

* * *

Bp. Pace and Albert F. Mathis came in with a bunch of sheep from Newcastle yesterday.

* * *

Alvin Kelsey is on the sicklist this week.

* * *

Stewart Thorley and Mr. and Mrs. Sam Stucki of the Thorley ranch were the guests of Mr. and Mrs. J. D. Neilson last Wednesday evening.

* * *

Clarence Inglestead has returned to his work in Hurricane Valley, after visiting with his family for a few days.

New Harmony, Feb 10 —Last week it was stated that there were 100 rabbits killed in the hunt. This is a mistake; there were 700.

Rulon and Karl Knell returned to their home in Pinto after spending a few days visiting friends and relatives here

Clair and Levi Gardner of Grass Valley were in town last Thursday on their way to Hurricane.

Meetings opened up again Sunday, the first there has been since the first of January.

Antone Prince went to St. George today to be gone indefinitely.

New HARMONY

New Harmony, Utah, Feb. 11, 1919.

Rulon and Carl Knell of Pinto were visitors here Saturday and Sunday.

* * *

County Agent Tipets held a meeting with the farmers here last Thursday night.

* * *

Mr. and Mrs. Gus Pingel of Kanarra were over yesterday on business.

* * *

Juanita Davis is in Kanarra visiting her sister, Mrs. Berry Williams.

* * *

Bro. Charles Cottam was up from St. George last week drawing up plans for a number of new homes to be built in the near future.

Washington County News
March 10, 1919

New Harmony, Mar 10 —Fern Timothy and Verna Pace returned from Newcastle yesterday where they have been the past three weeks

Rose and Eldon Schmutz went to Hurricane Friday where they will remain for a few days visiting friends

Mrs Frank Kelsey has recently returned from Grafton where she has been since December.

Mrs Antone Prince has returned from St George where she has been for several months

Washington County News
March 17, 1919

New Harmony, Mar. 17 —The new school house has been done for some time, but for some reason things have not been transferred there yet

Mr and Mrs. Donald Schmutz have gone to Beaver where Mr. Schmutz will teach school the remainder of the season

Andrew Schmutz returned from Lund yesterday where he went after a load of cement

Evlyn Prince has returned from St George where he has been the past few weeks

Stanley Snow of St. George was here yesterday transacting business

New Harmony, March 23, 1919.

E. L. Grant is in town today on business.

* * *

Mrs. Susan E. Pace has been quite ill with la grippe.

* * *

Mrs. William Chinn was on the sick list last week with the grip.

* * *

Schmutz Brothers will begin shearing their goats tomorrow.

* * *

Evelyn Prince, Golda Prince and Rose Schmutz went to the Goddard and Grant ranch yesterday on business.

* * *

Mr. and Mrs. Jake Denel and Mrs. Denel's mother, Mrs. M. O. Woolsey, were visiting relatives here last week.

* * *

Bp. Pace, George F. Prince, John Whipple and James L. Prince went to Kanarra yesterday on business.

New Harmony, Mar. 24 —Orson Hammond is having a new house built Work is being done on the basement now.

Miss Rose Schmutz entertained the seventh and eighth grades at a tea party Friday afternoon

Mr. and Mrs Jake Dual have been here visiting with Mrs Orson Hammond for a few days

William Zimmerman was in town last week on business.

New Harmony, Mar. 31.—School commenced in the new school house this morning. The meeting house having been vacated we can resume the ward meetings again.

Schmutz Bros are having their goats sheared the last week. Golda Prince and Fern Timothy are cooking for the shearers.

Co Supt. W. O. Bentley and Miss McAllister were here visiting school last Wednesday.

Edwin Higbee of Toquerville has been here for the past few days on business.

Lorenzo Prince has gone to St George to receive medical treatment.

Mitchell Bros of Parowan are here today buying cattle.

New Harmony, Apr. 7.—The Primary Assn gave a basket dance Friday night and sold lunches It was well attended and every one enjoyed themselves very much.

Forest Ranger Alex Macfarlane was here last Tuesday and Wednesday seeing about the cattle

Evelyn and Irving Prince returned from St George yesterday where they had been after furniture

Clarence Inglestead has gone to Nevada to herd sheep, expecting to be gone for some time

NEW HARMONY

New Harmony, Utah, Apr. 8, 1919. Eugene Leavitt has been in town the last three days on business.

* * *

Mrs. E. C. Grant is in St. George visiting her daughter, Gladys who is attending the D. N. C.

* * *

Bp. Pace went to St. George yesterday where he was called as one of the jurymen for this term of court.

* * *

Mr. and Mrs. Andrew Schmutz, Susan Pace and Amelia Schmutz went to St. George this morning to do ordinance work in the temple for a few days.

* * *

Mr. and Mrs. Evelyn Prince will make their home here this summer. Mr. Prince and his brother Irving went to St. George for their furniture last Friday, returning Sunday.

* * *

Mr. and Mrs. Berry Williams and family were visitors here Sunday.

* * *

The Primary gave a basket dance Friday night and every one reported a good time.

The infant son of Mr. and Mrs. J. L. Prince is quite ill with a bad cold on the lungs. He is three months old.

* * *

Leland and Rex Pace were over from their farm Friday night and attended the dance given by the Primary.

New Harmony, Apr 14 —Miss Minnie Pace was in town Saturday and Sunday from Hurricane visiting friends and relatives

Duane Leavitt of Gunlock is here working for Will Chinn.

Woodruff Tullis of Newcastle was in town last week on business

Mrs Susan E Pace and Cecil Schmutz are in St. George doing temple work

Washington County News
April 21, 1919

New Harmony, April 21 —Work commenced on the canyon road last Tuesday, Edwin Higbee supervising the work   There is a big force on at present   Eliza Kelsey and Golda Prince are cooking for the men

Miss Mildred Pace returned from Hurricane today where she has been engaged as clerk at the Petty Merc. store, for the past winter.

Otto Reeves of Kanarra is in town working for Reese Davis

Dr. Petty and family were down from Cedar yesterday visiting relatives.

Washington County News
April 28, 1919

New Harmony, Apr. 28 —Mrs Emma Grant was called to Hurricane to her husband who was suddenly taken critically ill Saturday night The last word received was that he was no better and that the nature of the disease had not been determined

Forest Sup Wm Mace was in town last Friday on business

Bp H A Pace and wife have moved to The Cliff View farm which is about a mile from town, for the summer.

Bruce Snow of Pine Valley was in town yesterday on business

We have had several showers the last three days, which have been greatly appreciated by the farmers

New Harmony, May 5 —May Day was observed by the school giving a dance Candy and nuts were sold and a good time was enjoyed by all

Yesterday Golda Prince, Fern Timothy, Clark Pace and Rulon Knell went to the hot springs A good time was reported

Mrs Susan E. Pace and Cecil Schmutz returned from St George yesterday, where they have been for some time

Mr and Mrs Elmer Taylor returned from St George yesterday where they have been since January.

Misses Mildred Pace and Rose Schmutz have gone to Hurricane to spend the week

Mrs Amelia Schmutz went to Beaver yesterday to stay for a few weeks

Bp Pace and Albert Mathis are having their sheep sheared this week

New Harmony, May 12 —Saturday night there was a dance under the auspices of the Relief Society Ice cream was sold and there was a bazaar. There was a large crowd in attendance and every one enjoyed themselves very much

Miss Minnie Pace returned from Hurricane Sunday where she has been teaching the past winter.

Miss Jean Isom of Hurricane is a guest of Mrs Laverna Inglestead this week

Ray Neagle of Toquerville has been in town the past two days.

Mr. and Mrs Lawrence Prince and Mr. and Mrs Frank P. Kelsey intend returning to their respective homes at New Harmony today after spending several days here. The ladies have been doing temple work.

Mrs Dawson Haycock left Wednesday morning for New Harmony to join her husband, who has been there for several weeks working.

Iron County Record
May 21, 1919

NEW HARMONY

New Harmony, Utah, May 21, 1919.
Claud Knell of New Castle is here visiting relatives.

* * *

The Sunday School will give a dance here this week.

* * *

A number of Kanarra young people were here Sunday.

* * *

Mr. Mace of the Forest Reserve was up from St. George last week.

* * *

J. Bert Snyder and Mr. McDonald of the Capitol Life Insurance Company were in town Saturday.

* * *

Mr. and Mrs. Jerry Leavitt spent the week end here with Mrs. Wm. Chinn, their daughter.

* * *

Mr. and Mrs. K. Booth and Lee Cox of St. George visited friends here Sunday and Monday.

* * *

Mrs. Evelyn Prince returned home Sunday from St. George, after visiting a few days there with her parents, Mr. and Mrs. Chas. Seegmiller.

* * *

Alton and Rose Schmutz, Fern Imothy and Mrs. A. W. Pace were visiting relatives and friends in New Castle Sunday.

* * *

Wilford Day held conference Sunday. Bro. Lyman of Wyoming was his companion down. They gave some timely instructions.

* * *

Mrs. E. C. Grant returned home Friday from Hurricane where she has been taking care of her husband who was operated on at the Wilkinson hospital two weeks ago. Mr. Grant is recovering nicely at this writing.

Washington County News
May 26, 1919

New Harmony, May 26 —There is still quite a force of men working on the canyon road and every thing is progressing nicely.

Mrs Amber and Amelia Schmutz have returned home from Beaver where they have been for some time

There has been several showers lately which have helped to freshen up things considerably.

Miss Lenora Ballard has returned to her home at Hurricane after being here for three weeks

Arch Ballard of Grafton was in town the latter part of the week on business

Miss Jean Isom has returned to Hurricane after being here for three weeks

John Whipple has purchased a new Ford car.

Washington County News
June 2, 1919

New Harmony, June 2 —Saturday night the S S gave a dance The Enoch orchestra being present. Lunches were sold and a thorough good time was enjoyed by all

Mrs. P. E. Harris and mother from St George are here to spend the summer. They are staying at Mrs Reese Davises'.

Mr. and Mrs William Taylor returned from Cedar City Saturday where they went on business.

Geary and Golda Page and Mrs Edwin Higbee were in town yesterday from ————.

Ray Neagle and Earl Jackson of Toquerville have come to work on the canyon road.

Donald Schmutz returned from Beaver Saturday where he has been teaching

Le Cox and Mrs Charles Seegmiller of St George were here yesterday.

Iron County Record
June 10, 1919

NEW HARMONY

New Harmony, June 10, 1919.

Mr. and Mrs. Mason Rencher spent the week end here.

* * *

Joseph W. Prince and daughter Velva were visitors here yesterday.

* * *

Maurice Whitehead returned to his home in St. George today after having spent a few days here visiting.

* * *

Born; a girl to Mr. and Mrs Donald Schmutz Sunday, June 8. They now have as many kinds as any one, their first being a boy.

* * *

Mrs. Maria Page and Nora Ireland who have been visiting their daughter and sister Mrs. LeRoy Grant, returned to their home in Panguitch yesterday.

New Harmony, June 16 —Cupid seems to have been busy lately in our town, his victims being Golda Prince and Lee Cox of St George They were married last Thursday in Parowan Their many friends are showering their congratulations upon them

Miss Berneice Gates of St George has spent the past two or three days visiting Miss Mildrod Pace

Mr and Mrs Donald Schmutz are wearing broad smiles over the arrival of a new daughter

The work on the canyon road has been discontinued for an indefinite length of time

Drs. Macfarlane and Bertstrum were here the latter part of the week

Mrs L Hall of Hurricane is here taking treatment from Dr Harris

The first crop of hay is principally all in the stack.

MARRIED

Mr Lee Cox and Miss Golda Prince were married at Parowan on the 12th inst The bride is a popular and very highly esteemed young lady of New Harmony, a daughter of Mr. and Mrs George Prince, highly respected residents of that place The groom is a son of Mr. and Mrs Warren Cox of this city, proprietors of the Arrowhead hotel, a pleasant and agreeable young man who is well respected by a host of friends

The News joins the many friends of the happy young couple in all good wishes.

New Harmony, June 23 — A shower was given for Mr. and Mrs Lee Cox at the bride's home last Friday evening A very pleasant time was enjoyed by all present

Primary ward conference convened yesterday there being a large crowd in attendance Some of the stake officers were present.

John - Whipple returned from Hurricane today where he has been since Saturday

Miss Minnie Pace left for Berkley, Calif, last Thursday to attend summer school.

Mr. and Mrs. Maeser Daily from Cedar City were town visitors yesterday.

Orson Hammond left for Parowan today for lumber

New Harmony, June 30 — Miss Fern Timothy has returned to her home at Vernal after being here the past year She was accompanied on her way back by Mrs Marvin Terry of Rockville

Church Historian Jensen was here last evening and held a meeting for the purpose of going over the ward records

John Whipple has gone to Logan, Nevada, to visit his parents, expecting to be gone several days

Several of our townspeople attened Stake Conference at Cedar City Saturday and Sunday.

Mrs Sophy Page of Little Pinto has returned home after spending the past week here

Will Taylor left for Parowan today for lumber, preparatory to building

NEW HARMONY ROAD FINISHED

Forest Supervisor W. M Mace writes The News from Cedar City as follows.

I note that your Correspondent at New Harmony stated last week that the road work in the canyon has been discontinued indefinitely. As a matter of fact the work we had outlined has been completed and the traveling public will be glad to know that there is now an excellent road from New Harmony to Page's ranch which can be traveled readily by cars or heavy loads. Approximately $5300 has been expended on this road during the past year, $1650 of which was furnished by co-operation from private citizens and Washington and Iron Counties, and the remainder by the Forest service. We hope later to abtain sufficient funds to complete a good road, via Pinto and the Meadows to connect with the Modena-St George highway

New Harmony, July 28 —The 24th was celebrated here with a meeting at 10 30 A very good program was rendered In the afternoon there were sports and a dance at night

Clarence Inglestead has bought John Whipple's farm John and his brother Reuben are expecting to move to Nevada.

Water and other convenience have been added to the school house The public will apppreciate this act very much

Antone Prince and Frank Kelsey have recently purchased new cars.

James Knell and daughter Iva, of Newcastle are here.

Iron County Record
August 5, 1919

NEW HARMONY

New Harmony, Aug. 5, 1919.
Threshing will begin here next week.

* * *

Tom Brown, a former resident of this place was in town yesterday.

* * *

Orson Hammond is hauling sand for the basement of his new home.

* * *

Jennie Reeves was a visitor here the fore part of the week.

* * *

J. G. Pace and family of Cedar were in town yesterday.

* * *

Thos. K. Holyoak of Parowan was a visitor to our Sabbath School and Sacramental meeting last Sunday.

* * *

Mrs. Verna K. Pace went to Cedar to spend a few days with her sister Miss Iva Knell who was operated on for appendicitis a few days ago.

* * *

Mr. and Mrs. Clarence Inglestead have moved to their new home which they purchased from John Whipple. Mr. Whipple will move to the Muddy country in September.

Mason Rencher came over from Grass Valley yesterday accompanied by Miss Rose Schmutz who has been visiting with her sister, Mrs. Rencher.

Iron County Record
August 25, 1919

HAPPENINGS OF THE PAST
WEEK AT NEW HARMONY

New Harmony, Aug. 25. 1919.
Miss Fern Davis of this place was operated on at the Macfarlane hospital Saturday for appendititis.

Melvin, the four year old son of Mr. and Mrs. Andrew Schmutz is quite ill at this writing.

Mrs. Frank Kelsey and Elmer Taylor returned home yesterday from Rockville and Gafton where they have been visiting relatives.
Thorley Thorley, the Missess Kate and Irene Thorley and Mr. and Mrs. Sam Stucki were visitors here Sunday.

Iron County Record
August 29, 1919

Mrs. Reese Davis of New Harmony, who has a daughter in the local hospital, has rendered valuable assistance to Miss Giles, the matron, by nursing among the several patients. Mrs. Davis is a very kind hearted and loveable woman, and has endeared herself to a numebr of the inmates.

New Harmony, Sept 1 — Miss Fern Davis was operated on for appendicitis a week ago at Cedar City. The last word received was that she was doing nicely.

Miss Iva Knell of Newcastle who recently underwent an operation for appendicitus is here, intending to stay for some time

There has been several showers lately which were very welcome as it has been hot and dry of late

Mr and Mrs Francis Dalton of Cedar City were here Thursday on business.

Vera and LeGrande Pace of Cedar City were in town yesterday.

Mrs Marie Prince went to St George Saturday.

HAND GRENADES FOR SCHOOL

This county has been apportioned 75 hand grenades to be given to the children for the purchase of War Savings Stamps during the 1919 campaign They have been apportioned to the various schools as follows.

Springdale 2, Rockville 2, Grafton 1, Virgin 2, Toquerville 3, La Verkin 2, Hurricane 12, Leeds 2, Washington 6, St George 24, Bloomington 1, Santa Clara 3, Gunlock 2, Veyo 1, Central 1, Pine Valley 1, New Harmony 1, Enterprise 6.

New Harmony, Sept 8 —Melvin Schmutz, the little son of Mr. and Mrs Andrew Schmutz, who has been ill with typhoid for the past two weeks, is getting along moderately well

Prof E M Hall of the D N. C is in town today on school business.

Alex Taylor who has been on the Kanarra mountains for the past month, is home again.

Miss Mary Urie of Hamilton's Fork is a town visitor today.

Several of our town people are contemplating attending the festival at St. George

Mrs LaVerna Inglestead and Miss Minnie Pace are in St George attending the school convention.

Mr and Mrs Mason Rencher of Grass valley returned home yesterday after a short visit here

Gotlieb Schmutz has recently purchased a new car.

After several hindrances, the threshing is finished

Handsome cards announce the marriage of Mr Ray Naegle and Miss Mildred Pace in the St George temple, Thursday, Sept 18. The bride is a daughter of Mrs Susan A Pace and the late L A Pace of New Harmony, a young lady who is held in the highest esteem by a large circle of friends The groom is a son of Mr and Mrs Heber Naegle of Toquerville, and is a young man who is very highly respected in that community, where he follows his occupation as farmer.

New Harmony, Sept 22 — A delightful wedding reception was held Saturday at the home of Mrs L A Pace for her daughter, Miss Mildred Pace, and Ray Naegle of Toquerville At 3 30 p m sixty guests were banqueted, there being members present from Cedar City, Newcastle, St George and Toquerville In the evening there were one hundred and fifty guests present The time was spent in playing games of various sorts interspersed with several musical numbers At 12 30 dainty refreshments consisting of punch and cake were served A thoroughly good time was enjoyed by all

Mr and Mrs Frank Kelsey and Mr and Mrs Elmer Taylor returned from the fair at Parowan Friday A very pleasant time was reported

Some of the Relief society stake officers were down yesterday and held meeting with the officers of this association

Miss Iva Knell, who has been here for some time has returned to Newcastle to assist in teaching the coming winter

John Whipple who recently moved to Logan, Nev, was here last week on business

Mr and Mrs Lee Cox of St George have been here for the past two days

School commenced on the 18th with LaVerna Inglestead as teacher

Mrs Sophia Cooper and Mrs Jane Whipple of Overton, Nev, spent several days here last week visiting relatives They left Sunday for New Harmony to visit there a few days

NEW HARMONY

New Harmony, Sept. 30, 1919.

Quite a number of our townspeople attended the carnival at Cedar City last week.

* * *

Mrs. Maggie Burk and children are here visiting relatives and friends.

* * *

Morris Whitehead of St. George is visiting a friend here this week.

* * *

Robert A. Kirker has been doing some development work at his coal mine north of here recently.

* * *

Lawrence and Antone Prince returned yesterday from Nevada where they have been for the purpose of locating a cattle ranch.

* * *

Mr. and Mrs. Gus. Permenter have moved to Cliff View Farm.

New Harmony, Oct 6 —Miss Rose Schmutz has gone to Cedar City to attend the B A C and Juaneta Davis has gone to Kanarra to attend the school there

Eldon Schmutz left to day for Salt Lake expecting to attend the state fair He was accompanied by his mother, Mrs Amelia Schmutz

Mr and Mrs J, G Pace of Cedar City were in town yesterday on business

Clark Pace went to Hurricane Saturday expecting to be gone some time

Jack Littlefield of Newcastle was in town today and yesterday on business

Ray Naegle of Toquerville is here expecting to remain for some time

Mrs Delta Hammond has gone to Salt Lake to attend the state fair.

Washington County News
October 14, 1919

New Harmony, Oct 14 —The addition to the home of George Prince (including a new post office) is now completed and is being painted.

Mr and Mrs Mitchell Smith of Quitchipaw have been the guests of Mr and Mrs Delbert Woolsey the past two days

Albert F Mathis went to St George yesterday on business He was accompanied by Charles Cottam

Eldon Schmutz and mother, Mrs Amelia Schmutz, have returned from Salt Lake

Mr and Mrs Mason Rencher of Grass valley were in town last week

Clinton and Vivian Milne of St George are here working

Lorenzo Prince has purchased a new touring car.

Albert Mathis of New Harmony was a business visitor here the fore part of the week

New Harmony, Nov 3 -- Mildred Naegle, Minnie Pace, Jean McAllister, Clark Pace and George Naegle, came up from Hurricane Friday, returning last evening. The boys came to hunt deer.

Some of the Y. L M I A stake officers were down from Cedar City a few days ago, and organized the young ladies mutual The first meeting was held last night

Last Tuesday a Relief society social was held at the home of Mrs Sarah Davis Dainty refreshments were served, a very pleasant time was enjoyed by all present.

Mr and Mrs Carl Phippan and family from Idaho are here to spend the winter. Mrs Phippan was formerly Miss Florence Kelsey of this place

A daughter was born to Mr. and Jedediah Woodard, Oct 23rd, and a son to Mr. and Mrs George Prince, Oct 24th

Heber and Clarance Cottam of St George are here plastering the new house of Albert Mathis'.

John Clark of Emery, Utah, was here last week visiting his sister, Mrs L A Pace

Elmer Taylor has gone off for the winter to work for H. A. Pace.

Iron County Record
November 4, 1919

NEW HARMONY

New Harmony, Utah, Nov. 4, 1919.

Mr. and Mrs. Karl Phippen of Carey, Idaho, are here visiting Mrs. Phippen's mother and grandparents, Mrs. Eliza Kelsey and Mr. and Mrs. Francis Prince.

* * *

Mr. and Mrs. Lee Cox of St. George returned home this morning after a few days visit with Mrs. Cox's parents, Mr. and Mrs. Geo. F. Prince.

* * *

Mrs. Ray Naegle of Toquerville, formerly Miss Mildred Pace of this place, Miss Minnie Pace, Miss Gean McAllister, all teachers in the district school at Hurricane, and George Naegle of Toquer, spent the week end in Harmony.

* * *

Mr. and Mrs. Walter Cottam, Antone Prince and Verna K. Pace went to Cedar City on business today.

* * *

Quite a number of our townspeople will attend the Chautauqua at Cedar City this evening.

Washington County News
November 10, 1919

New Harmony, Nov. 10 —Juanita and Fern Davis were operated on at Cedar City last Tuesday for the removal of tonsils

Mr and Mrs Delbert Woolsey and family have moved back to their home at the Woolsey ranch

Donald Schmutz has gone to the goat herd expecting to be gone some time

Edwin Higbee of Toquerville is doing some repair work on the canyon road

Clarance Inglestead has gone off for the winter to work for R. Watson.

County Agent Tippetts is in town on cattle business.

Glen Tullis was in town last week on business

Washington County News
November 20, 1919

Mr and Mrs Lee Cox returned Tuesday from New Harmony, where they had been about three weeks visiting relatives Melvin Cox came home with them after a short visit there

SPRY OLD GENTLEMAN

Francis Prince of New Harmony was here Tuesday paying the grazing tax on sheep which he has on the Arizona 'strip" Mr Prince paid the tax under protest, believing, as many others do, that the tax is unconstitutional

Mr Prince is in his 80th year, he being 80 years old next July. He is exceptionally spry and active for his years and still works on his farm

Mr Prince stated he saw a number of dead cattle being skinned near Bellevue that had died through eating poisonous weeds.

New Harmony, Nov. 25 —Clark Pace returned from St George yesterday, where he went on business

Some of our townsmen went to Modena last week to help deliver cattle there They are expected back today.

Mrs Susie Adair and family from New Mexico, are here to spend the winter with William P. Taylor, Sr.

Mrs Heber Cottam returned to St George Saturday after spending several weeks here

Miss Verda Stout has returned to Hurricane after being here for a few weeks

John Imlay of Panguitch is here visiting his sister, Mrs. Francis Prince

Mrs Donald Schumtz has gone to Cedar to have some dental work done

Lorenzo Prince and Albert Mathis went to Cedar yesterday on business.

NEW HARMONY

Mrs. Susie T. Adair of Durango, New Mexico, who is spending the winter here with her father, Independence Taylor, has been quite ill for a few days, with bronchitis, but is much improved at this writing.

* * *

Mr. and Mrs. Dan Barney are here visiting relatives.

* * *

Edwin Higbee and Walter Batty of Toquerville are in town today on business.

* * *

Mrs. Heber Cottam of St. George returned to her home after a short visit with her sister-in-law, Mrs. Antone Prince.

* * *

A crowd gathered at the home of Mr. and Mrs. J. D. Neilson last evening to listen to some of Dan Barney's good music on the violin. Among those present were Mr. and Mrs. Orson Hammond, Mrs. E. C. Grant, Miss Gladys Grant, Alex Taylor. Irving Prince, of this place; George Bacon, Stewart Thorley, Jack Pearson Hyrum Prince, Joseph Stucki, of Thorley; and Edwin Higbee and Walter Batty, of Toquerville; all enjoyed a musical treat.

Washington County News
December 8, 1919

New Harmony, Dec 8,—Fourteen inches of snow that fell about ten days ago has all vanished, but the weather as yet is unsettled.

Mrs. Frank Kelsey has returned from Grafton where she has been for the past two weeks.

The Cottam brothers have returned home after working here for several weeks

Miss Cora Williams of Kanarra is here working for La Verna Inglestead.

Mr and Mrs. Antone Prince have gone to St George to spend the win-

Miss Nora Ballard has returned to Grafton after several days visit here

Ed Grant is home again after several months absence.

Washington County News
December 14, 1919

Archie Ballard has just returned home from New Harmony He had the misfortune to cut his hand very badly.

Washington County News
December 18, 1919

Mr. Joseph W. Prince and Miss Belle Williams were married in the St George temple on Wednesday, Dec 10.

The bride is a daughter of Mr. and Mrs R J Williams, Sr, highly respected citizens of Kanarra The groom is the well-known son of Francis Prince of New Harmony, a prosperous sheep owner of this city, who is public-spirited and highly esteemed.

Washington County News
December 29, 1919

New Harmony, Dec. 29 —A generally good time is being had during these holidays On Christmas Eve the children participated in a Xmas tree, given under the auspices of the Primary. Old Santa Claus was as jolly as usual Saturday a base ball game was played between Harmony and Kanarra, the latter walking off with the honors

The following are home for the Christmas vacation. Minnie Pace, Eldon, George and Rose Schmutz, Rulon Taylor and Juanita Davis.

Mr. and Mrs Ray Naegle of Toquerville and Mr and Mrs Mason Rancher of Grass valley are spending the holidays here.

Our town people contributed willingly to the soldier fund, which they they were called upon to share

A number of our town's people have gone to St George to attend Soldiers' day and the carnival.

Frank and Annie Farr of Spanish Fork are here visiting their sister, Mrs Bert Grant.

Phil Blackburn of Salt Lake City is a guest of Mrs. L A Pace.

Washington County News
January 19, 1920

New Harmony, Jan 19 —Almost all the children in town have whooping cough, just how it got started no one knows At present there are only nine attending school

Mason Rencher returned to Grass valley last week after spending the holidays here Mrs Rencher will stay here for a while

Mr and Mrs LeRoy Grant returned from St George Saturday where they have been for some time visiting

Mrs A W. Pace has returned from Newcastle where she has been visiting for about a month

Donald Schmutz returned from Lund Saturday where he went after some freight

Mrs Sarah Davis has gone to Price to attend the funeral of her brother, Mr Redd

Ashby Pace, Lawrence Prince and Ezra Haden went to Cedar today on business

Albert Mathis and family have moved into their new home on the farm.

Washington County News
February 2, 1920

New Harmony, Feb 2 —An epidemic of influenza broke out here last week and at present there are about forty cases In some cases the entire family was down, but the situation was greatly relieved when young folks came from Enterprise to help Their kindness is surely appreciated

Rose, Eldon and George Schmutz came home last Tuesday to remain while the B A C. at Cedar City is closed

Mrs. Mildred Naegle came up from Toquerville last week expecting to remain for a while

Mrs. Mason Rencher returned to her home at Grass Valley last week

Levi Snow of Pine Valley was in town last Thursday on business

Iron County Record
February 2, 1920

New Harmony, Utah, Feb. 2, 1920. Mrs. Lurene Taylor is quite ill with rheumatism.

* * *

Wm. Chinn is home again after several month's absence with the sheep.

* * *

We had 83 cases of flu in our little town but we are thankful it is now a thing of the past.

* * *

Arch Ballard came up from Grafton yesterday to work for Frank Kelsey.

* * *

Evelyn Prince has bought the home of Lawrence Prince and will move in soon.

* * *

Our school started yesterday after being closed fo six weeks on account of whooping cough and flu.

* * *

The infant daughter of Mr. and Mrs. Donald Schmutz who has been ill for some time is much improved at this writing.

* * *

Miss Nora Ballard returned to her home in Grafton Saturday after a few days visit here with her sister, Mrs. Frank Kelsey. Mrs Kelsey accompanied her home and will visit there for a short time.

DEATH AT NEW HARMONY

Word has been received here that Mrs Lawrence Prince, who was critically ill with "flu," died of pneumonia last Sunday night Her husband was reported to be seriously ill of the same disease The News joins in sympathy with the bereaved relatives

NEW HARMONY STRUCK HARD

There are 93 cases of influenza in the little town of Kanarra, according to Dr. Macfarlane, who visited that place recently.

All but three homes in New Harmony are under quarantine for "flu." Mr and Mrs. Lawrence Prince of that place are both suffering with influenza-pneumonia, and as the lady was already in delicate health, her condition is most serious.

Influenza in Cedar City is rapidly subsiding, only one new case being reported yesterday, that of Mr. Hillman Dalley, who is living in close proximity to a family previously afflicted —Iron County Record.

Iron County Record
February 13, 1920

It is learned here with sincere regrets that Mrs. Lawrence Prince of New Harmony, who was reported last week to be seriously ill with influenza-pneumonia, succumbed to the attack. Her husband, also a sufferer from the disease, is slowly recovering.

Washington County News
February 16, 1920

New Harmony, Feb 16 — Mrs Ruth Prince died Sunday, Feb 8th, a victim of the ' flu," pneumonia and other complications She gave birth to a baby girl a day or two before her death. Her sister is taking care of it at present The bereaved husband and children have the sympathy of the community in their trouble

Mr. and Mrs Ed Whipple and Rulon Whipple, of Logan, Nev, and Mrs Mame Gardner of Wyoming were here at the death of Mrs Prince Mr and Mrs Whipple will leave tomorrow, the other two having previously returned

The infant son of Mr and Mrs George Prince passed away last week of whooping cough and the flu " The family have the sympathy of the people in the loss of their little one

The young people from Enterprise who have been nursing flu ' patients returned home Saturday Their assistance was greatly appreciated

Elmer Taylor who has been off working for H A Pace is in town for a few days visit

Rulon Taylor returned from St George Saturday where he has been attending school

Washington County News
February 23, 1920

New Harmony, Feb 23 — The ' flu" is about over now, there only being one new case in the last week The first ones that had it, with one or two exceptions are out again now.

It has rained almost constantly for the last four days, and now it looks as if it were going to end in a snow storm

Rose, George and Ellen Schmutz returned to Cedar City to resume their work at the B. A C.

Andrew Schmutz has returned from the goat herd where he has been for some time

Mrs Elmer Taylor returned from Rockville where she has been for the past two months.

Miss Lenora Ballard of Grafton is here visiting her sister, Mrs Lottie Kelsey.

New Harmony, Mar 1 — Mrs Donald Schmutz went to Cedar last week to take her baby that was suffering from an abscess and at this writing is still quite bad

Ray Naegle of Toquerville was in town last Friday and Saturday He came up to get his wife who recently has had the ' flu "

Evelyn Prince has purchased the house and lot of Lawrence Prince He expects to move in a short time

Mr and Mrs Evelyn Prince have returned from St George where they have been for the past two months

School commenced today after being closed for some time Most of the students are able to attend

Miss Cora Williams of Kanarra is here to work for LaVerna Inglestead

Rulon Taylor, Will and Irving Prince went to St George today

Elmer and Owen Taylor went south with the sheep last week

New Harmony, March 8 —Every one has recovered from the ' flu ' and are out well again with the exception of Mrs Rhoda Prince and Mrs Lurene Taylor, the former having had pneumonia, and the latter being left with rheumatism

David Spilsbury came up from Toquerville Saturday to attend Sunday school and meeting with the folks here, and also to bid them good bye, prior to his departure for Salt Lake City His visit was greatly appreciated

Andrew Schmutz is wearing a broad smile over the arrival of a baby girl born March 7th, mother and babe are doing nicely

The different auxilary organizations have commenced again, after having been closed for a month

Miss Jaunita Davis, who is attending school at Kanarra, has been in town for the past two days

Antone Prince returned home from St George last week, where he has spent the past winter

Miss Minnie Pace returned to Hurricane yesterday, after visiting here for a short time

The Schmutz Bros are going to commence shearing their goats tomorrow,

✦ NEW HARMONY ✦

New Harmony, March 9, 1920.

Mrs. Elmer Taylor is on the sick list this week.

* * *

The Schmutz brothers will begin shearing their goats tomorrow.

* * *

Antone Prince is home from St. George where he spent the winter.

* * *

Born—A girl to Mr. and Mrs. Andrew Schmutz, Sunday, Mar. 7. All concerned doing nicely.

* * *

Orven Taylor is home again after being away for some time with Bishop Pace's sheep.

* * *

Mrs. Frank Kelsey returned home from Grafton today after a week's visit with relatives there.

* * *

Eldon Schmutz returned home from Cedar City this week where he has attended the B. A. C. the past winter term.

William Chinn of New Harmony was a business visitor here last Friday He has sheep out south and came in to get supplies

OBITUARY—MRS RUTH PRINCE

Ruth Whipple, wife of George L Prince, died Feb 8, 1920, at New Harmony, Utah, of pneumonia following an attack of influenza

Mrs. Prince was a daughter of Mr. and Mrs. E. J Whipple of Logandale, Nevada, and was born Aug 12, 1889, at Pine Valley, Utah, where she resided until June 7, 1911, at which date she was married to George L Prince of New Harmony. Of this union there were four children, McKay age 7, Carol age 5, Rex age 2, and an infant daughter only two days old at the time of her death

Sister Prince was a faithful member of the Church of Jesus Christ of Latter-day Saints, having served as president of the ward Primary association for several years besides other duties of service in the Church, all of which she filled with honor and satisfaction to those in authority over her A characteristic of her disposition perhaps prominent above all others was her kind and loving ways, being always thoughtful of those around her,

Besides her parents, husband and children, Sister Prince leaves seven brothers and three sisters and a host of other relatives and friends to mourn her departure.

NEW HARMONY

New Harmony, March 22, 1920.

Edwin Higbee of Toquerville was a visitor here yesterday .

* * *

Miss Gladys Grant was on the sick list last week, but is much improved at this writing.

* * *

Mr. and Mrs. J. E. Farr of Spanish Fork are visiting their daughter Mrs. Bert Grant here for a few days.

* * *

J. E. Farr, Floyd Grant and Clair Young went to St. George Saturday to see George A. Grant.

* * *

G. L. and J. L. Prince, Ashby Pace, Alex Taylor and Evelyn Prince were business visitors at St. George last week.

* * *

Dr. and Mrs. P. E. Harris will make their home here for an indefinite period. The doctor has gone to Hurricane this week for a load of household goods.

Washington County News
March 23, 1920

New Harmony, Mar 23 — Mr and Mrs Farr of Spanish Fork motored down last week for their daughter Ann, who has been here for some time visiting with her sister, Mrs Clara Grant.

Dr E P. Harris and family have moved here Dr. Harris was here last summer. He intends renting Lorenzo Prince's farm this summer

There is about four inches of snow this morning and it is still snowing It looks like winter instead of spring

Morris Whitehead of St. George returned home Sunday after being here for several days

Mr Redd of Cedar City is here counting the cattle to go on the forest reserve.

Edwin Higbee of Toquerville was in town yesterday on business.

Washington County News
March 28, 1920

HARMONY HAS MUCH RAIN

Geo F. Prince, the weather observer at New Harmony has sent The News figures showing total precipitation at that place for February and March During February 5 74 inches fell, the number of days showing precipitation being 11. During March, to and exclusive of the 28th, the precipitaition was 4 42 inches and the number of days 14; a total for the two months up to the 28th ult, of 10.16 inches,

New Harmony, March 29,—A doctor was summond yesterday for Mrs Cecil Schmutz, who is critically ill with typhoid fever. Her condition is reported to be a little better to day and we truly hope that she will continue to improve

Miss Mary Giles, a trained nurse from Cedar City, came down yesterday to nurse Mrs Cecil Schmutz

Clarence Englestead returned from the sheep herd last week to resume work on his farm.

Dr Harris returned from Hurricane Saturday, where he went after a load of furniture.

George Schmutz has finished his winter course at the B A. C. and is now home again.

Floyd Grant has been a sufferer for the past week with quinsy.

New Harmony, April 5 —Mrs Cecil Schmutz who has had typhoid fever for the past three weeks is slowly improving Her sister, Mrs LaVerna Englestead, is a victim to the dread disease now, having come down with it a few days ago

Mr and Mrs Ed Whipple and Rulon Whipple of Logan, Nev, motored in last week to get Lawrence Princes baby They returned today

Friday evening the Y M M I A gave a dance and sold ice cream   A very pleasant time was enjoyed by all present

William Taylor returned from St George Saturday where he had been on business

Mr and Mrs Farr, and daughter Ann returned to Spanish Fork last week

Mrs Rhiner, instead of Miss Giles is nursing Mrs Schmutz

Mr and Mrs Frank Kelsey of New Harmony are here visiting the latters father, David Ballard

New Harmony, April 19 —Funeral services were held for Mrs Cecil Schmutz last Wednesday at 11 a m, who passed away Sunday the 11th The speakers were Elders John Schmutz, Albert Mathis, Wm Taylor and Bishop H A Pace All spoke highly of the departed sister She leaves a husband and two children, who have the sympathy of the entire community

We are having a great many storms lately, most too many to make it convenient for farming It snowed about four inches Saturday, and is cold and disagreeable today

Mrs Reese Davis has been over to Kanarra for the past week with her daughter, Mrs Berry Williams

Mr and Mrs Elmer Taylor have moved into Albert Mathis' house for the summer

Eldon Schmutz and Karl Phippan have gone to St George to shear sheep

Donald Schmutz is teaching school in La Verna Inglestead's place

Most of our townspeople are being inocculated for typhoid fever.

Frank Kelsey went to Hurricane today on business

Iron County Record
April 20, 1920

New Harmony. April 20.

W. S. Thorley was a business visitor here yesterday.

* * *

W. P. Taylor is on the sick list this week.

* * *

Mrs. Reese Davis is visiting her daughter, Mrs. G. B. Williams for a few days.

* * *

J. I. and G. E. Prince have gone to Dixie to shear sheep.

* * *

Mrs. Mary Prince is visiting her parents in St. George.

* * *

Funeral services were held here last Wednesday over the remains of Cecil Taylor Schmutz wife of Andrew G. Schmutz, who departed this life April 11. She was 29 years old last September and leaves a husband and two children, two brothers and one sister beside a host of relatives and friends to mourn her loss.

"None knew her but to love her
"Or named her but to praise."
Could we say more.

Washington County News
April 26, 1920

New Harmony, April 26 —A crowd of young folks met at the home of Mr and Mrs Francis Prince and had a social in honor of Mr and Mrs Karl Phippan who left for Idaho to day. A very pleasant time was enjoyed by all present.

Mr and Mrs Karl Phippan and family have returned to Idaho, after spending the winter here with Mrs Phippan s mother and grandparents

Mr and Mrs Frank Petty and Mrs Thomas Forsyth of Cedar City were town visitors yesterday

Miss Cora Williams returned to Kanarra today, after spending several weeks here

Mr. and Mrs John Williamson of Paragonah, are visiting Mr and Mrs Lorenzo Prince

Alvin Jones of Grafton is here working for H A Pace

WHITEHEAD-GRANT)

Mr. Morris Whitehead and Miss Gladys Grant were married at the home of Pres and Mrs George F. Whitehead at 1 o'clock p m Tuesday, Bishop James McArthur officiating

The bride is a highly respected young lady of New Harmony, a daughter of Mr. and Mrs Edgar C. Grant. The groom is the youngest son of Pres and Mrs. Geo F. Whitehead.

The News joins the many friends of the young couple in all good wishes,

New Harmony, May 10.—A shower was given last evening for Gladys Grant, who was married to Morris Whitehead of St George last Tuesday. They left for their home this morning

Bishop H A. Pace and Albert Mathis have been having their sheep sheared this past week.

George Naegle of Toquerville was in town last Friday on his way from Parowan.

Miss Minnie Pace has returned home from Hurricane where she has been teaching the past winter.

Miss May Dalton of Rockville returned home last week after spending several weeks here

Mr. and Mrs. Antone Prince have been to St George for the past two days visiting friends and relatives.

William C. Chinn is home again after being off the past winter with his sheep.

Mr and Mrs Morris Whitehead spent the week end in New Harmony

NEW HARMONY

New Harmony, May 11, 1920.

Miss Minnie Pace returned home last Friday from Hurricane where she has taught school the past winter.

* * *

Mr. and Mrs. Antone Prince were visiting at St. George Saturday and Sunday.

* * *

Wm. Chinn is in town again after an absence of two months with the sheep.

* * *

Mrs. Susie Adair and Mrs. Julia Barney, who have been quite ill the past two weeks are much improved at this writing.

* * *

A reception was given last Sunday night at the home of Mr. and Mrs. E. C. Grant in honor of Mr. and Mrs. Morris Whitehead who were married at St. George last Wednesday. The bride was formerly Miss Gladys Grant.

New Harmony, May 18 —William Taylor has gone to Dixie to look for a place to live   He is forced to live in a warmer climate on account of his health   We will regret very much to have him leave here

Mr and Mrs Frank Kelsey returned from Grafton Sunday where they had been to attend the wedding reception of Mrs Kelsey's brother.

Mrs Donald Schmutz returned from Rockville Sunday where she had been several days' visiting

Mrs Sarah Davis returned from Kanarra Saturday where she has been for the past month

Mrs Amelia Schmutz has gone to St George, expecting to be gone about three weeks

Elmer Taylor ,Antone Prince and Orson Hammond have gone to Lund to take wool

Mrs Mildred Naegle of Toquerville is here visiting with friends and relatives

William Chinn had a force of men employed last week to shear his sheep

Miss Leona Russell of Hurricane is here working for Mrs Susan E Pace

George Berry of Kanarra is having his sheep sheared here this week

Otto Reeves of Kanarra is here working for Bishop H A Pace.

Frank Kelsey went to Cedar today on business

Mrs Evelyn Prince and Miss Ruth Seegmiller of New Harmony are visiting here this week

Miss Velva Prince and Kuman Williams spent the latter part of last week visiting relatives at New Harmony.

NEW HARMONY

New Harmony, May 19, 1920.

Edwin Higbee of Toquerville was a business visitor here yesterday.

* * *

Mr. and Mrs. Frank Kelsey and Mrs. Donald Schmutz spent the week-end at Rockville and Grafton.

* * *

Wm. P. Taylor, who has been quite ill the past month has gone to La Verkin for a while.

* * *

Mrs. Alex Ireland who has been visiting her sister Mrs. Leroy Grant left for Salt Lake City this morning.

* * *

Lavena Englestead is quite ill at this writing, it was necessary to call Dr. Bergstrom down yesterday.

* * *

Orson Hammond, Oren Kelsey, Antone Prince and Elmer Taylor left this morning for Lund with Bishop Pace's wool.

* * *

Mrs. Susie Adair and family who have spent the winter here with her father, Independence Taylor, returned to their home in New Mexico last week.

New Harmoney, May 24 —Last Friday evening at the home of Mrs Amber Schmutz, the Y. L M. I A members entertained the Y. M M. I A members and partners The house was beautifully decorated with flowers An interesting program with refreshments, passed the time most pleasantly.

Lawrence and Lorenzo Prince returned from Dixie last Friday where they have been for some time shearing sheep.

Mrs Susie Adair and family have returned to their home in New Mexico after spending the past winter here.

Mrs La Verna Englestead is at the hospital in Cedar City being treated for ulcers of the stomach

Mrs. Susan A Pace and daughter Merle have gone to Toquerville to visit for a few days.

Miss Fern Davis returned from Kanarra last Friday where she had been for awhile.

Mason Rencher of Grass valley was in town yesterday on his way to St George

George Prince returned from Dixie yesterday where he has been shearing sheep

Mrs. Ray Naegle returned to Toquerville today after a week's visit here

Claude Knell of Newcastle was in town last week

New Harmony, May 31 —A social was given Mr and Mrs William Taylor Saturday evening at the home of Mr and Mrs Reese Davis as a farewell for them before moving to Hurricane Mr Taylor has been very poorly all spring and doctors advised his moving south He left Sunday morning The rest of the family will follow soon

Mrs Clarance Englestead underwent a critical operation for appendicitis and ulcers of the stomach last Friday She is getting along as well as can be expected

Avery Pace Elmer Taylor, Lorenzo Prince LeRoy Grant and Frank Kelsey went to Cedar City yeserday on busness

Mr and Mrs Elmer Taylor returned from St George Thursday where they had been to do temple work

Miss Juanita Davis returned from Kanarra Friday where she has been attending school the past winter

Miss Leona Russell has returned to Hurricane after being here for two or three weeks

Most of our townsmen are preparing to go on the cattle drive They will be riding all this week

A dance was given last Friday by the Primary Assn A pleasant time was enjoyed by all present

Mrs Sarah Jolly of Leeds spent the week end here as the guest of Mrs Susan E Pace

George Angell and family of Leeds were town visitors yesterday.

New Harmony, June 14 —The social given by the Y M M I A at the home of Clark Pace was a decided success There were 42 guests present The refreshments were delicious The young men did themselves proud in entertaining

A club was organized here today under the leadership of Rose Schmutz This is the extension club work of the A C of Utah

Mrs L A. Pace and daughter, Merle, have returned from Toquerville where they have been visiting with Mrs. Ray Naegle

Mrs La Verna Englestead, who has recently undergone a serious operation at a hospital returned home yesterday.

Two car loads of young people took a half hol'day Saturday and took a trip to the sulphur hot springs at La Verkin.

Miss Rose Schmutz has returned home from Cedar City where she has been attending school the past winter

Mrs. Verna K. Pace has gone to Newcastle to spend a few days with relatives and friends.

Mrs E C Grant is in St. George visiting her daughter, Mrs. Gladys Whitehead.

James G Knell spent a day or two here visiting his daughter, Mrs A. W. Pace

Mrs Moriah Page passed through town Thursday en route to Salt Lake City

Elders Wood and Leigh were home missionaries here Sunday.

The S. S club met at the home of Minnie Pace last Thursday.

Mrs Sadie Grant spent a day or two in town last week.

Iron County record
June 22, 1920

New Harmony, June 22, 1920.

Mrs. Annabelle Rencher is visiting her parents here for a few days.

* * *

Born—A daughter to Bishop and Mrs. Henry A. Pace June 15th.

* * *

The S. S. Club will give a character ball Friday night.

* * *

Mrs. Elmer Taylor is visiting relatives at Hurricane for a few days.

* * *

The S. S. Club met at the home of Lottie Kelsey Thursday.

* * *

Elmer Taylor and Antone Prince went to Hurricane Sunday on business.

* * *

Mrs. Donald Schmutz was operated on at the Macfarlane hospital last week and is getting along nicely.

* * *

Mrs. Eliza Kelsey and Miss Minnie Pace are cooking for the men who are working on the road near Page's.

* * *

Mr. and Mrs. Jeremiah Leavitt who spent the past week with their daughter, Mrs. Wm. Chinn returned home to Gunlock yesterday.

* * *

Mrs. Golda Cox returned to her home at St. George this week after a short visit here with her parents, Mr. and Mrs. George F. Prince.

* * *

Donald Schmutz returned home today from Cedar City after spending a few days with his wife who is in the hospital there.

New Harmony, July 12 —A farewell party was given for Donald Schmutz, last Friday, who left to go on a mission today The evening was spent in dancing, interspersed with a short program and refreshments

Some of the S S Stake officers were here yesterday to reorganize the S S Elmer Taylor was appointed to take Donald Schmutz's place as Supt , with Antone Prince and Parley Harris as counselors The rest of the officers and teachers were not released

Mr. and Mrs Frank Kelsey and family and Miss Nora Ballard of Grafton returned from Sevier county Saturday where they hal been on a fishing trip. A very pleasant trip was reported.

Anlone Prince was operated on at Cedar City for appendicitis about two weeks ago. He returned home last Friday.

Ray Naegle of Toquerville was in town today He was accompanied on his return by Mrs L A Pace

Mrs Mason Rencher returned to her home at Grass valley Thursday after being here for some time

Mrs Morris Whitehead of St. George is here visiting with her mother, Mrs. Emily Grant

Miss Ora Workman of Hurricane is here visiting friends and relatives

Mr. and Mrs. Lee Cox of St. George were in town yesterday.

New Harmony, July 19 —There are several cases of chicken pox in town in a very light form, It doesn t seem to be known just how they got started

The ladies social sewing club met at the home of Mrs Orson Hammond last Thursday A very pleasant afternoon was enjoyed by all members present

Frank Farr returned to Spanish Fork last week, after being here about two weeks

Rulon Taylor is home from the sheep herd where he had been for several months

George Schmutz has gone to Idaho expecting to remain for some time

Mr and Mrs J G Pace of Cedar City were in town yesterday

Forest Ranger Alex Macfarlane was in town yesterday.

Washington County News
July 29, 1920

Morris Whitehead returned Tuesday from New Harmony where he had been visiting for several days

Lee and Melvin Cox returned Sunday from New Harmony, where they spent the 24th

Washington County News
August 3, 1920

New Harmony Aug 3 —It has rained here every day for the last ten days and looks like we are going to get more today

The Milne brothers of St. George are here painting the meeting house

Miss Hortense Russell returned to Hurricane today atfer being here for several weeks

Some of the Y M and Y. L M. I A officers were here Sunday for meeting They gave us some good instructions

Eliza Kelsey and Minnie Pace returned from Pine Valley last week where they have been for some time

Miss Viola Armstrong spent the week end here as the guest of Alex Taylor and Susan D Pace

Miss Merle Pace went to Toquerville last Friday to visit with her sister, Mrs Ray Naegle.

Miss Iva Knell of Newcastle is here visiting with Mr and Mrs A W Pace

NEW HARMONY

New Harmony, Aug. 3, 1920.

The Misses Nora Ballard and Madge Jones of Grafton are visiting friends and relatives here for a few days.

* * *

Mrs. Melissa Hammond returned home Saturday from Cedar City, where she visited friends for a few days last week.

* * *

Floyd Grant and Clark Pace who have been visiting at Grafton and other parts of Dixie returned yesterday.

* * *

Mrs. Eliza Kelsey and Miss Minnie Pace are home again after six weeks absence cooking for the men who have been working on the road between Central and Pinevalley.

* * *

Stake Mutual officers visited us last Sunday afternoon giving some valuable instructions.

* * *

J. W. Prince of St. George was visiting his parents, Mr. and Mrs. Francis Prince here last Saturday.

Washington County News
August 9, 1920

New Harmony, Aug 9.—Edwin Higbee of Toquerville is in town today on his way to Panguitch where he will oversee some road work Mrs Eliza Kelsey and Minnie Pace will cook for the men

Mr and Mrs Parley Dalley and Jack Christensen of Cedar City were in town today on business

Iva Knell and Miss Rose Schmutz went to Cedar today expecting to be gone about a week

Royal Neilson of Monroe was in town last night on his way to St George

A baby girl was born to Mr and Mrs Lorenzo Prince, Aug 5th

Elmer Taylor has recently purchased a touring car

Washington County News
August 23, 1920

New Harmony, Aug 23 —Yesterday five of the S S Stake officers were here to hold S S ward conference A very interesting program was rendered

Mr and Mrs J D Neilson have returned from the Goddard and Grant ranch, where they have been for the past week

Mrs Wm Taylor returned to Hurricane last Friday, after spending several days here

Gotlieb Schmutz and Irving prince have gone to Grass valley to work for a few days

Rulon Taylor left for Fairview this morning, expecting to be gone for some time

Bishop H A Pace has gone to Nevada on business

NEW HARMONY

New Harmony, Aug. 24, 1920.

Threshing commenced here yesterday.

* * *

Gottleib Schmutz is in Grass Valley working.

* * *

Mason Rencher was in town last week on business.

* * *

Delbert Woolsey was in town Sunday for fruit.

* * *

Mr. and Mrs. Jacob Deuel were visiting Mr. and Mrs. Orson Sunday.

* * *

Mr. and Mrs. Antone went to Hurricane and St. George Sunday for fruit.

* * *

Rulon Taylor left yesterday for Fairview, Utah, where he will find employment for some time.

* * *

Miss Rose Schmutz will leave Saturday for Spanish Fork country where she will teach school this winter.

Iron County Record
August 30, 1920

New Harmony, Utah, Aug. 30.

Mrs. A. F. Mathis was on the sick-list last week, but is much improved at this writing.

* * *

William Pace of Delta passed thru here Sunday en route to Washington, Utah, to visit his mother, Mrs. H. M. Jolley.

* * *

Stake Pres. Henry W. Lunt, his 1st Counsellor, Myron D. Higbee, and Elder Jed Jones were visitors at our Sunday School and Sacramental meeting Sunday.

* * *

Mr. and Mrs. A. W. Pace, Eldon Schmutz and Iva Knell returned yesterday from Pine Valley mountain, where they spent the week end sightseeing.

* * *

Mr. and Mrs. Hyrum Prince from Thorley, were here after fruit yesterday.

* * *

Claud Knell was a visitor here yesterday.

Mrs. Frank Kelsey and Mrs. Elmer Taylor have gone to Grafton to put up fruit.

Washington County News
August 30, 1920

New Harmony, Aug 30 —Frank Kelsey and Clark Pace left for Grafton today

J C Knell of Newcastle was in town yesteiday He and his sister, Miss Lva, left today for Panguitch, expecting to go to Bryces canyon on their return

Iva Knell, Verna Pace, Ashby Pace and Eldon Schmutz returned from a trip to the Pine Valley mountain yes terday A very pleasant trip was reported

Miss Rose Schmutz left for the northern part of the state last Saturday where she will teach school the coming winter

Bishop H A Pace, Will Pace and Bert Grant left for Salt Lake city today

New Harmony, Utah, Sept. 14, 1920.

Mr. and Mrs. Berry Williams of Kanarra are here today for fruit.

* * *

Mrs. Bert Grant returned home last week from Spanish Fork, where she has been visiting her parents, Mr. and Mrs. John Farr.

* * *

Wm. P. Taylor is in town for a few days.

* * *

Heber Cottam of St. George, is plastering Wm. Chinn's new house.

* * *

Mrs. Susan A. Pace returned home Saturday from Toquerville where she has been visiting her daughter Mrs. Ray Naegle.

* * *

Elmer Taylor is in St. George attending the Teacher's Institute. He will teach school here this winter.

* * *

Mrs. Evelyn Prince, Mr. and Mrs. Antone Prince, Mrs. E. C. Grant, Mr. Eldon Schmutz, Mrs. Donald Schmutz and Gottlieb Schmutz were at the Festival in St. George.

* * *

Clark Pace and Orren Taylor have gone to Zion Canyon.

* * *

Minnie Pace has gone to Hurricane where she will teach school this winter.

* * *

Fern and Juanita Davis went to St. George Sunday, where they will attend the "Dixie" this year.

Mart Woolsey left last Saturday for his home at New Harmony after spending several weeks here recovering from injuries received in an automobile accident.

Washington County News
September 27, 1920

New Harmony, Sept 27 —Those who attended the Iron county fair at Cedar City from here were Mr and Mrs A F Mathis, Mr and Mrs Elmer Taylor, Mr and Mrs H A Pace Mr and Mrs Frank Kelsey, Mr and Mrs A W Pace, Eldon Schmutz, Emily Grant, Mrs Susan E Pace, and Antone Prince

Mr and Mrs Delbert Woolsey of Woolseys ranch have moved here for the winter, so that their children can attend school Miss Ada Slack, Mrs Woolsey's sister, came with them

Bp H A Pace, Mesdames Susan E Pace, Emma Neilson, Amber Schmutz, Melissa Hammond, Verna Pace, Sarah Davis and Elmer Taylor attended conference at Parowan

Edwin Higbee of Toquerville has a force of men employed repairing the canyon road

Heber Cottam of St George is here plastering William Chinn's new residence

Iron County Record
October 5, 1920

New Harrmony, Oct. 5, 1920.

Born, a son to Mr. and Mrs. Delbert Woolsey, Sept. 30.

* * *

Mrs. Donald Schmutz has gone to Vernal to spend the winter with her parents.

* * *

Gotlieb Schmutz left for Salt Lake yesterday to attend the fair.

* * *

Emma Neilson entertained the married people at a chicken supper Saturday evening.

* * *

Pole Pollock was a business visitor here today.

* * *

Mr. and Mrs. Frank Prince of Middleton were here with a load of grapes and molasses yesterday.

* * *

Heber Cottam has finished his work here and will return to his home at St. George tomorrow.

New Harmony, Oct 5 — A party was given for Mrs Donald Schmutz Saturday evening, who left yesterday for Vernal expecting to spend the winter there

Gottlieb Schmutz left for Salt Lake City yesterday to attend the state fair He was accompanied by Mr and Mrs John Schmutz of St George

A baby boy was born to Mr and Mrs Delbert Woolsey Sept 30, all concerned doing nicely.

Ezra Haden returned from Toquerville yesterday where he had been on business

Rulon Platt of Kanarra is in town on business

New Harmony, Utah, Oct. 19, 1920. Gotleib Schmutz returned home last Friday from Salt Lake City, where he attended the State Fair and Confrence.

* * *

Miss Rose Schmutz is home for a few days from Lake Shore, Utah, where she is teaching school this year.

* * *

Mr. and Mrs. Lee Cox and their brother Melvin, came up from Saint George Sunday. Mrs. Cox is visiting her parents, Mr. and Mrs. George F. Prince, and the boys are hunting deer.

* * *

Dr. Frank Petty of Cedar City and Heber Cottam of St. George, with their wives, are visiting Mr. and Mrs. Antone Prince. The Doctor and Bro. Cottam are doing some hunting, also.

* * *

Mr. and Mrs. Berry Williams of Kanarra were over here Sunday.

* * *

Miss Madge Jones and sister of Grafton are spending a few days here with friends.

Washington County News
October 25, 1920

New Harmony, Oct 25 —Irving and Will Prince returned home last week from the northern part of the state, where they have been for several weeks

Ethel Schmutz, Merle Pace and Pearl Pace, who are attending the B A C. of Cedar City, spent the week end here

Rulon Taylor has returned home from the northern part of the state where he has been working for some time.

Bishop H. A Pace returned from Lund Saturday where he had been on business for a week

Mr and Mrs Lee Cox of St George are here visiting friends and relatives.

Mrs Sadie Woolsey of Woolsey's ranch has moved here for the winter

Madge and Fern Jones of Grafton are here visiting friends.

Washington County News
November 8, 1920

New Harmony, Nov 8 —Mrs Albert Taylor of Price arrived here last week to be with her mother, Mrs Woolsey, during her sickness

Lawrence Prince and children left here yesterday for Logan, Nev, where they will spend the winter.

Mrs Morris Whitehead of St George is here visiting with her parents, Mr. and Mrs Ed. Grant.

Mrs Sarah Woolsey has been bed fast for two or three weeks and at this writing is not any better.

Frank Kelsey returned from Toquerville yesterday where he had been on business

Roy Grant is in from the ranch the past two days on business

New Harmony, Nov 15 —Last Wednesday Mrs Ed Grant was operated on at Cedar City for diseased gall bladder She is reported to be getting along fairly well

Some of the stake presidency were down yesterday from Cedar City to hold ward conference with us Some primary and mutual officers were present also and held meeting with us last night.

Lawrence Prince has returned from Logan, Nev , where he took his children who will stay with Mr. and Mrs F J Whipple this winter

Edwin Higbee of Toquerville and Arch. Batty of Bellevue were in town yesterday on business

Mrs J D Neilson is in Cedar City with her mother, Mrs. E Grant, during her operation.

Miss Nora Ballard of Grafton is here visiting with Mr. and Mrs Frank Kelsey

Mrs Alex Taylor has gone to Enoch expecting to be gone for a week or two

Ezra Haden left last week for Esclante, where he will remain this winter

A very good program is under way here for a Thanksgiving celebration

NEW HARMONY

New Harmony, Utah, Nov. 23, 1920.

Funeral services were held here last Friday for Mrs. Sarah Woolsey, wife of Martin O. Woolsey, who departed this life Nov. 17, 1920, of heart and liver trouble. She was born Mar. 12, 1862, and was the mother of eight children, three of whom preceded her to the great beyond. Those living are, Jake Deuel of Tonopah; Mrs. Albert Taylor of Price; Mrs. Orson Hammond, Mrs. Jed F. Woodard and Delbert Woolsey, of this place. She had been to the house of the Lord, and was a faithful Latter-day Saint, but as she lived on a ranch nearly all of her life was unable to take active part in the church work, as she would liked to have done.

At the service the choir sang "Rock of Ages." Prayer was offered by Bro. Francis Prince. Vilate Prince sang the solo, "I Have Read of a Beautiful City." The speakers were Gotleib Schmutz, James E. Taylor, Wm. P. Taylor, Albert F. Mathis and Bishop Henry A. Pace. James L. Prince offered the closing prayer and Albert F. Mathis dedicated the grave.

* * *

After having the central telephone office for 15 years, Mrs. Gotleib Schmutz has resigned and Mrs. Geo. T. Prince has charge of same.

* * *

We are anticipating a good time on Thanksgiving. There will be a public dinner at 2 p. m. with program following; a children's dance at 4 p. m. and one for the adults at night.

* * *

Dr. A. N. Leonard and Edwin Higbee were visitors here yesterday.

* * *

The plumbers from St. George are here doing some work for Gotleib Schmutz.

New Harmony, Nov. 29 —We had a fine time here on Thanksgiving. A hot dinner was served for every one after which a short, but very good program was rendered. There was a dance in the evening.

Mr. and Mrs R B. Naegle and Mr. and Mrs Wm. Taylor have returned to Toquerville after visiting a few days here with relatives and friends.

Mrs Alex Taylor returned home Saturday from Enoch where she has been visiting with her parents.

Mr. and Mrs Frank Kelsey have returned from Grafton where they went to spend Thanksgiving.

Jauneta and Fern Davis returned to St. George yesterday where they are attending the D. N. C.

Mr. and Mrs. Charley Mosdell of Hamilton's Fort have moved here for the winter.

Geo. F. Thompson of St George is here doing some plumbing for Gottlieb Schmutz.

Mrs Kenneth Hirschi of St. George is here visiting with Mr. and Mrs. Elmer Taylor.

Miss Minnie Pace, who is teaching school at Hurricane, spent the week end here.

Miss Hortense Russell of Hurricane is here as the guest of Irving Prince.

Mr. and Mrs William Chinn and family have moved into their new home.

Clarence Englestead went to Hurricane today on business.

Mrs. Delta Hammond has moved into her old home.

Ashby Pace went to Cedar City today on business.

New Harmony, Dec. 8.—The children are out selling Christmas seals today. They reported each family buying its full quota at all the houses they had visited. Yesterday some very good talks were made on that subject.

Mrs Emily Grant returned from Cedar last Wednesday where she had been for the past three weeks. She was operated on for a diseased gall bladder and is getting along nicely

Mr. and Mrs Elmer Taylor returned from St George Saturday where Mr. Taylor went to attend the teachers' institute

Evelyn Prince has returned home from the sheep herd where he has been working for some time.

Mrs Evelyn Prince has returned from St George where she has been for several weeks

Seth Harper of Cedar City was in town today on business.

Ashby Pace went to Toquerville today on business.

Iron County Record
December 21, 1920

NEW HARMONY

New Harmony, Utah, Dec. 21, 1920.

Mrs. Susan E. Pace has been quite ill but is much better at this writing.

* * *

The Misses Pearl and Merle Pace and Ethel are home for the holidays. They are attending the B. A. C. this winter.

* * *

Mr. and Mrs. Antone Prince have gone to St. George to spend the winter.

* * *

John and George Tullis passed through here last week enroute to Dixie with a load of potatoes.

* * *

Bp. Henry A. Pace attended Priesthood meeting at Cedar City Saturday.

* * *

George L. Prince is going to the Muddy to spend the Holidays with his children who are living with their Grand parents M. and Mrs. Ed. Whipple.

At the services the choir sang 'Rock of Ages." Prayer was offered by Bro Francis Prince Vilate Prince sang the solo, I Have Read of a Beautiful City" The speakers were Gotleib Schmutz, James E Taylor, Albert F. Mathis and Bishop Henry A Pace James L Prince offered the closing prayer and Albert F Mathis dedicated the grave —Iron County Record

FUNERAL OF MRS. SARAH WOOLSEY OF NEW HARMONY

New Harmony, Utah, Nov. 23, 1920. Funeral services were held here last Friday for Mrs Sarah Woolsey, wife of Martin O. Woolsey, who departed this life Nov. 17, 1920, of heart and liver trouble She was born Mar. 12, 1862, and was the mother of eight children, three of whom preceded her to the great beyond Those living are, Jake Deuel of Tonopah; Mrs· Albert Taylor of Price, Mrs Orson Hammond, Mrs Jed F. Woodard and Delbert Woolsey, of this place She had been to the house of the Lord, and was a faithful Latter-day Saint, but as she lived on a ranch nearly all of her life was unable to take active part in the church work, as she would have liked to have done.

New Harmony, Utah, Jan. 11, 1921.

Miss Nora Ballard returned to her home at Grafton today after a short visit here with her sister Mrs. Frank Kelsey.

* * *

Eldon Schmutz is home from the herd.

* * *

Olive Slack is on the sick list this week.

* * *

Wm. P. Taylor and family are home again after spending some few months in Dixie for the benefit of his health. He is now well and glad to get back.

* * *

Anna Bell Rencher spent a part of the Holidays here with her parents, Mr. and Mrs. Gottlieb Schmutz, returning to her home at Grass Valley, Saturday.

* * *

Mr. and Mrs. Evlyn Prince returned home last week from St. George where they spent the Holidays.

* * *

Bert Grant is home from the herd for a few days.

* * *

Ranger Macfarlane was a business visitor here yesterday.

Iron County Record
January 25, 1921

New Harmony, Jan. 25, 1921.
Born to Mr. and Mrs. Frank Kelsey, a son, January 20th.

* * *

Mrs. Sam Radliffe of St. George is here visiting.

Mr. Asby Pace went to Newcastle Saturday after his wife who has been visiting relatives there.

* * *

A. F. Mathis has been quite ill with the measles but is better.

* * *

Two children of Mr. and Mrs. Orson Hammond and three of Mr. and Mrs. Delbert Woolsey have the measles.

* * *

A surprise party was given Bishop Henry A. Pace last Wednesday evening. A large crowd enjoyed a very pleasant evening.

Washington County News
February 1, 1921

New Harmony, Feb. 1 —Shortly after holidays a few people broke out with the measles but were put under strict quarantine and no others have taken it.

Mrs Flora Radliff of Parashaunt, Ariz, is here visiting friends. She was formerly Mrs Brown of this place.

Mrs R. B. Naegle of Toquerville is here visiting during her husband's absence in Idaho

Mrs Robert Platt of Newcastle is here visiting with her sister, Mrs. Wm Chinn.

Mrs. E. O. Grant has gone to St. George to spend the remainder of the winter.

New Harmony, Feb 14 —Albert Mathis has received word that his wife and children who are at Logan, Nev, are all victims of the "flu." Mr Mathis himself is just recovering from the measles

Levi Taylor of Kaysville has been in town for the past two days He talked to us yesterday in meeting and gave us some good instructions along genealogical lines. He went to St George today where he expects to work in the temple for some time

Misses Merle and Pearl Pace who are attending the B. A C. have been spending the week end here.

Mrs Charley Mosdell returned from Cedar City Wednesday where she had been for a few days.

Lawrence Prince left for Logan, Nev, last week where he expects to remain for a while.

Bishop H. C. Pace and Elmer Taylor went to Parowan today on business.

Mrs. Elmer Taylor is in St. George visiting with her parents.

Mrs Elmer Taylor of New Harmony is here visiting her parents, Bishop and Mrs David Hirschi

Iron County Record
February 15, 1921

New Harmony, Feb. 15, 1921.....
Mrs. Reese Davis is on the sick list this week.

* * *

Lawrence Prince went to Overton last week to take care of his folks who have the "flu".

* * *

Frank Kelsey, James I. Prince, E. L. Grant, James L. Prince, Elmer Taylor and Bp. Henry A. Pace went to Parowan today on business.

* * *

Mrs. Francis Prince is in St. George visiting her son Joseph W. Prince.

* * *

Mrs. Robert Platt returned to her home at Newcastle last week after a short visit with her sister, Mrs. Wm. Chinn.

* * *

The Misses Pearl and Merle Pace spent the weekend here with their parents. They are attending the B. A. C. this winter.

* * *

Levi Taylor of Harrisville visited relatives here last week.

Washington County News
February 21, 1921

New Harmony, Feb 21 —Some of the young folks went to Kanarra Friday to attend the play that was put on by Hurricane They said they felt well paid for their trip

Mrs Francis Prince returned from St George yesterday where she has been visiting with Mr. and Mrs J. W. Prince

Some of the Y. L and Y. M M. I A. officers were down from Cedar City and held meeting with us last night.

Mr. and Mrs Delbert Woolsey and Ada Slack returned from Toquerville yesterday after a short visit.

Mrs. Susie H Taylor has returned from St. George where she has been visiting with her parents.

George Esplin and Jos. Fife of Cedar City were here yesterday as home missionaries

Ashby Pace, LeRoy Grant and M Woolsey are in Parowan on business.

William Chinn left for his sheep herd this morning.

New Harmony, Mar 1 —Last Tuesday the infant son of Mr and Mrs Frank Kelsey passed away after being sick only two days Short funeral services were held at the home Wednesday at 3 p m The bereaved parents have the sympathy of the community in the loss of their little one

Mrs Albert Mathis and children returned home from Logan, Nev, where they have been for some time Two of her brothers, Ruben and Wilford Whipple accompanied them home

Lawrence Prince returned from Logan, Nevada, last Thursday where he has been for the past two or three weeks He brought his children back with him

We have been enjoying real spring weather for the past two weeks Winter commenced early and indications now are that spring will come early.

Mrs Josephine Hale and children from Darlington, Idaho, are here visiting with Mrs. Hale s parents, Mr. and Mrs Orren Kelsey.

Mrs Nancy Prince and Susan E Pace have gone to St George to work in the temple for a few days.

Eldon Schmutz returned from the goat herd last week where he has been for some time.

New Harmony, March 8 —Antone Prince went to St George last week and returned with his wife and children who have been there the past few months

We had home missionaries here Sunday, Elders Mitchell and Adams from Parowan We always appreciate visits from home missionaries.

A baby girl was born Mar. 1 to Mr and Mrs Agustus Permenter, mother and baby are doing nicely.

W O Bentley of St George was here in interest of the school last week

Delbert Woolsey of Woolsey's ranch has been in town the last two days.

Mrs Mary Prince has gone to St George expecting to be gone for some time

Mr and Mrs LeGrande Pace of Pace s ranch, spent Sunday here

HEALTH OFFICERS APPOINTED

Appointments made by order of the board of county commissioners, and approved by F. B Beatty, M D, state health commissioner, of registrars of vital statistics and health officers for the following precincts:

Harold Russell,	Springdale
Liddia B Hastings,	Virgin
Rebecca Dennett,	Rockville & Grafton
R E Fletcher,	La Verkin
Walter H Slack,	Toquerville
Lizzie McQuaid,	Leeds & Harrisburg
George F. Prince,	New Harmony

WILLIAM BAKER, M D, Hurricane and all above Precincts

F J. WOODBURY, M D, St George and all precincts mentioned hereunder.

Vivian Frei,	Santa Clara
F. O Holt,	Gunlock
Mrs James Cottam,	Veyo
Leroy Holt,	Central
Walter J. Knell,	Pinto
P. E. Beckstrom	Pine Valley
Julia F. Campbell,	Enterprise
Frank Stahell,	Washington
L J. Larson,	Bloomington

New Harmony, Mar. 21 —Yesterday afternoon a doctor of Cedar City was summoned for Mrs Lurene P. Taylor who was suffering terribly with gall stones She will be taken to Cedar to morrow to be operated on

The Relief Society gave a social on the 17th Refreshments were served and a very pleasant time was enjoyed by all.

Orson Hammond who has been herding sheep in Nevada the past winter is home for a few days

Grant Hale of Darlington, Idaho, arrived here yesterday expecting to remain for some time.

George and Laurence Prince have gone to the Muddy valley to shear sheep

Mr. and Mrs. Charley Mosdell went to Cedar City last Wednesday on business.

Clark Pace returned from Newcastle today where he went to take grain

Washington County News
April 4, 1921

New Harmony, Arizona, April 4 — Miss Myrtle Butler, health inspector for Washington county schools, was here last week Her visit was appreciated and we think that much good will be the result of the same.

Mrs. Wm. P. Taylor, who was operated on for gall stones and appendicitis about ten days ago at Cedar City will be able to come home in a few days.

Mrs. Viola A. Taylor returned from Enoch Saturday where she has been the last two weeks. She was accompanied home by her father and sister.

Mrs R. B. Naegle has returned to Toqueryille after being here a week caring for the children of Mr. and Mrs. Wm. P. Taylor.

Forest Ranger Alex Macfarlane of St. George was here Friday and Saturday counting cattle on the reserve.

Max Pace has returned home from Cedar City where he has been attending the B. A. C. the past winter.

Herbert Knell of Newcastle who has been here shearing for two weeks, returned home Saturday.

Melissa Hammond has gone to Hurricane to visit relatives for a few days.

Washington County News
April 18, 1921

New Harmony, Apr. 18 —Mrs. Lurene P. Taylor has returned home from Cedar City where she recently underwent an operation. She is recovering nicely.

George Prince, Charley Mosdell, Jim Prince and Ashby Pace have gone to Hurricane to shear sheep

Orson Hammond is having a new house built Mr. Woolsey of Salt Lake has the contract.

Miss Mamie Perkins was in town Sunday visiting her sister, Mrs Maggie Mosdell.

Mrs Clarence Englestead went to Hurricane Thursday to visit for awhile.

Miss Hortense Russell of Hurricane is here working for Mrs. Wm. Taylor.

Bp H. A Pace returned from the sheep herd last week

Iron County Record
May 9, 1921

New Harmony, May, 9, 1921.

Miss Minnie Pace is home from Hurricane, where she taught school the past winter.

* * *

Mrs. George F. Prince, who was operated on at the Macfarlane hospital last Friday, is getting along nicely.

* * *

The recent storm has done much good for the crops.

* * *

Bishop Pace began shearing at Cliff View farm this morning. He is having his sheep sheared with the blades this spring.

* * *

Alvin Kelsey, who has been very ill for some time, is much improved at this writing.

* * *

Mr. and Mrs. Antone Prince and Lawrence Prince went to Saint George Friday, returning home last night.

* * *

Nora Ballard returned to her home at Grafton last Wednesday after visiting here a few days with her sister, Mrs. Frank Kelsey.

Washington County News
May 30, 1921

New Harmony, May 30.—Mrs. George Prince has returned from Cedar City where she was operated on for ulcers of the stomach. She is getting along nicely.

Mrs. Donald Schmutz and children have returned from Uintah county where they have been for several months.

Jaunita and Fern Davis have returned home from St George where they have been attending the D. N. C.

Merle Pace, Pearl Pace and Ethel Schmutz are home again from attending the B. A C. at Cedar City.

A baby boy was born to Mr. and Mrs Charley Mosdell of this place at Cedar City, May 16th.

Mrs. Gladys Whitehead of St. George is here visiting with her parents.

Work is progressing nicely on Orson Hammond's house.

◆ NEW HARMONY ◆

New Harmony, May 30.

Alex Taylor, who has been dangerously ill with pneumonia for the past two weeks, is still dangerously ill.

* * *

Mrs. Lamar Terry and children are visiting her sister, Mrs. Donald Schmutz, here this wee

* * *

Mr. Jed Adair and of Salt Lake City, relatives here yesterda

* * *

Miss Rose Schmutz home last week from where she taught sch winter.

* * *

Mrs. George T. Prin the improve.

* * *

Lee Cox of St. Ge town today.

Bishop Pace went to 1 today to meet a woolbuyer.

* * *

Mrs. Eliza Kelsey has gone to

her daugh-

Messrs. Will Woolsey and Geo. Worthen are building a bungalow for Mrs. Orson Hammond.

New Harmony, June 20 —Funeral services were held here last Wednesday for Mrs Sarah Richardson, who passed away Monday morning after a brief illness She came here last winter from Idaho to be with her brother, Independence Taylor She was 79 years old The speakers were Elders James D Taylor, Gottlieb Schmutz and Albert F. Mathis

The Stake Presidency and other members of the board were here yesterday and held Sunday School and meeting with us. Bro. Albert F. Mathis was released from being first counselor to Bp Pace and James E Taylor was chosen in his place.

Mrs Susan A Pace and daughter, Miss Merle, have gone to Toquerville to visit for a few days.

Miss Iva Knell of Newcastle has returned home after visiting here for the past two weeks

Alex Taylor is around again having been ill for some time with pneumonia

Miss Minnie Pace has gone to Salt Lake City to attend summer school

LeRoy Grant was in from his ranch Saturday on business.

New Harmony, June 27 —Mrs Amelia Schmutz has gone to Oregon on a pleasure trip She was accompanied by her daughter, Miss Rose

Several of our towns people went to conference at Cedar City yesterday Apostle Ballard was in attendance

Mrs Evelyn Prince has returned from St George where she has been for some time

Mr and Mrs LeGrande Pace of Cedar City were here yesterday

Miss Pauline Adams of Parowan is here visiting friends

Clarance Englestead is home from the sheep herd

New Harmony, July 11 —A crowd of young folks left this morning for Grass valley on a fishing trip They expect to be gone several days.

Last Tuesday evening the S. S gave a dance and sold ice cream. A very good time was enjoyed by all.

Mr. and Mrs Clarence Englestead have gone to Mt Carmel to live on their homestead for a few months

Waldon Ballard and sister, Miss Nora, have returned to Grafton after spending the Fourth here.

Miss Hortense Russell of Hurricane has returned home after spending several weeks here.

Charley Mosdell and Grant Hale have gone to Lund to get freight.

Mr. and Mrs Berry Williams of Kanarra were in town yesterday.

New Harmony, July 18 —Mrs. Eliza Kelsey has returned home from Carey, Idaho, where she has been visiting for the past two months.

The farmers are busy heading grain. There is an unusually good crop this year.

Miss Pauline Adams has returned to Parowan, after being here for some time.

Alvin Kelsey went to Cedar last week and had his tonsils removed.

Bp H. A. Pace went to St. George last week on business.

Grant Hale has gone to Lund to work for J. D. Leigh.

Washington County News
August 8, 1921

New Harmony, Aug 8.—Mr and Mrs. Wm Taylor and family, Mrs L A Pace and daughter, Miss Merle, spent last week on the Kanarra mountains A very pleasant trip was reported

Mrs. Walter Spencer of Babbitt, Minn , and J. C. Knell and sister, Miss Iva, were here last Monday visiting Mr. and Mrs Ashby Pace

Mr and Mrs A B Prince, Jauneta and Fern Davis and Bp H. A Pace and family have gone to the Kanarra mountains for a few days.

Mrs Amelia Schmutz returned from Rockville Saturday where she had been for several days

Forest Ranger E. J. Storm was here last week on business.

Mrs. Alex Taylor has gone to Enoch to visit for a while.

Washington County News
August 25, 1921

Mrs William Branch, Mr and Mrs Henry C Pace and two children, of Price arrived here last Friday to visit relatives They left for return home Tuesday, intending to visit relatives in New Harmony and Cedar City enroute.

New Harmony, Aug 29 —Mr. Eldon Schmutz and Miss Eva Buys of Salt Lake were married on the 10th of this month, returning from Salt Lake last week A wedding reception was given in their honor Friday evening A very pleasant time was enjoyed by all.

Verna Pace returned from Newcastle yesterday where she had been visiting for the past week

Mrs Susan E Pace has returned from Spanish Fork, where she has been visiting for a week

Miss Minnie Pace has returned from Toquerville where she has been visiting for a few days

The men are busy threshing. The grain crop is good this season.

Mr. and Mrs Albert Bryner of St. George are here

Olive Oviatt of Santa Clara is here visiting friends

Mr. and Mrs. Eldon Smoots of Harmony were in Cedar Tuesday on business. Mrs. Smootz was formerly Miss Eva Buys and taught at the B. A. C. and in the Cedar district school during the past four years.

Andy Schmutz of New Harmony spent several hours in Cedar Wednesdaf. The gentleman reports that several floods have visited that section, but no great amount of damage was done.

New Harmony, Oct 3 —Mrs L A. Pace went to Cedar Sunday where she will remain this coming winter so that her family can attend the B. A C

Misses Junita and Fern Davis and Ethel Schmutz have gone to St George to attend the D N. C. this winter

Mr. and Mrs Delbert Woolsey of Woolsey a ranch have moved here for the winter to send their children to school

Clark Pace, Irving and Will Prince have returned from Lund where they have been working for some time

Mrs Walter Spencer has returned to Newcastle after visiting here for the past two weeks

Born, a daughter to Mr. and Mrs. Bert Grant, Sept 26, mother and babe donig nicely.

Clarance Englestead has gone to Mt Caimel expecting to be gone for some time

School commenced Sept 19th with Mr. and Mrs. Elmer Taylor as teachers.

Wm. Woolsey and Lawrence Prince have gone to Hurricane on business.

Alex Taylor left this morning to work on the Lund and Cedar road

Mr. and Mrs Wm Chinn have gone to Gunlock for a few days

Albert Mathis and family have moved in to town for the winter.

Forest Ranger E V. Storm was here last week on business

A daughter was born to Mr. and Mrs Alex Taylor last week

Miss Pearl Pace has gone to Cedar to attend the B A. C

Will Pace of Delta was in town last week.

Iron County Record
October 7, 1921

NEW HARMONY.

Baby girls have recently arrived at the homes of the following: Mr. and Mrs. Alex Taylor, Sept. 21; Mr. and Mrs. Bert Grant, Sept. 26. All concerned doing nicely.

Mrs. Ann Willard of Spanish Fork, is here visiting her sister, Mrs. Bert Grant.

Mrs. Mary Spencer has returned to Newcastle after visiting here with her sister, Mrs. Verna Pace, for several weeks.

Mr. and Mrs. Delbert Woolsey have moved in from their ranch to send their children to school.

Alex Taylor left recently to work on the Lund road.

Frank Kelsey and Irving Prince have spent the past few days visiting in Grafton and bathing in the sulphur springs at LaVirkin.

Bp. H. A. Pace has gone to the Lund desert to look after his sheep.

M. O. Woolsey of Woolsey's ranch, motored into town yesterday.

Mrs. L. A. Pace has moved to Cedar City. for the winter, where her son, Max and daughter, Merle, are attending the B. A. C.

Miss Pearl Pace is in Cedar City, attending the B. A. C.

The Misses Juanita Davis, Fern Davis and Ethel Schmutz are in St. George attending the D. N. C.

Iron County Record
October 14, 1921

HARMONY.

County Supt. W. O. Bentley of St. George was here Friday visiting the school.

Orren Taylor has returned from the sheep herd where he has been for the past several months.

Mrs. Lee Cox of St George is here visiting her parents, Mr. and Mrs. G. F Prince, while her husband is in Cedar City threshing grain.

Melvin Cox of St. George was a town visitor yesterday.

Mrs. Evelyn Prince has gone to St. George to spend the winter with her parents, Mr. and Mrs. Chas. Seegmiller.

Evelyn, Irwin and Will Prince are on the desert trapping predatory animals.

Local hunters are all excitement these days as the deer season approaches. Cleaning and oiling of guns seems to be the order of the day.

Washington County News
October 24, 1921

New Harmony, Oct 24.—Mr and Mrs Guss Permenter and family left here Saturday for Spirrel Oklahoma where they intend making their future home

Mrs Wm Chinn returned from Gunlock last Sunday where she had been for some time

Charley Mosdell H A Pace and Wm Chinn have gone to Lund on business

J C Knell and Iva Knell of New Castle were in town Sunday and Monday

Several of the forest rangers were in town Saturday on business

Seve al cattle buyers were here last week buying cattle

Iron County Record
October 28, 1921

NEW HARMONY.

Forest Supervisor Wm. M. Mace with Rangers Macfarlane and Storm, and an Ogden official, were here Saturday looking over the range.

Local sheepmen have been at Lund the past week selling lambs.

Mr. Covington and Miss Velva Prince of St. George spent the week end here visiting relatives and friends.

A birthday social was given Wednesday afternoon to some of the elder ladies of the ward at the home of Mrs. Donald Schmutz in honor of Mrs. Amelia Schmutz.

Alex Taylor, who is working on the Cedar-Lund road, spent Sunday at home.

Mr. and Mrs. Lee Cox of St. George have returned home after visiting here for some time.

Mr. Evelyn Prince has returned home from St. George where she has been visiting her parents.

Miss Pearl Pace, who is attending the B. A. C., came home last evening for a short stay.

Stockmen are busy gathering cattle for a sale in the near future.

Local hunters have been very successful this year. Nearly every one brought home a deer.

Washington County News
November 21, 1921

New Harmony, Nov 21 —Some of the M I A, officers were here from Cedar yesterday. Their visit was much appreciated

Mr. and Mrs Grant Hale have moved to Lund for the winter where Mr. Hale has employment.

Mrs Orson Hammond and Emily Grant have gone to Cedar to have their tonsils removed

Mrs Alex Taylor has gone to Enoch to visit with her parents for awhile

Mr and Mrs Tom Mosdell of Hamilton's Fort were in town yesterday

I. G Pace of Cedar City was in town Saturday buying cattle.

Mrs Emma Grant and son Roy of New Harmony spent last week here with Mrs Grant's daughter, Mrs. Gladys Whitehead.

Washington County News
December 12, 1921

New Harmony, Dec 12 —Mrs Lottie Kelsey has been very ill the last few days She was taken to Cedar today where she will receive medical treatment

Mr and Mrs. Eldon Schmutz returned home today from the goat herd where they have been for the past three weeks

Mrs Morris Whitehead of St. George is here visiting with her parents, Mr and Mrs Ed Grant

Albert Mathis returned from Rockville yesterday where he had been on business

Mr. and Mrs Lee Cox of St George were in town yesterday.

Alex Taylor has gone to Loa on business

Washington County News
December 29, 1921

PRINCE-REBER

Mr George Lawrence Prince and Mrs Rhoda Oviatt were married in the St George temple Tuesday Dec 27 1921

The bride is a daughter of Mr and Mrs Frederick Reber of Santa Clara an accomplished young lady who is very highly esteemed she has been teaching in the county schools during the past ten years and is at present teaching at Hurricane The bridegroom is a son of Mrs Reese Davis of New Harmony an industrious farmer and stock raiser of exemplary character

Handsome cards announce that they will be At Home at New Harmony Utah after June 1 1922

The News joins in all good wishes for the happiness of the newly wedded pair

The death of Mrs Frank Kelsey of New Harmony December 17th following an operation at the local hospital was a shock to the community Her husband and two children and other relatives remain to mourn her loss The many friends of the family in Iron county extend heartfelt sympathy to the bereaved ones — Iron County Record

NEW HARMONY.

Our local government weather observer reports over 12 inches of rainfall during the last three weeks.

The Misses Juanita and Fern Davis were home from school to spend the Christmas holidays. Also Orren Taylor and Pearl Pace.

The holidays passed off very quietly here. Stormy weather put the damper on everything except a few dances.

Mrs. Antone B. Prince slipped on the linoleum and fell last week, fracturing her right knee very severely. She has been in much pain, but is better at present.

Irving Prince. Clark Pace, Will Prince and Evelyn Prince are spending the holidays in Dixie.

Lawrence Prince of this place and Mrs. Rhoda Oviatt of Santa Clara, were married in St. George at the temple, on December 27. Mrs. Prince is at present teaching school at Hurricane. However, handsome cards announce that their place of residence after June 1 to be New Harmony. We welcome them to our community and wish the happy couple a joyful and prosperous married life.

New Harmony Jan 9—Vilate Prince who met with the misfortune to break her leg about three weeks ago is recovering slowly

Mr and Mrs Charley Mosdell returned from Cedar City last Tuesday where they had been visiting for a few days

Mr and Mrs Batty of Idaho are here visiting with their daughter, Mrs J L Prince

Bert Grant and Ezra Haden went to Parowan last week to get bounty on their furs

William Taylor returned from Cedar Thursday where he had been on business

Mr and Mrs Berry Williams of Kanarra were in town yesterday.

EXPOSURE MAY COST MAN S LIFE

Price Jan 12—John A Mathis one of the best known cattlemen in this part of the state will probably lose his left leg and may die as the result of freezing and exposure for two days in the Coal Creek canyon region above Sunnyside

After having been lost for two days in a blizzard with nothing to eat but a loaf of bread Mr Mathis was rescued last evening shortly before dark by J D Critchlow and E D Lee a Nine Mile rancher When discovered he was staggering along half frozen and was in such a state of exhaustion and bewilderment that he did not recognize his rescuers

Mr Mathis was quickly conveyed to the Lee ranch where it was found that his feet and hands were frozen his left leg as far up as the knee As soon as word reached Price physicians were sent to his aid It is understood tonight that his condition is critical and that he will lose his left leg if not his life

Mr Mathis left Price last Friday by horseback with J D Critchlow also of Price to round up cattle in the Coal Creek canyon country At Coal creek pass they separated agreeing to meet next day in the park at the head of Soldier canyon Mathis continued on but Critchlow turned back later and remained all night at the Young ranch The next morning Critchlow reached the point where he and Mathis had agreed to meet but Mathis was not there Critchlow then went back twelve miles to follow the trail of Mathis from the point where they had separated but the snow had covered the trail and the task was hopeless Critchlow then returned to Price and reported the matter after which thirty five men in automobiles enlisted in the search for the missing man

The country was scoured on both sides of the mountain but no trace of Mathis was found until early last evening when Critchlow and Lee discovered him more dead than alive stumbling along in the direction of Whitmore park some miles from the Lee ranch When found Mr Mathis still clutched a piece of dry frozen bread in his hand It is not known what became of his horse

Mr Mathis who is 44 years of age has ranged stock in Carbon county for thirty years He is a nephew of President Henry G Mathis of Carbon stake and has a wife and eight children —Salt Lake Tribune

The unfortunate man is a son of Henry Mathis of New Harmony and a cousin of Wallace B Mathis of St George He was married to Rachael Cottam a daughter of Pres Thomas P Cottam of this city, who died some time ago

Washington County News
January 19, 1922

OBITUARY—LOTTIE B KELSEY

Lottie Ballard Kelsey wife of Frank Kelsey of New Harmony died Dec 17 after a short illness

Besides her immediate family her husband and two little boys Verl and Merlin she leaves a father David Ballard Brothers and sisters and a host of friends who deeply feel the great loss

In her death the New Harmony ward lost one of its most energetic and conscientious workers one who was always willing and ready to help the sick the needy and aid in ward enterprises She was an officer in the Relief Society and the Primary at the time of her death

Her cheerfullness frankness and thoughtfulness of others won the love of everyone who knew her

New Harmony Jan 23 —Mrs Karl Phippan of Carey Idaho who came here to attend the funeral of her sister in law Mrs Frank Kelsey has returned home

Miss Madge Jones of Grafton is here working for Krank Kelsey

Mrs LeGrande Pace of Cedar City is here visiting for a few days

The weather has been extremely cold for the last week but has moderated now which is a welcome change

Wilford Bastian has returned from Dixie where he has been for some time

Walter Spencer of Denver Colorado was in town Saturday

Elder Donald Schmutz of New Harmony has been appointed president of the West Iowa conference He sends greetings to his many friends in this section Elder Schmutz has been 14 months in the mission field and is enjoying his labors immensely

FROM NEW HARMONY.

William Chis is home from the sheep herd for a short visit.

Fred Slack of Toquerville is in town.

Miss Madge Jones of Grafton is here working for Frank Kelsey.

Mr. and Mrs. Legrande Pace of Cedar City are visiting here.

Mr. and Mrs. Reese Davis attenled the funeral of Mr. Davis' brother of Myron F. in Kanarra last week.

A benefit social and dance was given Friday night in which $35 was collected to send to our missionary.

G. L. Prince as returned from Dixie where he has been on a business and pleasure trip.

Messrs. Alex Taylor and Wilford Bastian have been to St. George on business.

Mrs. Florence Phippen of Idaho, who has been ere for several weeks visiting with relatives and friends, has returned home.

Iron County Record
February 10, 1922

NEW HARMONY.

Mrs, Anthon Prince has gone to St. George to visit her parents,

The Misses Nora Ballard and Edna Russel of Grafton are here visiting.

Mr. G. L. Prince is in Hurricane visiting with his family

Mr. and Mrs. Chas Mosdell spent last week in Cedar visiting relatives.

Mr. and Mrs. Wm. Chinn are the proud parents of a fine baby boy that arrived January 28th.

Mrs, Wilford Bastian has gone to Grafton to visit her sister, Mrs. Lamar Terry.

The Y. M. and Y. L. association entertained the community with a very pleasing drama called "All Tangledg Up." The play was a success.

Washington County News
February 21, 1922

New Hatmony Feb 21 — Funeral services were held yesterday for Mrs Delta Hammond who died on Feb 18th of pneumonia after a brief illness of only a few days   The speakers were Albert F Mathis James E Taylor and Wm P Taylor Her children who survive her are Mrs Mary Duffin of Idaho Mrs H A Pace Orson Hammond and William Chinn all of this place She will be greatly missed as she was loved and respected by all

Mrs Myrtle Andreason of Salt Lake who came to see her grandmother Mrs Hammond during her illness is still here visiting friends

Mr and Mrs Orren Kelsey have returned from Overton Nev where they have been for some time

Mrs Josephine Hale of Lund is here visiting with her parents Mr and Mrs Orren Kelsey

Miss Iva Knell of Newcastle has been here for several days visiting with relatives

Miss Pearl Pace who has been attending the B A C came home last week

Mrs Emily Grant and Vilate Prince are in St George

Iron County Record
March 3, 1922

NEW HARMONY.

Miss Iva Knell is here visiting with relatives.

Mr. Charlie Mosdell is out of town for a few days.

Albert Mathis and George Schmutz have gone south with their sheep.

Mrs. Clarence Englestead spent two days in Hurricane last week.

Orson Hammond came home from Nevada to be with his mother during her illness.

Mrs. Mary Dufton from Idaho, is here for a short visit with relatives and friends.

Vera Dennet of Grafton has returned home after visiting here a few days.

Mrs. Myrtle Anderson of Salt Lake City came to attend her grandmother's funeral, Mrs. Delta Hammond.

On the morning of the 18th Mrs. Delta Hammond passed away, after being sick six days with pneumonia. She leaves four children, twenty-four grand-children, and four great grand-children. She will be missed very much in the Ward, and we all mourn our great loss.

Iron County Record
March 10, 1922

NEW HARMONY

John Condie is recovering from a bad case of pneumonia.

Mr. Clarence Englestead has gone to work for H. A. Pace in Dixie.

Although being very careful and the quarantine law enforced the "flu" has found its way in two homes.

Mrs. Rhoda Prince is here for a few days while school in Hurricane is closed on account of "flu".

Alex Taylor and Ezra Haden have returned from Dixie where they have been on business.

Mrs. Anthon Prince is back after spending several weeks in St. George with her parents.

Our school teacher Mr. Elmer Taylor has recovered from a bad case of lagrippe.

Evelyn Prince and family are home after spending the winter in St. George, and are now bed-fast with the "flu."

Mrs. Emma Grant has returned home after spending some time in St. George with her daughter, Mrs. Morris Whitehead.

Iron County Record
March 17, 1922

NEW HARMONY.

Miss Mamie Grant is up and around again after having an attack of appendcitis.

Mr. Eldon Schmutz has returned home from the goat herd.

Mr. Lawrence Prince has gone to Hurricane on business.

Mr. Delbert Woolsey has gone back to his ranch after being here with his family a few days.

Andrew Schmutz has returned to his goat herd.

The New Harmony drama troup is going to put on a drama here next Saturday, March 18th.

Washington County News
March 20, 1922

New Harmony Mar 20 —The M I A staged a comedy All A Mis take to an appreciative audience Saturday night They will take the play to Kanarra Friday and Enoch Saturday night

William Chinn has moved back to his old home James E Taylor has purchased his new home and is now living in it

Mrs Morris Whitehead of St George is here visiting with her parents Mr and Mrs E Grant

Mr and Mrs Wilford Bastian have returned from Dixie where they have been for some time

J D Neilson returned from St George Friday where he went on business

Lee Cox of Cedar City was in town today on business

Washington County News
March 27, 1922

New Harmony Mar 27 —The Dra
matic Company went to Newcastle
Saturday and presentd the comedy
All a Mistake, returning yesterday
They will play it tonight in Kanarra

County Assessor A B Andrus of
St George was in town today on business

Charley Mosdell has returned from
Dixie where he has been for some
time

Jas G Knell of Newcastle returned
home today after spending a few days
here

Mr Timothy and Mrs Wilford Bas
tian have returned to Vernal

Bp H A Pace and Alex Taylor
have gone to the sheep herd

Alex Urie of Hamiltons Fort was in
town today on business

Antone Prince went to Cedar today
on business

Washington County News
April 3, 1922

New Harmony April 3 —A W
Pace has returned home from
Toquerville and Hurricane where he
has been on business

C B Pace made a business trip to
Hurricane and St George last week
He says that end of the county looks
like summer

Mrs Ashby W Pace is spending a
few days in Newcastle visiting
friends and relatives

Clark Pace is in town for a few
days   He is attending the B A C
at Cedar City

Will Prince has returned home af
ter spending the winter in Cedar City

Herbert Knell is here shearing
goats for Schmutz Bros

The weather is unusually cold for
the time of year   There were light
frosts Sunday and Monday mornings
which did some damage to fruit al-
monds and apricots principally   It
rained here all last night and is rain
ing this morning   It is snowing in
the northern part of the county
Burgess Ranch reporting six inches
of new snow and New Harmony 14
inches at 8 o clock this morning and
still snowing

Iron County Record
April 7, 1922

NEW HARMONY

Mr. Henry A. Pace spent Monday in Cedar on business.

Mrs. Verna Pace is at Newcastle visiting friends and relatives.

Mr. Clarence Englestead has gone to Salt Lake City on business.

The Schmutz Bros. are here shearing their goats.

Mr. John Condie and family moved to Cedar for an indefinte time.

March 31, Mr. Will Prince of this place and Miss Lida Cox of St. George were married.

Mrs. Alex Taylor is in Enoch visiting with her parents, Mr. and Mrs. John M. Armstrong.

Miss Pearl Pace who is attending the B. A. C. at Cedar spent the week end here visiting her parents.

Mrs. Delbert Woolsey and family have returned to their ranch after being here all winter.

Mr. Berry Williams and family of Kanarra spent Sunday here with Mrs. Williams' mother, Mrs. Reese Davis.

On March 31 the town gave Mr. and Mrs. James E. Taylor and famly a house warming. Everyone present had an enjoyable time, in playing games, and playing music.

Washington County News
April 17, 1922

New Harmony April 17 —Will Prince and Miss Lida Cox of St George were married in Parowan Apr 1st Mrs Prince returned to St George to finish the school year Mr Prince is a well respected young man of this place and his many friends wish them much happiness

Ashby Pace Charley Mosdell Geo Prince Bert Grant Evelyn Prince and Irving Prince have gone to Dixie to sheer sheep

Mrs Amber Schmutz and William Taylor went to Cedar today to have Mrs Schmutz s little girl operated on

Some of our townsmen are work ing on the county road about two miles from town

Mrs Viola Taylor is in Enoch vis iting with her parents

Mrs Charley Mosdell has gone to Cedar City

New Harmony Apr 24 The appricot trees are in bloom now and we are hoping that the fruit will not get killed this year like it did last

Last Monday evening the Primary Assn gave an entertainment, the different parts being very well taken

Clark Pace and Lawrence Prince have returned from Hurricane where they spent the week end

A baby girl was born to Mr and Mrs Clarance Englestead, Apr 22

Mr and Mrs Will Prince went to St George yesterday

John Armstrong of Enoch was in town Saturday

Mrs Eldon Schmutz has gone to Salt Lake City.

PRINCE-COX

Married at Parowan April 1 Mr William Prince and Miss Lida Cox

The bride is a daughter of Mr and Mrs Warren Cox of this city a charming and vivacious young lady who is very highly esteemed by a large circle of friends The groom is a highly respected resident of New Harmony

The News joins the many friends of the young couple in all good wishes

NEW HARMONY

Miss Leon Russell is in Hurricane visiting with her mother.

* * *

Miss Nora Ballard is here visiting with friends.

* * *

Miss Irene Ford is here for a few weeks working.

* * *

Mr. John Armstrong spent a day here visiting with his daughter Mrs. Alex Taylor.

* * *

Mr. and Mrs. Henry A. Pace spent two days in Cedar last week on business.

* * *

Mr. and Mrs. Clarence Englestead are the proud parents of a fine baby girl, which arrived at their home April 22th.

NEW HARMONY

Mr. Harry Leigh was a town business visitor to-day.

* * *

Mrs. Evelyn Prince is home again from St. George.

* * *

Lawrence Prince and Clark Pace made a trip to Hurricane last week.

* * *

Will Prince is back after spending a few days in St. George with his wife.

* * *

Mr. Alex Taylor is home from Dixie where he has been for sometime.

* * *

Mrs. Amber Schmutz left Sunday for the mission field where she will join her husband.

* * *

Roy Grant and family have moved back to their ranch after being here all winter.

* * *

Will Woolsey of Hurricane was here last Friday and took part in the farewell party that the town gave to Mrs. Aamber Schmutz.

* * *

DASTARDLY POISONING AT NEW HARMONY

Co Atty Geo R Lund Sheriff Wilford Goff and Jos W Prince went to New Harmony Sunday to investi gate an alleged attempt to poison a family and the killing by the same means of two valuable horses

It appears from what the county officials learned that Mrs Kelsey was preparing breakfast at the home of her father Francis Prince one of the best known and most highly re spected residents of New Harmony She made some coffee and on tasting it noticed it was bitter She threw it out and made some more when Mr Prince came in, he tasted the freshly made coffee and said at once strych nine the poison having apparently been placed in the kettle

After breakfast they went to the stable to water the horses out of a trough Twenty minutes after drink ing the horses died apparently of poisoning

Mr Prince then notified the coun ty officers

Sheriff Goff obtained a sample of the water from the horse trough Unfortunately the kettle and coffee pot had been emptied into a slop bucket which in turn had been emp tied onto the ash heap, samples of this heap where the water had been thrown were obtained and the sam ples were then sent to state chemist Harms for analysis

Sheriff Goff believes it was a pre meditated attempt to kill the Prince family, consisting of Mr and Mrs Francis Prince and their daughter, Mrs Kelsey He has no clue to work on as Mr Prince is not known to have an enemy Mr Prince is so well liked that it is hard to believe that anyone would attempt to do him or his an injury

Investigations are being continued

FRANK P. KELSEY IS HELD FOR POISONING

Frank P Kelsey of New Harmony was brought before Justice Ellis J Pickett Monday charged with having attempted to poison Francis Prince and members of his family and poisoning two horses particulars of which were given in The News last week

Defendant waived a hearing and sufficient evidence being offered to justify holding him over Justice Pickett bound him over to the district court fixing bonds at $6 000 in two bonds one of $5 000 the other $1 000 Up to time of going to Press bondsmen had not been secured

KELSEY RELEASED ON BONDS

Frank P Kelsey who is held to the district court for alleged poisoning of two horses and attempting to poison Francis Prince and members of his family at New Harmony was released last Friday afternoon on $6000 bonds furnished by David Ballard of Grafton and William Chinn of New Harmony.

Iron County Record
May 26, 1922

NEW HARMONY.

Edwin Higbee of Toquerville was a town visitor last week.

* * *

Miss Vern Davis is home. She has been at St. George going to school.

* * *

Miss Juanita Davis is in Kanarra visiting her sister, Mrs. Berry Williams.

* * *

Miss Minnie Pace is home again after having spent the winter in Hurricane teaching school.

* * *

Miss Velva Prince of St. George is here visiting with her grandparents Mr. and Mrs. Francis Prince.

* * *

Misses Pearl and Myrtle Pace are home. They have been at C___ tending the B. A. C. the ____ar at____ past winter.

* * *

Albert Mathis and family have moved back to their field after being in town all winter so the children could attend school.

New Harmony May 22 —Miss Minnie Pace and Mrs Lawrence Prince have returned from Hurricane where they have been teaching school the past winter

The Misses Juanita and Fern Davis have returned from St George where they have been attending the D N C

Mrs L C Pace and daughter Merle have returned from Cedar City where they have been the past winter

Mr and Mrs Albert Mathis and family have moved to their farm on the flat for the summer

Yesterday was Primary Ward Conference Some of the Stake officers were in attendance

Miss Pearl Pace is home again after attending the B A C at Cedar City

Some of the S S Stake officers from Parowan were here yesterday

Mrs Lorenzo Prince has gone to Idaho to see her father, who is ill

Miss Velva Prince of St George is here visiting relatives

New Harmony June 5 —Last week the young women met at the home of Olive Chinn and organized a club Vilate Prince being president and Minnie Pace Susie Taylor and Eva Schmutz amusement committee

The young folks had a chicken supper at the home of Antone Prince last night A very pleasant time was enjoyed by all

A baby girl was born to Mr and Mrs J D Neilson May 28th Mother and babe doing nicely

Will Chinn returned from his sheep herd Thursday where he has been for some time

Mr and Mrs LeGrande Pace of Cedar City were in town yesterday

Some of the Stake Presidency from Cedar were here Sunday

Mr James Irving Prince of New Harmony and Miss Mary Edna Russell of Grafton were married in the St George temple June 8

NEW HARMONY

——oo——

The little infant daughter of Mr. and Mrs. James Neilson is quite ill.

——oo——

On June the second a fine baby girl arrived at the home of Mr. and Mrs. Delbert Woolsey.

——oo——

Mr. James E. Taylor has been bed fast the past two weeks with kidney trouble.

——oo——

Mr. and Mrs. David Hurchi and Mr. and Mrs. Claude Hurchi were visitors of Mr. and Mrs. Elmer Talyor.

——oo——

Mrs. Antone Prince has gone to St. George to visit with her mother Mrs. Rachel Cotton.

——oo——

Mrs. Elmer Taylor has gone to Hurricane to visit with her parents Mr. and Mrs. David Hurchi.

——oo——

Mr. Irving Prince of this place and Miss Edna Russel of Grafton were married in the St. George Temple June 5.

——oo——

Lost Sun. night the young married and single people had a chicken supper at Mr. and Mrs. Antone Prince's farm.

——oo——

Last week Mr. and Mrs. George Prince gave a wedding reception for their sons Irving and William H. and Edna Russel and Lida Cox. A large crowd was present, and a plesant evening was spent by everyone. At a reasonable hour a dainty lunch was served.

Washington County News
June 26, 1922

New Harmony June 26 —Mrs James E Taylor has returned home from the hospital where she has been for several days in a critical condition She is now much improved

Mrs Elmer Taylor a member of a fishing party was badly burned in the face while opening a can of beans

Mrs A W Pace has returned from Newcastle after spending two weeks with her father Jas G Knell

W W Pace and family from Thatcher Ariz was here Tuesday the guests of Mrs L A Pace

Mr and Mrs Wm Chinn have gone to Newcastle to visit the latter s sister Mrs R Platt

Grant Hale and J David Leigh from Lund were here last week on business

Mr and Mrs Lee Cox from Cedar City are here visiting relatives and friends

Mrs R B Naegle from Toquerville is here visiting her mother Mrs L A Pace

A number of our townspeople attended conference at Cedar City Sunday

Mr and Mrs William H Prince from Cedar City are here visiting

Bp Henry A Pace is having the plumbing done in his house

Mrs Lawrence Prince has gone to Santa Clara to visit

A W Hall from Enterprise spent the week end here

Mrs Bert Grant has gone to Spanish Fork to visit

Washington County News
July 10, 1922

New Harmony July 10 —The celebration here on the 4th was very successful There were cannons and serenading at day break a splendid program at 10 30 sports and refreshments in the afternoon and a dance at night There was a dance the following night On the 6th there were horse races between Kanarra and Harmony

The Boy Scouts and their leaders Wm P and Elmer Taylor are intending to go to Pine Valley for the M I. A. outing the 19th

Mr and Mrs John Humphries and Mr and Mrs Harvey Dalton of Hurricane were here yesterday on business

Mr and Mrs Alex Taylor have returned from Cedar City where the former has been for some time

Mr and Mrs Antone Prince Mr and Mrs Reese Davis went to Hurricane Wednesday on business

Mr and Mrs Delbert Woolsey and family of Woolsey s ranch were in for the 4th celebration

Miss Merle Pace has gone to Toquerville to visit with her sister Mrs R B Naegle

Mrs Evelyn Prince has returned from St George where she has been for a while

Mr and Mrs Berry Williams of Kanarra were town visitors last week.

Mr and Mrs Wilson Imlay of Hurricane were in town today on business

Mrs Chas Walker and daughter Miss Ruth of St. George are here

Mr and Mrs Irving Prince went to Grafton for the 4th

George Platt of Mountain Meadows was in town last week

Washington County News
July 18, 1922

New Harmony July 18 —Thurs day evening the Ladies club enter tained at a lawn party for the club members and pratners Refresh ments were served and a very pleas ant time was enjoyed

A most pleasant surprise party was sprung on Miss Minnie Pace yester day by a number of friends the oc casion being her birthday A very enjoyable time was had

Mrs Clara Grant and children have returned from Spanish Fork where they have been for some time

Mrs Jas Jennings who is suffering from a goitre has gone to Cedar to consult a physician

Orren Taylor has returned from Cedar where he has been working for some time

Antone Prince and Elmer Taylor went to Hurricane yesterday on busi- ness

Mrs Susan B Pace has gone to Lehi to attend a family reunion

Iron County Record
July 21, 1922

NEW HARMONY

—oo—

H. A. Pace and Albert Mathis spent a day in Cedar on business.

—oo—

The Club members gave Miss Min- nie Pace a surprise party July 17. A jolley time was had.

—oo—

Last Thursday evening the ladies Club entertained their partners at a party at the home of Miss Minnie Pace. A very enjoyable time was had

—oo—

Mrs. Susan E. Pace is back after at- tending the Jolley family reunion held at Saratogo Hot Springs Resort in Utah County.

Washington County News
July 31, 1922

New Harmony, July 31 — William P Taylor had the misfortune to be thrown from a horse recently and hurt his back   He has not been able to get about much but is improving

Our missionaries, Mr and Mrs Donald Schmutz, who are laboring in Council Bluffs Iowa, report the work progressing nicely in that field

Scout Master Elmer Taylor with his Scouts have returned from a fishing trip to Grass valley   They had an exceedingly pleasant time

Some of our pleasure seekers took lunch and spent the 24th in Sawyer s canyon   They returned very enthusiastic over their outing

Mrs Alex Taylor entertained the club at her home last Thursday   All enjoyed the afternoon   Refreshments were served

A number of our town s people attended the Carnival at Enterprise and report a most splendid time

Mrs Reber of Santa Clara is here spending a few days with her daughter, Mrs Lawrence Prince

Mr and Mrs A W Pace have gone on Kanarra mountain to spend a few days

The ward has recently purchased a piano for the meeting house

Washington County News
August 15, 1922

New Harmony   Aug 15 — Last Thursday evening all club members and partners had a chicken supper at the home of Bp Pace   A splendid time was enjoyed

Mr and Mrs Jesse Whipple and family of Overton Nev, were here last week on their way to Idaho

Clarence Englestead has returned from Mount Carmel where he has been for some time

Miss Merle Pace has returned from Toquerville where she has been for some time

R A Kirker has returned from Price where he has been on business

Some of the D N C teachers were here yesterday on business

A W Hall of Enterprise was here a few days last week

Washington County News
August 21, 1922

New Harmony, Aug 21—Last week Rulon Taylor had the misfortune to get his jaw bone broken while coming from Minersville

Yesterday some members of the Cedar Com were down and gave us some musical numbers during Sunday school which was very much enjoyed

Mr and Mrs Antone Prince went to Cedar City today on business

Dr F H Petty and family of Cedar City were in town yesterday

Mr Chas Allen of Orderville was in town last week on business

Washington County News
September 4, 1922

New Harmony, Sept 4—James Knell of Newcastle and Mrs J D Cox of Cedar City were in town the last of the week

Yesterday some of the Stake officers were down from Parowan for S S ward conference

Mrs Minnie Pace has returned from Toquerville where she had been for a few days

Mrs Elmer Taylor went to Hurricane last week, intending to stay for a while.

Mrs Mary K Spencer of Newcastle is here visiting friends and relatives

Thos Carlott of Provo is in town on business

Mr and Mrs Charles Walker returned Monday from New Harmony where Mrs Walker has been spending the summer.

NEW HARMONY LON BEATEN

In the case of the State vs Charles Hollis and Samuel Barwick heard before Justice of the Peace Geo C Murdock Tuesday the defendents charged with assault and battery on Vernon Taylor of New Harmony employed as a guard at the railroad shops in Milford entered a plea of guilty and each was fined $25 00 — Beaver City Press

Iron County Record
September 13, 1922

NEW HARMONY.

——oo——

Mrs. Ed. Grant has gone to Salt Lake City to visit with her daughter, Mrs. Morris Whitehead.

——oo——

Mr. and Mrs. Antone Prince, Mr. and Mrs. Elmer Taylor and Miss Minnie Pace went to Hurricane last week to attend the "Peach Day" held there.

——oo——

Mr. ond Mrs. Claude Knell and sister were here a few days last week visiting Mr. and Mrs. Ashby Pace.

——oo——

Mr. Will Taylor and family are over their attack of throat trouble.

——oo——

Recently several of our cattle men sold a large number of steers. Mr. Elmer Taylor took the animals to Salt Lake City.

All roads lead to Cedar City September 13-14-15.

——oo——

The Baseball game during the Meet will be between Milford and Cedar. It will be a real baseball battle.

——oo——

Have you ever seen a man dropping hundreds of feet thru the air? Take it from us, there's a kick in it. See this at the Legion Race Meet.

——oo——

We know you are thinking about this Race Meet as well as talking about it. Well, "the thought that is father to the wish" and we are prepared to satisfy that wish.

COURT ORDERS BODY TO BE EXHUMED

The case of the State vs Frank P Kelsey was called in the district court last Thursday morning before Judge Wm F Knox

The charge is felony it being alleged that the defendant did knowingly mingle strychnine with water on May 15 1922 with the intention that the same should be taken by Eliza Kelsey, Francis Prince and Elizabeth Prince (mother and grandparents respectively of the accused)

Pros Atty W B Higgins stated that he had been unable to locate one important witness Wm P Boyce for the state and asked for a continuance of the case

Atty David H Morris for defendant resisted this motion and asked the court to proceed with the case

Court adjourned until 2 p m and upon resuming the attorney for the State presented a sworn affidavit that the State had used the utmost diligence to prepare the case but was unable to furnish much needed evidence and asked for a continuance of the case

Atty Morris again resisted the motion for a continuance After arguments of attorneys Judge Knox ordered the case continued for the term the case being set for hearing on Dec 12

Pros Atty Higgins for the State presented request to the Court asking it to authorize the Justice of the Peace of New Harmony precinct to disinter the body of defendant s wife and secure proper assistance in having the stomach removed and sent to the state chemist to ascertain if death resulted from poison

Judge Knox issued an order on the Precinct Justice at New Harmony to act if unable, then the work to be done by Justice Ellis J Pickett of St George with instructions to send the stomach etc , by special messenger to the state chemist.

The substance of the affidavit presented by Atty Higgins to Judge Knox is as follows:

Since the beginning of this session of the Court I have had conversations with certain witnesses in this case in behalf of the State and was informed and believe that Lottie Kelsey, deceased wife of the defendant immediately prior to her death was taken suddenly ill with violent convulsions and extreme pain in her stomach and kidneys and showed many symptoms of poisoning That prior to her death defendant wrote a letter to Dr A N Leonard of Salt Lake City, requesting said Dr Leonard to sign a statement as physician to the Intermountain Life Insurance Co stating that said Lottie Kelsey was eligible as far as her health was conserned for a life insurance policy In his letter to Dr Leonard Frank P Kelsey falsely stated the condition of health of his wife, stating she was not then in a pregnant condition knowing full well that she was in such a condition, in said letter to Dr Leonard Frank P Kelsey offered to pay the said Dr Leonard $25 if he would sign said certificate embodying these falsehoods and convey the same to the said life insurance company, Dr Leonard in response to said letter said he would not comply with the request That at the time of death of said Lottie Kelsey said Frank P Kelsey had already taken out some sort of life insurance policy upon the person of Lottie Kelsey, and at the time of writing to Dr Leonard was seeking to take out more life insurance on Lottie Kelsey

Justice Ellis J Pickett Sheriff Wilford Goff, Dr D A McGregor and George F Whitehead chairman of county commissioners and Miss Mary Whitehurst went last Saturday to New Harmony where they were joined by Dr Menzies Macfarlane of Cedar City Dr H H Wilkinson of Hurricane and Dr D A Leonard of Salt Lake City The body of Mrs Lottie Kelsey was disinterred from the grave where it had lain for about a year, and the stomach and some other organs were removed and sent by special messenger to the State chemist for analysis

New Harmony Sept 25 —The peo ple here were greatly schocled at the sudden illness and death of the in fant daughter of Mr and Mrs Walter Spencer Mrs Spencer being here on a visit from Newcastle The baby was taken to Cedar and operated on for telescoping of the bowels but on- ly lived a few hours afterwards The funeral was held at Newacstle and the remains were taken to Pinto for burial We all feel to sympathize with the bereaved parents

Juanita and Fern Davis, Pearl Pace and Reed and Marion Prince have gone to St George to attend the D N C this winter

Mrs L A Pace and daughter Merle have gone to Cedar for the winter where the latter will attend the B A C

Mr and Mrs Delbert Woolsey of Woolsey s ranch have moved here for the winter to put the children in school

Mrs LeRoy Grant has moved in from the ranch to send her children to school

Alex Taylor is home again after being with the sheep herd for some time

Max Pace has gone to Cedar City for the winter

New Harmony Oct 19 —The Y L M I A was organized Sunday with Rose Schmutz as president, Sadie Grant and Eva Schmutz counselors Amber Schmutz as class leader and Emma G Neilson secretary

Mr and Mrs R B Naegle of Toquerville were here the fore part of the week They were guests of Mr and Mrs A W Pace

Mrs Morris Whitehead has return ed to her home in Salt Lake City af ter being here for the past month

Mr and Mrs A B Prince have re turned home from Salt Lake where they have been to the State Fair

Mr and Mrs Chas Burke of Vir gin are here visiting relatives and friends

Born a son to Mr and Mrs Henry Prisbrey, mother and babe doing nicely

Mrs Alex Taylor has gone to En och expecting to be gone for some time

Orren Taylor left Sunday for Cedar City to attend the B A C

E C Grant has returned to his work in Hurricane.

KELSEY CHARGED WITH FIRST DEG. MURDER

Frank P Kelsey was arrested at New Harmony yesterday on a charge of murder in the first degree it being alleged that he administered arsenic to his wife from the effects of which she died

The defendant was brought before the district court Sept 7 on a charge of felony it being alleged that he did mingle strychnine with water on May 15 1922 with the intention that the same should be taken by Eliza Kelsey Francis Prince and Flizabeth Prince (mother and grand-parents respectively of the accused) This case was continued At the same time the prosecuting attorney presented a request for the exhuming of the body of the wife of accused giving reasons in an affidavit Judge Knox made the order and directed that the organs be sent to the state chemist for analysis The returns from the state chemist showed that arsenic was found in the organs of Lottie Kelsey, deceased wife of the accused and Co Atty Geo R Lund Sheriff Wilford Goff and Deputy Sheriff F R Bentley went to New Harmony and arrested Kelsey on a capital charge Kelsey was out on $6000 bonds at the time He is now in the jail here

Miss Velva Prince returned Satur day from New Harmony where she spent some time visiting relatives

Washington County News
November 6, 1922

New Harmony Nov 6 —Word has
been received here recently that John
Pace of Price who was stricken ill
here about three weeks ago died of
Bright s disease

Mrs Rhoda B Prince returned
home from Salt Lake City last week
She was operated on there for goitre
and is getting along quite well

William Chinn is home from the
sheep herd where he has been for
some time

Mrs Josephine K Hale and children have gone north for the winter

Bp H A Pace and family have
gone to St George for the winter

Mr and Mrs Eldon Schmutz have
gone to Salt Lake for the winter

Henry l richrey went to St George
a few days ago on business

Washington County News
November 20, 1922

New Harmony, Nov 20 —Mrs
Sarah E Davis spent a few days in
St George last week on business
She was accompanied back by Mrs
Nancy Redd from Price

Mr and Mrs Antone Prince and
Mrs Elmer Taylor went to Cedar City
last Tuesday on business

Elmer and Rulon Taylor went to
Grass valley Saturday after cattle

Benj Williams of Kanarra was in
town last week on business

The preliminary hearing of Frank
Kelsey of New Harmony on suspic
ions of having administrated poison
to his wife will be held tomorrow
morning

New Harmony Nov 27 —Word was received here this morning that Henry Mathis of Price had passed away Bro Mathis was among the first settlers of this place The last few years he has been at Price with his children The remains will be brought here for burial

Frank Staheli of Washington and others have been here the past week threshing We were fortunate in having a streak of good weather while it was done

A town dinner was being planned for Thanksgiving but on hearing of the death of Bro Mathis it was given up

Reed and Marion Prince who are attending the D N C are home to spend Thanksgiving

Mrs Florence Phippan of Carey Idaho is here visiting with relatives

Mrs Edna R Prince has gone to Grafton to visit for a while

KELSEY TO BE TRIED, FIRST DEG. MURDER

Frank G Kelsey of New Harmony was brought before Justice Ellis J Pickett last Friday at 10 a m charged with first degree murder in that he did administer arsenic to his wife Lottie Kelsey on the 5th day of December 1921 from the effects of which she died Dist Court Stenographer Wm H Keller was present and took full notes of the proceedings The prosecution was conducted by W B Higgins district attorney and Geo R Lund county attorney Defendant was represented by Atty Schulder of King & Schulder Salt Lake and Atty D H Morris of this city A plea of not guilty was entered by defendant s counsel

No witnesses were produced by the defense Witnesses for the prosecution were Dr M J Macfarlane Cedar City, Dr D A McGregor St George, Dr Leonard of Salt Lake City State Chemist Herman Harms James F Taylor Mrs Reese Davis Mrs La Verna Englestead and Mrs Sadie Grant, all of New Harmony

Witnesses testified to the symptoms of the illness of Lottie Kelsey immediately after dinner on Dec 5 which had been prepared by the husband The doctors described the symptoms of arsenical poisoning and told of the exhumation of the remains of Lottie Kelsey and the parts sent to the state chemist

Mr Harms testified to receiving the organs and described the tests to which he subjected them in detail He described the Goodside test and the Marsh test both of which were used He made five different tests and found arsenic present each time in sufficient quantity to kill a person He made a final test to separate antimony from arsenic and was absolutely sure arsenic was taken into the stomach before death

At the conclusion of the taking of testimony, defendants s counsel moved that the case be dismissed

Justice Pickett held the defendent over to the district court without bail

[Note —We had intended to give a fuller account of the preliminary hearing and had taken a full report for that purpose But later decided not to do so because it appears that there may be difficulty in securing a jury to try the case That being so the best interest of the public is served in giving the brief synopsis as above —Ed]

Washington County News
December 4, 1922

New Harmony Dec 4 —Funeral services were held for Henry Mathis Thursday afternoon The speakers were Gottlieb Schmutz James D Taylor Orson Hammond and Bp H A Pace All were long acquaintances of Bro Mathis and spoke highly of him He is survived by four children James and John Mathis Mrs Mary Pace of Price and Albert Mathis of this place All of his children were in attendance at his funeral

Clarence Englestead has returned from his homestead near Long valley where he has been for sometime

Mrs Reese Davis is in Kanarra with her daughter Mrs Berry Williams who is very ill

Mrs Viola A Taylor has been here from ——— for a few days visiting relatives

Miss Fern Davis has returned to St George after spending a few days here

Lawrence Prince has gone to Hurricane on business

Washington County News
January 4, 1923

Born a son to Mr and Mrs William Prince of New Harmony in this city this morning

Washington County News
January 8, 1923

New Harmony January 8 —The Christmas holidays were spent here very pleasantly every one expressing themselves as having had an extra good time

Mr and Mrs Ashby Pace have returned from Newcastle where they spent the holidays

Mrs Alex Taylor returned from Enoch Friday where she has been for some time

Earl Clark of Kanab has been in town for the past two days

Mrs Reese Davis has been to Kanarra the past few days

Mrs Vilate Prince is in St George visiting relatives

Mrs Morris Whitehead of Salt Lake is here

Mrs Susan E Pace is in St George visiting relatives.

Washington County News
January 16, 1923

New Harmony Jan 16 —M D Higbee and J M Urie of Cedar City were missionaries at our Sunday services Their talks were very much enjoyed

George Millet of Cedar City was in town yesterday on business

Miss Iva Knell of Newcastle is here visiting relatives

Miss Stella Hammond returned from Cedar City yesterday where she has been for the past few days

Mrs Morris Whitehead was operated on at Cedar City last Wednesday She is getting along fairly well

Washington County News
February 6, 1923

New Harmony Feb 6 —Friday evening Jan 27 the M I Assns debated the subject of Income Tax Sarah Grant and LaVerna Englestead taking the affirmative and Albert Mathis and Elmer Taylor the negative It was very interesting

The young men chose sides and had rabbit hunts Friday and Saturday the losing side giving a dance Saturday night

Mrs Reese Davis has gone to Kanarra to visit her daughter Mrs Berry Williams who is very ill

It seems our winter weather is just commencing There is a foot of snow and it is very cold

A cottage meeting was held at the home of Jas E Taylor Jan 28 Ward teachers officiating

Susan E Pace has returned from St George where she has been visiting

Iron County Record
February 16, 1923

NEW HARMONY
——oo·——

There is now about eighteen inches of snow here, on the level and good prospects for more.

Bp. Henry A. Pace is in St. George visiting for a few days with his family.

Miss Estella Hammond, who was operated on for appendicitis on the 6th. is reported doing nicely.

The storms and extreme cold weather seems to be very hard on the livestock in this section.

Mrs. Gladys Whitehead is here visiting her parents and convalescing after an operation.

Mr. Vern Slack of Toquerville is here visiting his sister, Mrs. Delbert Woolsey.

Mr. Geary Page and others passed through here on their way home from Toquerville, where they had been visiting.

The little eight months old daughter of Mr. and Mrs. James D. Nielson, who has been very ill with an abcess in the head, is reported to be slowly improving.

FRANK P KELSEY DENIED
BOND PRIVILLGE ON APPEAL

Frank P Kelsey, 29, farmer of New Harmony is denied release on bail and remanded to the custody of the sheriff of Washington county to await trial for the alleged poisoning of his wife in an order issued by the state supreme court this morning

After Kelsey was denied bail by the Fifth district court the case was appealed to the supreme court on a writ of habeas corpus Mrs Kelsey died in December 1921 and the attending physician signed a warrant certifying death to have been caused by uremic poisoning Ten months later Kelsey s mother and grandparents became ill and several horses died after drinking from a neighboring spring

Coffee grounds which were thrown out after the mother and grandparents had complained that the coffee was bitter were collected and on examination declared to have contained strychnine

These circumstances led to suspicion concerning the death of Mrs Kelsey The body was exhumed and State Chemist Herman Harms on examination reported arsenic present in the stomach in quantities sufficient to have caused death A few weeks later Kelsey was bound over to the district court on a charge of murder in the first degree —Deseret News

New Harmony March 6 —Relatives of Jos Taylor had a party Thursday evening in his honor, at the home of Jas E Taylor A very pleasant time was enjoyed by all present

Virginia Prince a daughter of Mr and Mrs Antone Prince was operated on for appendicitis She is recovering nicely

Mrs Reese Davis is in Kanarra with her daughter Mrs Berry Williams who has recently been operated on

Orson Hammond has returned from Nevada where he has been working for some time

The Mutual staged their play "Blundering Billy at Kanarra Thursday night

George Millet of Cedar City has been in town for the past three days on business

Joseph Taylor of Idaho is here visiting relatives and friends

Mrs Limer Taylor has gone to Hurricane on business

J D Neilson has gone south to work for awhile

Mrs Eliza Kelsey is in St George on business

Washington County News
March 12, 1923

New Harmony Mar 12—Miss Mary Tolbert has returned to Paragonah after spending three weeks here

Evelyn Prince has returned from Salt Lake where he has been for some time

Albert Mathis went south last week with his sheep

George Tullis of Newcastle was in town last week

Antone Prince has taken his sheep to Dixie

Edd Grant has gone south to work

Iron County Record
March 16, 1923

NEW HARMONY

Orson Hammond has returned from Nevada, where he has been for some time with sheep.

Mrs. Reese Davis is home, having spent a number of weeks with her daughter Mrs. Berry Williams of Kanarra.

Antone Prince, Rulon Taylor, Reese Davis, James D. Nielson, and Albert Mathis have gone south with sheep.

The Mutual staged their play, "Blundering Billy", to an appreciative audience in Kanarra.

Mrs. Lee Cox of St. George is here visiting her parents Mr. and Mrs. George F. Prince.

Relatives of Joseph A. Taylor entertained in his honor at the home of James E. Taylor. Twenty five of his relatives were present. Cake and ice cream were served and all spent a pleasant evening.

New Harmony, March 19 — Mrs
Elmer Taylor has returned from Hurricane where she has been for the
past three weeks

Marion Prince, who is attending
the D N C was in town for a day or
two last week

Max Pace who is attending school
at the B A C is in town on business

Several of the townspeople went to
Cedar yesterday to attend conference

Mr and Mrs Will Prince of St
George are here visiting relatives

Judge D H Morris of St George
is in town on business

Mrs Lee Cox and children have returned to St George

Berry Williams of Kanarra was in
town yesterday.

Monroe Russell of Grafton is here
visiting.

KELSEY MURDER TRIAL STILL OCCUPIES COURT

After the jury was secured at noon
last Thursday in the case of the state
against Frank P Kelsey charged
with the murder of his wife Lottie
Kelsey as reported in last week s is
sue of the News the court took a
recess until 3 p m at which hour
district attorney Higgins began his
opening statement for the prosecu
tion It was set forth that it expect
ed to prove that about Dec 5 1921
Frank P Kelsey had asked his wife
to lie down while he prepared dinner
and that while partaking of this meal
she was taken violently ill, and continued to vomit intermittently for
several days, after which defendant s
mother had called Dr McFarlane,
and that he had treated her for toxemia pregnancy Also that defendant had previous to this taken out a
joint life insurance policy for himself and wife and had attempted to
take out a second policy The physician had refused to sign papers for
him on account of his physical condition and his wife had refused to be
examined for more insurance claiming that they already had enough insurance Defendant had then written to Dr Leonard asking him to
sign a certificate to the effect that
himself and wife were in fit physical
condition for an insurance policy, but
that Dr Leonard had refused to do
so stating that he could not do so
without examining them That after

the death of his wife defendant had sent the life insurance policy to Dr McFarlane asking him to collect the insurance and take out of the money received the pay for his professional services in attending his wife during her illness The prosecution expected to show that if Mr Kelsey had obtained the insurance that he attempted to obtain, it would have given him something like $20,000, and that he had made the claim that he would soon be on Easy street He proposed to show that prior to the death of his wife Kelsey had shown special affection for Miss Nora Ballard, and that on the death of his wife he had had the ring taken from his wife a finger and placed on the finger of Nora Ballard It was also proposed to show that the body was afterwards taken up by order of the court and parts of the organs sent to State Chemist Herman Harms who had discovered the presence of sufficient quantities of arsenic to cause her death and that no other kinds of poison were found

The first witness for the state was James B Taylor of New Harmony, who had known Frank P Kelsey and his wife since before their marriage He had seen Mrs Kelsey at Sunday school and meeting on Sunday, Dec

4 when she seemed well and cheerful Had been called to her home next day, when he found her quite ill, her face being flushed and she complaind of being thirsty and could keep nothing on her stomach Mrs Eliza Kelsey had told him that Frank and his wife had done a washing that morning and that when they finished Frank had told his wife to lie down and he would get dinner, which he did and while she was eating dinner she was taken ill Mrs Lottie Kelsey complained of pains in her head and back He next saw her when called to assist in placing her in the coffin after her death

The witness was cross examined by Mr King and stated that George Prince had asked him to visit Mrs Kelsey the first time, that he had talked about the conversation quoted prior to the time the body was exhumed but could not remember the exact date, had repeated the symptoms described prior to being told the symptoms of poison could not remember when he first mentioned that she was thirsty, had made no memorandum of the conversation, and could not tell the size of the bed room only that it was crowded

Wm B Taylor of New Harmony, had seen the dead body of Mrs Lottie

Kelsey the day of the funeral He was at her home the day before she was taken to the hospital Was called to administer to her and asked her if she would take some oil, and

Fix your fences, sidewalks, etc.

she said she could not keep anything on her stomach. Her face was flushed. He attended her funeral and went to the cemetery but defendant remained at home instead of accompanying his wife's remains to the burial ground.

The court then adjourned till 10 a m Friday when Wm B Taylor was cross examined by Mr King who brought out the fact that the day of the funeral was stormy and only a few people went to the cemetery.

Mrs Emma Grant the next witness told of Mr Kelsey coming to her home to borrow a thermometer to take his wife's temperature stating that he had assisted his wife with a washing on Monday and then told her to lie down while he got dinner which she did and that during the meal she was taken very ill though she was well in the morning.

Cross examination of witness pertained to the exact date of the sickness fo Mrs Kelsey.

Dr N Leonard of Salt Lake City testified to having been present with Drs Wilkinson of Hurricane McGregor of St George and Macfarlane of Cedar City, when portions of the vital organs of Mrs Kelsey were removed and placed in jars, and that he carried these parts to Salt Lake City and delivered them to State Chemist Harms. He testified to having received a letter from Frank P Kelsey inclosing certain papers and asking him to sign them certifying to the health of himself and wife in order to take out life insurance stating that he had not been able to pass the examination by local doctors; that he would pay him $25 for the service and stating that Lottie was feeling fine and was not pregnant. The witness refused to sign the papers without an examination. Had talked with Mr Kelsey about the letter later in his office and again in St George at which time the latter had said unless he could produce the letter, he proposed to deny it.

On cross examination it was brought out that witness had attended Mrs Kelsey during her first two confinments, had been the family physician until about five years ago, and had found no organic trouble in 1921 Mr Kelsey was treated by witness, after having been refused life insurance on account of his physical health and had told him that he thought he would soon be in a condition to pass the examination. Witness was also questioned as to the contents of the letter recived from defendant and as to his first attempt to repeat the contents of the letter, as well as his conversations with the defendant. Court then took recess until 2 p m.

At 2 p m the cross examination of Dr Leonard was continued. He stated that no portion of the brain, lungs or any portion of the clothing were taken from the body of Mrs Kelsey. He had prescribed for Mrs Lottie Kelsey about Dec 6, 1921, on a written request of defendant's mother. On redirect examination witness said the office girl heard the conversation with defendant in his office Also that the vital organs taken from the corpse were placed in two fruit jars one of which was taken by Dr Macfarlane and the other was delivered by witness to Mr Harms

State Chemist Herman Harms was called to the stand and detailed an account of the toxological examination made of the portions of the organs of Mrs Lottie Kelsey delivered to him by Dr Leonard Examination of Mr Harms was not completed at the time of adjournment of court

Saturday at 10 a m Mr Harms was again called to the witness stand and most of the morning session was occupied in the direct examination by the prosecution

Mr King then began the cross-examination of Mr Harms and asked if he had not refused to make a joint test with some reputable chemist, to which the state objected The jury was excused while counsel presented arguments to the court who sustained the objection giving Mr King permission to state as a matter of record what he expected to prove by these questions Under redirect examination witness further detailed symptoms of arsenic poisoning, and gave his opinion as to the amount of arsenic contained in commercial fly-paper.

Washington County News
April 6, 1923

Born in this city, a daughter to Mr and Mrs Evlyn Prince, of New Harmony, March 30

Washington County News
April 16, 1923

New Harmony Apr 16 —Mr and Mrs Ashby Pace returned from Newcastle last Thursday where the latter had been for two weeks

A daughter was born to Mr and Mrs Irving Prince Mar 25 at Cedar City

Mr and Mrs Kenneth Hirschi of Rockville are here visiting relatives

Mrs Viola Taylor has gone to Enoch to visit with relatives

Mrs Emma Neilson went to Cedar last week for medical aid

Mr and Mrs Albert Mathis went to Cedar today on business

Orren Kelsey went to Provo last week on business

Warren Taylor of Loa was in town yesterday

KELSEY ACQUITTED OF MURDER CHARGE

After the News went to press last Thursday the statement by Mrs Eve lyn Prince who is ill was read into the record to the effect that she left New Harmony for St George on Tuesday about three weeks before Christmas and that Frank Kelsey worked all day the Monday previous sawing wood

Dr S G Colange of Salt Lake de scribed symptoms of acute and chron ic cases of arsenical poisoning and those of eclampsia and toxemia of pregnancy and expressed the opinion after hearing symptoms described by Dr Macfarlane that Mrs Kelsey died of the latter complaint

Mrs Eliza Kelsey was recalled and again denied that she had told var ious parties that Frank got dinner Dec 5 and that after eating it Lottie was taken sick

Dr George E Robinson of Salt Lake also described symptoms of ar senical poisoning and eclampsia and declared that the body of Mrs Kelsey could have absorbed arsenic from the moisture in the ground through the principal of osmossis because of the coal iron and copper deposits within a few miles of the burial ground

Edwin Higbee testified to the pres ence of coal iron and copper within four to ten miles of the New Harm ony cemetery

Evelyn Prince was recalled by the state and asked if he told Mrs Gladys Whitehead that his grandpa and aunt Eliza wanted him to testify that Frank ate dinner at grandpa s the day they sawed wood and that was the day Lottie took sick but that he couldn t do it because it wasn t true, to which he replied only in part but denied saying they wanted him to testify to anything that wasn t true

Defense then rested and court took a recess till 9 30 a m Friday, at which time the state called Wm P Taylor one of the six witnesses by which it was proposed to impeach Mrs Eliza Kelsey The defense objected to the introduction of such testimony The jury was excused and after argument by counsel the court took it under advisement until the afternoon session at which time the objection was sustained

Wm W Taylor of Loa Utah was then called by the state in rebuttal, and testified to visiting New Harmony the week after Thanksgiving 1921 to place headstones at graves in the cemetery that he arrived there Sunday Nov 27, visited Francis Prince Monday or Tuesday when the wood was being sawed and left Friday, Dec 2 for Kanarra where he gave Riley D Williams a check dated Dec 4, to pay freight on headstones for graves there

James E Taylor testified to visiting the home of Francis Prince with his brothers W W Taylor and Penn Taylor the week following Thanksgiving when Frank Kelsey, Will and Evelyn Prince were sawing wood

Mrs James E Taylor also testified that the wood was sawed the Monday or Tuesday following Thanksgiving

Elmer Taylor remembered that W W Taylor came to New Harmony Sunday Nov 27 and left the latter part of the week prior to Lottie Kelsey s sickness On cross examination said he fixed the date by two checks written by him the day Mr Taylor came

Wm P Taylor testified that the inner walls of the Kelsey home were of adobe (Miss Leone Russell had described them as being of lighter material)

Gladys Grant Whitehead said that in November 1922 Evelyn Prince had told her that his grandma and aunt Eliza wanted him to testify that Frank ate dinner at his grandpa s the day they sawed wood and that was the day Lottie was sick but that he couldn t do it because it wasn t true

At 7 30 p m Riley G Williams testified that Warren Taylor came to Kanarra from New Harmony and that as they never came he still had the check uncashed

W P Taylor said Warren Taylor came to New Harmony Sunday, Nov 27 and left Friday, Dec 2 1921 Independence Taylor testified to the same dates

The state closed at 8 30 p m and Attorney King asked the court to instruct the jury for a verdict of not guilty

Judge W F Knox refused to take the case away from the jury as Defense Attorney S A King had asked be done Sufficient testimony had been introduced to warrant decision by the jury Judge Knox said and he ordered the arguments in the case be started

District Attorney William Higgins opened the argument for the state The greatest emphasis was laid upon the fact that Kelsey had prepared the last meal which Mrs Kelsey had eaten before she became violently ill and ten days later died in a hospital in Cedar City The symptoms of arsenical poisoning as described by experts and the symptoms of Mrs Kelsey's illness as told by neighbors and attending physicians coincided, Mr Higgins claimed

That three attempts had been made by Kelsey to obtain life insurance polices upon Mrs Kelsey's life against her will as stated by insurance agents was emphasized

Stress was laid upon the claim that Kelsey had had associations with Nora Ballard sister of Mrs Kelsey, which the relation of brother in law did not sanction

The prosecution also argued that Kelsey had taken out an unusually large life insurance policy for a man of his means upon his mother's life and that shortly thereafter she was poisoned with strychnine in a mysterious manner and that Kelsey attempted to have the event hushed up, claiming it would cause trouble if investigated

Former Judge D H Morris opened the argument for the defense He claimed that testimony had shown that Kelsey was not at his home when his wife took sick and therefore could not have prepared the meal which resulted so fatally for Mrs Kelsey Numerous New Harmony neighbors had testified that Kelsey was engaged in sawing wood at the home of his grandfather Judge Morris stated

That Kelsey had obtaind the life insurance policies in a legitimate manner and that it was legitimate for a man to own life insurance policies was alleged by Mr King who continued the argument for the defense

Kelsey's relations with Miss Ballard were at all times proper and legitimate he claimed and no undue conduct between them had at any time taken place

Attorney General Harvey Cluff presented the final argument for the prosecution He attempted to establish a motive for the crime in claiming that Kelsey was in financial difficulties had heavily insured his wife's life and was greatly enamored of Nora Ballard

Judge Knox then delivered his charge to the jury which was a very lengthy one Part of his charge to the jury follows In this case if you should find and believe from the

evidence beyond a reasonable doubt that arsenic was found in the body of the deceased Lottie Kelsey and that she died as a result of arsenical poisoning it would be your duty nevertheless to acquit the defendant unless you should further find and believe from the evidence beyond a reasonable doubt that the defendant administered said arsenic to her and that he did so with the specific intent of wilfully and feloniously with premeditated malice aforethought of killing her and unless this is proven to your satisfaction beyond all reasonable doubt then you must acquit the defendant

No evidence has been offered or received in this case from which you will be warranted in finding that the defendant ever at any time or place possessed arsenic or that he knew of its use purpose or its deadly poisonous effect and before you would be warranted in convicting the defendant the state would have to prove to your satisfaction that the defendant did possess arsenic and that he actually caused it to be administered to the deceased Lottie Kelsey, for the purpose of taking her life

The case was given to the jury at 8 30 Saturday night after lasting nearly three weeks and creating intense excitment

NEW HARMONY NEWS

—OO—

A large number of our towns people have been witnesses at the court in St. George.

—OO—

Word has reached here of the acquittal of Frank P. Kelsey of the first degree murder charge.

—OO—

A baby girl was born to Mr. and Mrs. Irving Prince at the Iron County Hospital March, 23. All concerned have gotten along nicely.

—OO—

Carel Prince, the small daughter of Lawrence Prince, who was recently operated on for appendicitis at the Washington County Hospital is convalescing nicely.

—OO—

The family of Bishop Henry A. Pace have been quite ill in St. George with what they called the flu.

—OO—

Albert Mathis has returned from St. George while there he was quite ill with the flu.

—OO—

Word has reached here that Mrs. Josephine K. Hales is very ill in Provo. Her father Orren Kelsey has gone there. She is reported as improving some.

—OO—

The men are all behind with their work on account of a large number of them having to attend court in St. George, the past three weeks.

Washington County News
April 24, 1923

New Harmony Apr 24—Bp H A
Pace brought Mrs Pace and children
up from St George Saturday   They
spent the past winter there   Their
daughter Pearl will remain there until school closes

Mrs LaMar Terry of Rockville was
here last week visiting with her sister Mrs Donald Schmutz

Mrs Florence Phippan has returned to Carey, Idaho after visiting here
about a month

James Parry and Thos Carlott of
Cedar City were here Saturday on
business

George, Evelyn and Jim Prince
have gone to Hurricane to shear
sheep

Elwin Ballard and Merrill Russell
of Grafton are here visiting relatives

Will Prince brought a load of
freight from St George Saturday

Joseph Taylor has gone south to
work

———————

Iron County Record
April 27, 1923

NEW HARMONY NEWS.

——oo——

Bishop Henry A. Pace has moved
his family home from St. George.
Pearl stayed there to finish her school
year.

——oo——

Will and Evelyn Prince hav been
home on a short visit. At present they
are both making there home in St.
George.

——oo——

Warren Taylor of Loa, Utah and
John Taylor from Arizona have been
here on a short visit, after having
attended the court in St. George.

——oo——

Orren Kelsey has returned from
Provo, bringing with him his daughter Josephine's five children. He reports her as being slightly improved
in health.

——oo——

Mrs. Florence K. Phippen of Carey,
Idaho is here visiting relatives and
friends.

——oo——

Joseph A. Taylor left here this
morning for St. George expecting to
be gone for some time.

——oo——

Mrs. Gladys G. Whitehead is now
in St. George for a short stay with
her husband's parents.

——oo——

Mr. and Mrs. Kenneth Hirschi and
Mrs. Marvin Lerry and children all
from Rockville have been here on a
visit with their sister Mrs. Elmer
Taylor and Mrs. Donald Schmutz.

Washington County News
April 30, 1923

New Harmony April 30 —Mary Marsden Relief Society Stake Pres was here yesterday She gave a very timely talk in the Sacramenttal services and held a special meeting with the Relief Society officers afterwards

Albert F Mathis went to St George today to see about having his sheep sheared

R A Kirker returned from California Saturday where he has been for a while

Mrs Viola Taylor has returned from Enoch where she has been for two weeks

Mrs Delbert Woolsey and children have gone back to their ranch for the summer

W W Cannon of St George has been here the past two days on business

Lawrence Marker of Cedar City was in town yesterday on business

Mrs Amelia Schmutz went to Salt Lake City last week

Washington County News
May 7, 1923

New Harmony May 7 —Mrs Morris Whitehead who has been here for some time convalesing from an operation has gone north, where her husband is working

Mrs Amelia Schmutz has returned from Salt Lake where she has been for two weeks

Mrs Eldon Schmutz has returned from Salt Lake where she has been the past winter

Antone Prince and Elmer Taylor are having their sheep sheared here this week

Mrs LeRoy Grant and Marie Page have gone to Toole county to visit relatives

Mr and Mrs Berry Williams of Kanarra were in town yesterday

Vernon Hall of Harmony a sophomore at the Agricultural college will be one of the thirty-four men from the college to attend the reserve officers training camp at the Presidio near San Francisco this summer Mr Hall will leave for the camp on or about June 10 and will receive basic training in military tactics for six weeks After that he will return to Harmony —U. A. C. Publicity

NEW HARMONY NEWS

Our school closed Friday after a very successful school year with Elmer Taylor as Principal.

Miss Emma Prisby has returned to her home in Washington after spending the past winter here.

Mrs. Amelia Schmutz and Mr. and Mrs. Eldon Schmutz returned yesterday from Salt Lake City.

Antone Prince, Gotlieb Schmutz and Elmer Taylor are having their sheep sheared at the Schmutz corral.

R. A. Kirker returned last week from a two weeks business trip to California. He has had some repair work done on his mine the past week.

Mrs. Gladys G. Whitehead has gone to Salt Lake City to join her husband there, after visiting here for a few months.

Mrs. Sadie Grant, accompanied by her two children and mother Mrs. Maria Page left yesterday for a visit in Salt Lake City and Ogden. Mrs. Page has spent the past winter here and will return to her home in Panguitch for the summer.

Washington County News
May 14, 1923

New Harmony May 14 —Juanita and Fern Davis and Pearl Pace came up from St George today They have been attending the Dixie college the past winter We will be glad to have all of the young folks home again

William Palmer and Frank Wood of the Stake Presidency were down from Cedar yesterday and talked to us in Sunday school and Sacrament meeting

The Relief society members gave a birthday party for Sarah E Davis R S president Saturday afternoon Refreshments were served and a pleasant time enjoyed by all

Mr and Mrs Wm Pace of Delta were here last week They had been to Washington and were on thei way home

Reed and Marion Prince have returned from St George where they have been attending the D C

Mr and Mrs Antone Prince took their daughter Virginia to Cedar today for medical treatment

J D Neilson has returned from Dixie where he has been working for some time

Albert Mathis returned from Lund Saturday where he had been on busi ness

Mrs Francis Prince has been at Hurricane visiting relatives

Mrs Evelyn Prince of St George is here visiting relatives

Bert Grant has gone to Panguitch to shear sheep

Elmer Taylor has gone to Lund on business

Washington County News
May 17, 1923

Mr and Mrs I ving Prince I rank Kelsey and son Verle are here from New Harmony, visiting

Merrill Russell has gone to New Harmony to work

Iron County record
May 25, 1923

NEW HARMONY NEWS

———oo———

Jaunita and Fern Davis, Pearl Pace and Reed and Marion Prince have all returned from St. George where they have been attending the D. N. C.

Wm. H. Pace of Delta and his mother and sister, Mrs. Hannah Jolley of Washington and Mrs. Maggie Hartley of Leeds were here last week visiting relatives.

Last week a birthday party was given our Relief Society President, Sarah P. Davis by the Relief Society members. Refreshments were served and a good time was had by all.

James D. Nielson is home after being gone for some time in Dixie.

Elmer Taylor has returned from a business trip to Lund.

———oo———

Washington County News
May 29, 1923

New Harmony, May 29 ——There will be a cattle sale here today The cattle men have been gathering the cattle the last week to put on the upper range Forest Ranger Alex Mac farlane is here counting the cattle

Mrs. LeRoy Grant has returned from Toole county where she has been for some time

Orren Kelsey and Rulon Taylor went to Cedar last week on business

Mr and Mrs LeGrande Pace of Pace s ranch were here yesterday

Mr and Mrs J W Prince of St. George were in town yesterday

Mrs. Ashby Pace went to Cedar last Thursday on business

Forest Ranger D V Storm of Leeds was here Saturday

Nora Ballard of Grafton is here visiting relatives

New Harmony, June 4 —Mrs L A Pace and daughter Miss Merle have returned from Cedar City where the latter has been attending the B A C

Miss Minnie Pace is home again after teaching school in Enterprise the past winter

Mr and Mrs LeRoy Grant and family have moved to their summer ranch

Frank Kelsey and Evelyn Prince have gone to Salt Lake City on business

Miss Juanita Davis has been visiting friends in Kanarra the past week

Max Pace has returned from Glendale where he has been working

Orren Taylor went to Summit yesterday on important business

Wm Kelsey of Minersville has been here visiting relatives

Iron County Record
June 10, 1923

NEWS FROM NEW HARMONY.

——oo——

June 10, 1923

——oo——

Orren Taylor is home after attending the B. A. C. the past winter.

——oo——

Miss Lenora Ballard of Grafton has been here for some time visiting friends.

——oo——

Miss Rose Schmutz has returned from Salt Lake City where she has spent a number of months.

——oo——

Frank Kelsey has returned from a trip to Salt Lake City, bringing with him a new car.

——oo——

Miss Minnie Pace has returned home after teaching in Enterprise the past winter.

——oo——

Mr. and Mrs. LeRoy Grant have moved to their ranch for the summer.

——oo——

Mrs. Susan A. Pace and son and daughter, Clark Max and Merle, have returned from Cedar City where the latter have attended the B. A. C.

——oo——

James E. Taylor and Mr. and Mrs. James D. Nielson and daughter Bernice were in Cedar City Saturday on business.

——oo——

Mr. and Mrs. Albert Mathis, Ashby Pace, Mrs. Rhoda Prince and son Lyle made a business trip to Cedar City Saturday.

——oo——

Mr. and Mrs. James E. Taylor, Wm. P. Taylor, Mrs. Emeretta Kelsey and Mrs. Jas. D. Neilson spent Wednesday in St. George working in the temple.

——oo——

Bp. and Mrs. Henry A. Pace and Minnie and Merle Pace have gone to Salt Lake City to attend conference and the Pace reunion, which is to be held there.

Washington County News
June 11, 1923

Mr and Mrs Jim Prince of New Harmony were visitors Saturday and Sunday at the home of Frank Russell and family

Merrill Russell left yesterday to go to his work at New Harmony

Washington County News
June 18, 1923

New Harmony June 18—Our town was greatly shocked to learn of the death of Mrs Nellie Pace of Cedar City Twenty eight people went up yesterday to attend her funeral She leaves a large circle of friends here who mourn her death The bereaved family have our sympathy

Jeff Pace and sons Leslie and Marion of Delta and Miss Eva Clark of Salt Lake City were here visiting friends yesterday

W W Cannon of St George was here Saturday checking up on the water and stated that he found it surprisingly low

Mr and Mrs Elmer Taylor and Mr and Mrs Antone Prince have gone to Grass Valley on a fishing trip

Lawrence Prince was called to Santa Clara Saturday on account of sickness

Clark Pace has gone to Toquerville for awhile

Washington County News
July 2, 1923

New Harmony July 2—Efforts are being made the past few days to improve on present water system By everyone following instructions a very marked change will be noticed

Bert Grant who has been off working for some time returned yesterday

Misses Minnie and Merle Pace Mrs L A Pace and Clark Pace returned from Toquerville yesterday where they had been for some time

Most of our towns people went to Cedar Wednesday and had the honor of seeing Pres and Mrs Harding

Mr and Mrs J C knell of New castle were in town Thursday and Friday on business

A splendid program has been arranged for the 4th and a very good time is anticipated

Mrs Mason Rencher and children of Grass valley are here visiting relatives

Miss Alice Allen of Summit is here visiting friends

NEW HARMONY NOTES.

Mrs. Mason Rancher and children are here visiting relatives.

Mr. and Mrs. Claud Knell of New-castle have been here visiting rela-tives for a few days.

Mr. and Mrs. Jas. E. Taylor and Mr. and Mrs. Reese Davis spent Fri-day in St. George working in the temple.

LeRoy Grant and Sid Goddard have been in town for a few days on business. They are spending the summer on their ranch.

Mrs. Susan A. Pace and daughters Minnie and Merle and son Clark have returned from Toquerville where they have been visiting rela-tives.

A large percent of our townpeople attended the reception given Presi-dent Harding and his company at Cedar City. A few went to Kanarra and Toquerville.

Mr. and Mrs. James E. Taylor and Mr. and Mrs. Orson Hammond at-tended the funeral for their Uncle, Samuel Kelsey, which was held in Cedar City.

New Harmony July 9 —Leonard the little son of Mr and Mrs Wm Chinn had the misfortune to be kicked by a horse today breaking his arm He was taken to Cedar City to receive medical treatment

The Fourth celebration was a success in every sense of the term and the dance at night was good in spite of the fact that our music failed us at the last moment

Mr and Mrs Owen W Clark and daughters Rose and June of Cannonville were visiting the former's sister Mrs L A Pace the latter part of the week

Messrs Rulon Knell and Miff Kleinman have returned to their homes after spending a day or two here visiting friends

Clarence Englestead has gone to Salt Lake City where he intends being operated on for diseased tonsils

Mr and Mrs Mason Rencher of Grass valley are spending a short time visiting the latter's parents here.

After spending a short time here visiting friends Miss Alice Allen has returned to her home at Summit

Mrs Sarah Davis who has been confined to her bed for several days is able to be about again

Mr and Mrs Lee Cox and Mr and Mrs Wm Prince of St George were town visitors recently

Mrs A W Pace has gone to Newcastle to spend a few days visiting relatives and friends

Mr and Mrs R B Naegle of Toquerville spent the Fourth here

Miss Elizabeth Snow of Pine Valley is a guest of Miss Minnie Pace

NEW HARMONY NOTES.

July 10, 1913.

Bert Grant is home after being gone for some time shearing sheep.

Clarence Englestead left Monday for a business trip to Cedar and Salt Lake.

Albert Mathis, Lorenzo Prince and son Lyle made a trip on business to Cedar yesterday.

Our milk cows were recently tested for tuberculosis. Not one was found to be affected.

Mrs. Susan E. Pace and daughter, Mrs. Geo. F. Prince leave this morning for a visit to Salt Lake, Price and Emery County.

Mr. and Mrs. Leroy Grant, Mr. and Mrs. Delbert Woolsey, Sid Goddard, Clarence Englestead, Alvin Kelsey and Ed. Grant all came home to help celebrate Independence day.

Leonard, the little son of Mr. and Mrs. Will Chinn was unfortuately kicked by a horse and his arm broken. Dr. Macfarlane set the limb and the boy is getting along nicely.

We had a very good time here on Independence day. A large number of visitors helped to make the day a success. Among those present from other towns were Mr. and Mrs. Ray Naegle, Mifflin Kleinmann, Mr. and Mrs. Mason Rancher, Alice Allen, Rulon Knell, James Thornton, Geary Page, Earl Woodard, Miss Snow, Mr. and Mrs. Lee Cox, Mr. and Mrs. Will Prince, Merril Russell and Miss DeMills.

Washington County News
July 16, 1923

New Harmony July 16 — Miss Elizabeth Snow has returned to Pine Valley after spending a short time here She was accompanied back by Miss Minnie Pace of this place

Ashby Pace went to Pinto yesterday to get his wife who has been to Newcastle the past week

Mrs Harvey Pace and Mrs Nancy Prince have gone to Emery county for a short visit

Mrs R B Naegle of Toquerville is here expecting to stay for a short visit

Ray Naegle and Miff Kleinman of Toquerville were here yesterday

Relatives of Mrs Amelia Schmutz are visitors here from Oregon

Eldon Schmutz is commencing to build on the upper Mathis lot

Mrs Francis Prince has gone to Panguitch to visit relatives

Ray Dalley of Cedar City was in town today on business

Washington County News
July 23, 1923

New Harmony July 23 — Mr Alvin Kelsey of this place and Miss Thelma Edwards were married at Parowan last week

Relief Society conference was held here yesterday Three of the Stake officers from Parowan were in attendance

Mr and Mrs John Mathis of Price were here last week visiting friends and relatives

Mr and Mrs Jeremiah Leavitt of Gunlock are here visiting relatives

Harmony is going to join with Kanarra for the 24th celebration

I W Thornton of Cedar City was here last Thursday on business

Mrs Emily Grant has gone to Ophir to visit relatives

J D Neilson has gone to Ophir to seek employment

Washington County News
July 31, 1923

New Harmony July 31 —Bp H A Pace and family have returned from Fish Lake and other points of interest where they spent a week

Mr and Mrs Len DeLong and Mrs Joseph DeLong of Salt Lake City are here visiting friends and relatives

Miss Mona Hirschi has returned to Hurricane She has been here two or three weeks

George Cottam is here from St George visiting his daughter Mrs A B Prince

Miss Emma Prisbrey of Washington came up to spend the 24th here

Mrs Lee Cox and children of St George are here visiting relatives

Wilford Whipple of Overton Nev is a town visitor

Washington County News
August 6, 1923

New Harmony August 6 —Mrs Reese Davis and daughter Miss Fern have gone to Fish Lake with Mr and Mrs Berry Williams of Kanarra

Mr and Mrs Ed Whipple of Overton Nev were here Thursday night on their way to Yellowstone park

Mrs Olive Chinn and children have been to Quitchipau for a few days Mr Chinn is working there

Miss Wanda Armstrong of Enoch is here visiting her sister Mrs Alex Taylor

Mr and Mrs LeGrande Pace of Cedar City were here Saturday

Jesse Kleinman and Vern Slack of Toquerville are here working

Miss Juanita Davis has been in Kanarra for the past week

NEW HARMONY NOTES.
August 6th., 1923.

Mr. and Mrs. Len DeLong of Salt Lake and Mr. and Mrs. Joseph De-Long and children of Ogden were here last week visiting relatives and friends.

—OO—

Ray Neagle is in town, having come for his wife who has spent some time here with her mother.

—OO—

Mr. and Mrs. Lee Cox are here visiting, also Mr. Evelyn and Will Prince.

Evelyn has recently returned from Salt Lake where he has attended the university of Barbers.

—OO—

Mr. and Mrs. Leroy Grant and Mr. Del Woolsey were in town Sunday.

—OO—

Eldon Schmutz and Elmer Taylor are having some nice homes built.

—OO—

Bishop Henry A. Pace and family recently returned from a visit to Fish Lake and Price.

Washington County News
August 13, 1923

New Harmony Aug 13 — Relatives of Miss Rose Schmutz entertained at a shower in her honor Thursday evening Games were played and refershments were served A very pleasant time was enjoyed by all

Mrs Harvey Pace Mrs Amelia Schmutz and James E Taylor went to Leeds today to attend the funeral services of Mr Olsen

Last week an error was made in regard to some boys that are working here They were Jesse Naegle and Vern Slack of Toquerville

The Misses Juanita Fern and Vilo Davis and Miss Ethel Schmutz have gone to the Kanarra mountains to spend a few days

G G Pace and children Mrs Stanley Parry and Mrs LeGrande Pace of Cedar City were here yesterday

Mrs Nancy Watts and grand children and Grant Condie of Cedar City spent the week end here visiting

Lee Cox of St George and others were here Wednesday locating a site for a saw mill

Elmer Taylor is commencing to build on his farm above town

Mrs Pearl Pace went to St George Thursday to spend a few days

Washington County News
August 27, 1923

New Harmony Aug 27 — Miss Rose Schmutz and Benj Jobb of Salt Lake City were married last Friday at St George leaving the same day for Salt Lake We extend our best wishes for a joyous and prosperous life

Reed and Sylva Prince Pearl Pace and Florence Prince were operated on a few days ago for removal of tonsils

A daughter was born to Mr and Mrs Eldon Schmutz Saturday at Cedar City all concerned doing nicely

Primary Ward conference was held here yesterday Three of the stake officers were in attendance

Mr and Mrs Ashby Pace returned from Pinto Saturday where they went to attend a home coming

Mr and Mrs Ed Whipple of Overton Nev are here visiting Mr and Mrs Albert Mathis

Glen Olsen of Leeds was here yesterday

Washington County News
August 30, 1923

Mr Ben Eugene Jobb of Salt Lake City and Miss Rose Schmutz of New Harmony were married August 23 by President Snow in this city

Iron County Record
August 31, 1923

————00————

NEW HARMONY NEWS

————00————

Miss Rose Schmutz and Mrs. Ben Jobb of Salt Lake City were married in St. George yesterday. The young couple left for Salt Lake where they will make their home. They leave with the best wishes of a host of friends.

Mr. and Mrs. Eldon Schmutz are rejoicing over the arrival of a daughter which came to them at the Iron County Hospital August 25th.

Miss Minnie Pace spent the past three weeks with her sister, Mrs. Ray Naegle, in Toquerville.

Mr. and Mrs. Ashby W. Pace are attending the home coming in Pinto.

Bp. and Mrs. Henry A. Pace, Geo F. Prince and Mr. and Mrs. James — Prince spent Friday in Cedar City where Miss Pearl Pace and Florence Sylvia and Reid Prince had their tonsils removed at the County Hospital. All are getting along nicely

Mrs. Amelia Schmutz, Mrs. Melissa Hammond and Mrs. Sarah P. Davis were visitors in Cedar City today.

New Harmony Sept 3 —Mrs Or
1en Taylor of this place and Miss
Alice Allen of Summit were married
Saturday at Summit   Mr Taylor is
an exemplary young man and has a
large circle of friends who wish them
a joyous and prosperous life

Myron Higbee Frank Wood and
Miss Catherine Webster members of
the stake presidency were here yes
terday and talked in Sacrament meet
ing

Orson Hammond Ashby Pace and
Bert Grant returned from the God
dard and Grant ranch where they
have been putting up hay for a week

Miss Minnie Pace has returned
from Toquerville where she has
been for the past three weeks

Mrs Emma Neilson has gone to
Ophir for a few days where her hus
band is working

Miss Bessie Davis of Kanarra is
is here working for Mrs   Albert
Mathis

Mrs Walter Spencer of Newcastle
is here visiting Mr and Mrs Ashby
Pace

Ray Naegle of Toquerville was in
town the fore part of the week

New Harmony Sept 10 — A wed ding reception was given for Mr and Mrs Orren Taylor Thursday evening at the bridegroom s home Dainty refreshments were served and a pleasant time was enjoyed by all

Lester Taylor who has been at Park City the past year working came to attend his brother s recep tion He returned yesterday

For the past two weeks Bp H A Pace has had several teams at work excavating a fish pond on his farm southwest of town

Mrs Nora Island of Juaraz Mexi co is at the Goddard and Grant ranch visiting with her sister Mrs LeRoy Grant

The Misses Fern and Juanita Davis have gone to St George where they will attend the Dixie college

Donald Schmutz has returned from Mount Trumbull Ariz where he had been on business

Mrs Eldon Schmutz has returned from Cedar City where she has been for two weeks

Miss Kate Isom of Hurricane is here working for Mrs Wm Taylor

Mr and Mrs LeGrande Pace of Cedar City were here yesterday

Max Pace has gone to Cedar City where he has employment

Elmer Taylor is having his house plastered

NEW HARMONY NOTES.

Mrs. Eva B. Schmutz has returned home bringing with her a new baby.

Mrs. Mary Spencer of Newcastle has been here visiting relatives.

Miss Bessie Davis of Kanarra is here working for Mrs. Albert Mathis.

Miss Kate Isom of Hurricane is here working for Mrs. Wm. P. Taylor.

Lester Taylor, who has spent the past year in Park City, came home to attend his brothers wedding.

Reese Davis left for St. George today taking his daughter Juanita and Fern with them where they can attend the Dixie College. —

Mrs. Emma G. Neilson is in Ophir on a visit with her husband, mother and sister. Her husband, James D. Nielson, has been there working for some time.

Mr. Orren Taylor of this place and Miss Alice Allen of Summit were married September 1st. Orren is the son of Mr. and Mrs. James C. Taylor and all are highly respected residents of New Harmony. The many friends of the young couple wish them a happy and prosperous life.

New Harmony Sept 17 — Fern the seven year old daughter of Mr and Mrs James L Prince met with an accident last week. She was cutting a thick piece of cloth when the scissors slipped and struck her right eye. She was rushed to the hospital at Cedar City where her eye was treated but the sight cannot be restored.

Mrs Emma Neilson and Mrs Emily Grant have returned from Ophir where they have been for a while visiting relatives

The Misses Merle and Pearl Pace have gone to Cedar City where they will attend the B A C this winter

Most of our town s people attended the rodeo at Cedar City last week and reported having had a very good time

George Schmutz returned home last week. He has been off most of the summer working

Mrs LeRoy Grant has moved in from the ranch so that her children can go to school

Miss Minnie Pace has gone to Enterprise where she will teach school this winter

District school opened this morning Elmer Taylor teaching

New Harmony Sept 24 — A daughter was born to Mr and Mrs Wm P Taylor on the 20th all concerned doing nicely

Miss Estella Hammond has gone to Cedar City where she will attend high school this winter

Several of our towns people attended conference at Cedar Saturday and Sunday

James Knell and Miss Iva Knell of Newcastle are here on a short visit

Vilate Prince health officer went to St George last week on business

The weather is disagreeable and cold lately

Clarence M. Englestead was in Cedar City last week on business.

— OO—

Mr. and Mrs. Leroy Grant have moved down from their ranch to send their children to school.

—OO—

School started September 17th with Elmer Taylor as principal. This is four years he has held that position.

—OO—

Mr. and Mrs. Orson Hammond went to Cedar City last week taking their daughter Annetta to have her tonsils removed.

—OO—

Miss Merle and Pearl Pace are in Cedar attending the B. A. C.

—OO—

Leslie and Estella Hammond are attending the Junior High School at Cedar City.

—OO—

Ethel Schmutz and Fern and Juanita Davis are attending the St. George Academy.

NEW HARMONY NOTES
(Too late for last issue)

—OO—

Mrs. Emma A. Grant and daughter Mrs. Emma Nielson have returned from Ophir and Salt Lake City where they have been visiting.

—OO—

Born a daughter to Mr. and Mrs. Wm. P. Taylor, September 20th. All concerned doing nicely.

—OO—

Mr. and Mrs. Wm. Worthen and Mr. and Mrs. Alma Jensen all of Terron, Utah have been here visiting Mrs. Worthen's sister, Mrs. Susan E. Pace.

New Harmony Oct 8 —Estella Hammond Leslie Pearl and Merle Pace who are attending school at Cedar City spent the week end here

Alex Taylor has returned from Bryce canyon where he has been working for some time

Mrs Irving Prince has returned from Grafton where she has been visiting relatives

Max Pace who has been working at Cedar City the past month is here for a few days

E C Grant is home for the winter He has been off working for some time

Mrs Alex Urie of Hamiltons Fort was in town yesterday on business

Mrs Ashby Pace spent a few days at Iron Springs last week

Washington County News
October 15, 1923

New Harmony Oct 15 — Mrs Reese Davis went to Kanarra a few days ago to see her daughter Mrs Berry Williams who was very ill

W E Spencer water commission er of Salt Lake was here a few days last week transacting business

Miss Minnie Pace spent the week end here She is teaching school at Enterprise

Mr and Mrs E G Hale of Fairview are here visiting relatives

Mr and Mrs Elmer Taylor went to St George Friday on business

Mr and Mrs LaGrande Pace of Cedar City were here Friday

Forest Ranger S A Macfarlane was here Saturday

Bp H A Pace went to Cedar today on business

Washington County News
October 22, 1923

New Harmony Oct 22 — Mrs L A Pace who had gone to Cedar for the winter was called back when her daughter Mrs Taylor was taken sick

Miss Iva Knell of Newcastle Mrs Vera Parry of Cedar City and Earl Clark of Kanab spent the week end here visiting friends

Mrs Wm P Taylor had a severe spell of sickness last week She is now somewhat better

John Benson of Enterprise brought cattle here last week They were delivered at Modena

Mr and Mrs Claud Hirschi of Hurricane spent the week end here

John Brown of Hamilton Fort was here Saturday transacting business

Miss Irene Ford of Kanarra is here working for Mrs Donald Schmutz

Mrs Maria Page of Panguitch has come here to spend the winter

Mrs Hazel Sorensen of California was here on business Saturday

Jos E Taylor has purchased a new Ford touring car

The M I A meetings commenced last night

New Harmony, Oct 29 —James L Prince and daughter Fern left for Salt Lake today where the little girl will be operated on for her eye She accidently stuck the sissors in it a few weeks ago It is believed by operating that partial sight will be restored

Pres Henry W Lunt and Wm Palmer of Cedar City were here for Sunday services Mrs Bateman of the B A C faculty was also down in the interest of teachers training work

J D Nielson has returned from Ophir where he has been working for some time

Lee Cox and Wm Prince of St George spent the week end here

Mr Timothy of Vernal is here visiting relatives

Orson Hammond has gone to Modena to work

DEER ARE PLENTIFUL

Deer are more plentiful than for many years in this section and a goodly percent of the hunters have been successful

Among those who succeded in getting a deer each are Dean A Clark John Smith Jack Evans Lee Cox Bill Prince Melvin Cox Bob Seaman Rex Cannon Ammon Lake Roy Atkin Willie Baker Lee Hafen Vivian Frei Andrew Laub Max Hafen Glen Frei Fred A Reber Walter Pace Newell Frei Oliver Graf Ross Barton Ed O Hamblin Charles Starr D C Watson Bert Covington and Welden Graf John M Higgins and Joseph W Judd got one between them as also did David O Woodbury and Lorenzo Mc Gregor

Several others were brought in but we have not learned the names of the hunters

Dean A Clak John Smith and Jack Evans got theirs in the Kanab country The Cox boys Prince and some others got theirs somewhere about New Harmony Others were brought in from Bull valley and the Jackson country

Anton B Prince of New Harmony shot a fine buck weighing 245 pounds dressed last week

Iron County Record
November 20, 1923

NEW HARMONY NEWS

Nov. 20, 1923.

The Mutuals gave a splendid program Friday evening in honor of the "Home."

Mr. and Mrs. Orren Taylor spent the week end here visiting relatives Mrs. Taylor, formerly Miss Alice Allen of Summit, is teaching in her home town.

Mr. and Mrs. Morris Whitehead are here visiting the latter's parent's, Mr. and Mrs. E. C. Grant.

Miss Ethel Schmutz spent Saturday and Sunday here. She is attending the D. N. C.

James E. Taylor was operated on at the Iron County Hospital last week and is getting along nicely. He had a great deal of trouble from tuberculosis of the bone of his leg and had other operations. It is hoped that this will be pefmanent cure.

Mrs. Maria Page is here spending the winter with her daughter Mrs. Leroy Grant.

Mr. and Mrs. Grant Hale are here ending the winter with the latter's parents, Mr. and Mrs. Orren Kelsey.

Mrs. Edna Prince is visiting with her parents at Grafton.

Irving Prnice, Orson Hammond, Alex Taylor, Clarence Englestead, and Jr. Dostalek are all working at Molena.

Andrew Schmutz has sold his home to John Sorenson and they have moved here for the winter.

Washington County News
November 26, 1923

New Harmony Nov 26 — S S has been organized with Donald Schmutz superintendent Antone Prince and Andrew S Schmutz counselors Marion Prince secretary and Susie Taylor organist

Mr and Mrs Orren Taylor spent the week end here visiting relatives Mr Taylor is working at Iron Springs and Mrs Taylor is teaching school at Summit

Mrs Morris Whitehead is here visiting relatives She has been at Ophir for some time where her husband has been working

James E Taylor underwent an operation last Wednesday at the Iron county hospital He is getting along nicely

John Sorensen and family have moved here from Thorley s ranch They have bought Andrew Schmutz s house

Ethel Schmutz returned to St George yesterday after spending a few days here

Miss Bessie Davis of Kanarra is here working for Mrs Donald Schmutz

Mrs Lulu Pollock has returned to Kanarra after working here for a short time

Clarence Englestead and Alex Taylor have gone to Modena to work

Reese Davis went to Hurricane Friday on business

Max Pace of Cedar City spent the week end here

Iron County Record
December 2, 1923

— oo —

New Harmony, Utah, Dec. 2, 1923. Thanksgiving day was fittingly celebrated here by a Town Dinner. A meeting in the morning and dances for children and adults. All spent a very pleasant day.

Miss Minnie Pace and Forest Ranger, Alex McFarlane of St. George were here on Thanksgiving day. Minnie is teaching in Enterprise.

Bp. Pace has moved his family to Cedar for the winter.

Pearl and Leslie Pace, Estella Hammond, and Fern and Juanita Davis all came home from school to spend Thanksgiving.

Mrs. Hunt, from New Mexico, a sister of Gotlieb Schmutz is here visiting relatives.

Mrs. Reese Davis is spending a large part of her time with her daughter's family in Kanarra while her daughter Mrrs. Berry Williams is in Hurricane taking treatment from Dr. Wilkinson.

Mr. and Mrs. Evelyn Prince spent Thanksgiving here with Mr. and Mrs. Geo.F. Prince.

Irving Prince came home last night after working in Modena for some time. He was accompanied by Monroe Russell of Grafton.

KELSEY TO BE TRIED AT FILLMORE DEC. 13

The case of the State of Utah vs Frank P Kelsey, charged with poisoning his mother and grandparents and also causing some horses to be killed with strychnine which the defendant is said to have placed in the drinking water at the residence of Francis Prince at New Harmony came on for hearing in the District Court Wednesday, on the application of the defendant for a charge of venue on the ground that public sentiment in this county as he alleges would prevent him getting a fair and impartial trial here

Although this defendant was tried for the murder of his wife through poisoning her with arsenic at the March term of court here the present year and acquitted he claims that the jury who tried him on the murder charge, and the court who tried the case have been so severely criticized by the people of this county, and there has arisen such a sentiment against him that it will be impossible for him to recieve a fair trial on the poisoning charges now against him in Washington County and therefore asks that it be changed to some other county in the district

The court after hearing and examining the affidavits presented for and against the motion for change of venue agreed to grant the change to another county in the district with the understanding that the case would be tried during the present term of court.

This morning the Court granted the motion for the change and entered an order transferring the case to Millard county for trial The case was set for hearing on Friday Dec 13

The defendant s application was supported by the affidavits of 71 persons, the state presenting counter affidivits of 84 persons

An open venue would have been necessary to procure a jury to try the case here and sentiment is so strong in the county against the defendant that we believe Judge Burton was just and right in granting the change of venue

SALE OF ANIMALS FOR DAMAGES

State of Utah County of Washington In the New Harmony precinct of said county I have in my possession the following described animals which if not claimed and taken away will be sold at public auction to the highest cash bidder at my corral in New Harmony precinct on the 11th day of December 1923 at the hour of 4 p m

One red cow branded O on right hip and shoulder marked crop off left ear and under slope in right

One red brockle faced cow branded Z on left ribs marked slit in left ear and upper slope in right ear

One spotted four year old steer branded AL on left ribs marked crop and two slits in right ear and crop off left ear

The two first described animals are held by me to secure the payment of $2 00 damages done by said animals upon the premises of Henry A Pace on the 27th day of November 1923 The latter animal is held by me to secure the payment of $6 00 damages done by said animal upon the premises of James E Taylor on the 1st day of December 1923

Elmer Taylor

Washington County News
December 10, 1923

New Harmony Dec 10 —Orson Hammond Manuel Dossick and Alex Taylor who are working at Modena spent the week end here

Irving Prince came home last week from Modena where he has been working

Mrs H A Pace and children have gone to Cedar for the winter

Iron County Record
December 16, 1923

NEW HARMONY

——oo——

December 16, 1923.

Alex Taylor is home after working for some time in Modena.

Elders Fisher and Grimshaw of Enoch, were here last week laboring in our ward. Two cottage meetings were held at the home of James E. Taylor. Both were well attended. They visited each home. The people enjoyed and appreciated their visits.

The little infant daughter of Mr. and Mrrs. Eldon Schmutz has been quite ill for a few days with the croup.

James E. Talor is recovering nicely from his recent operation.

Mrs. Vioa A. Taylor has been called to Enoch, as her mother has recently been operated on for appendicitis.

Albert Mathis spent a number of days in St. George last week, where he was called as a juryman.

Ashby Pace has returned from a trip to Grass valley.

James D. Neilson and William P. Taylor are working on the state road.

Mr. and Mrs. Orren Taylor are spending the week end with relatives.

MACFARLANE PACE

Announcement has been received by The News of the marriage of Mr Samuel A Macfarlane and Miss Minnie Pace at Salt Lake City Dec 22

The bride is a daughter of Mrs L A Pace of New Harmony a very highly respected young lady who for several years has been engaged in school teaching The groom is a son of Mrs E J Macfarlane of St. George a young man who for a number of years has served the government as forest ranger on the Dixie reserve He is also very highly respected

The News joins the many friends of the happy twain in hearty wishes for a happy married life

Iron County Record
December 30, 1923

NEW HARMONY

—oo—

December 30, 1923.

Senator and Mrs. David Hirschi and their two daughters spent Christmas here with their daughter Mrs. Elmer Taylor.

—oo—

Mr. and Mrs. Morris Whitehead and Andrew Schmutz are visiting with relatives in St. George.

—oo—

Irving Prince has returned from Grafton, bringing his wife who has spent a few months there with her parents.

—oo—

Mr. and Mrs. Alex Macfarlane are here visiting.

—oo—

Mrs. Susan A. Pace, and daughter Merle and son Max are home for a few days visit.

—oo—

Mr. and Mrs. Ray Naegle are here visiting relatives and friends.

— oo—

Mrs. Amelia Schmutz and grand-daughter Cecil are visiting relatives in Salt Lake City.

—oo—

Mr. and Mrs. Orren Taylor are spending a few days here with the formers parents, Mr. and Mrs. Jas. E. Taylor.

—oo—

Cards are out announcing the marriage of Miss Minnie Pace to Alex Macfarlane of St. George, in Salt Lake City, Dec. 22nd. Their many friends here wish them a long and happy life.

40620887R10279

Made in the USA
Charleston, SC
08 April 2015